Sari Oikarinen
A DREAM OF LIBERTY

CW00971475

BIBLIOTHECA HISTORICA 34

Sari Oikarinen

....

"A Dream of Liberty"

Constance Markievicz´s Vision of Ireland, 1908–1927

Suomen Historiallinen Seura ■ Helsinki

Cover drawing by Jari Asikainen

ISSN 1238-3503

ISBN 951-710-091-4

Tammer-Paino Oy

Tampere 1998

◼ Contents

■ Acknowledgements

I first read about Constance Markievicz twelve years ago and since then she has been present in my life, sometimes more, sometimes less. I don't know whether now it is time to say a final goodbye to her, but at least it is time to thank all you who have helped in making this dissertation possible.

First I would like to express my warmest thanks to my former Professor Olli Vehviläinen for his support for my ideas, which was a crucial factor in starting post-graduate studies at all. Professor Marjatta Hietala has been an enthusiastic supporter for the last years of my work. I also warmly thank the examiners of my manuscript, Professor Emerita Aira Kemiläinen and Doctor Margaret Mac Curtain. During the process of the work many people have made valuable comments on my plans and manuscript on different occasions, be it in Ireland or in Finland. I thank them all. However, I would especially like to thank Doctor Rosemary Cullen in Ireland and the participants in the Nordic Women Historians' Meetings in 1993 and 1996. The staff in various libraries and archives have without exception been helpful, prompt and well-informed, which has made my task easier.

The History Department at Tampere University has been a pleasant place to work. I am grateful to Lic. Phil. Kirsi-Marja Tuominen and Doctor Pirjo Markkola for their encouragement through the years and the chance they have given me to work with them. Doctor Markku Hyrkkänen saw my earliest tentative pages about Markievicz and his analytical insight as well as common sense have helped me from thereon.

Over the years I have been lucky to get financial support for my work. It is a pleasant duty to thank the Finnish Academy, the Finnish Cultural Fundation, Emil Aaltosen Säätiö, the University of Tampere, H. Weijolan Säätiö, and The Graduate School on Cultural Interaction and Integration. I thank Tampereeen Kaupungin Tiederahasto for giving me a grant for correcting my English and for publishing my dissertation. It is a joy that the Finnish Historical Socity has accepted my thesis in the series Bibliotheca Historica. Doctor Robert Bell has patiently corrected my English with skill and taste for which I am grateful. Jari Asikainen contributed to the making of this book by planning and drawing the cover picture .

People near my heart have given me strength to do this work by just being who they are. I would like to thank my family and parents-in-law for their patience and encouragement. In the course of the work Doctor Virve Manninen has always been there, and her original sense of humour as well as her intelligence have often increased my joys and diminished my sorrows. Life would be dull without friends, laughter and talk. So, here's to you, too, Paula, Sari, Pia, Minna and Kirsti!

I dedicate this book to my husband Jarmo Oikarinen and our daughter Mona. Sharing my life with them is the best thing that ever happened to me.

Tampere, September 1998

Sari Oikarinen

■ Introduction

Constance Markievicz and Irish politics at the beginning of the Century

> *"Every cause that men and women die for must be based on fundamental principles, and strike some note that is in tune with all that is deepest and strongest in their natures...A dream of liberty can light a flame in every human soul...men and women of all ages have given martyrs in the cause of liberty for thought of person, sex, class, religion or country."* [1]

The writer of these words was Constance Markievicz (1868-1927), an Irish Republican politician, who was centrally involved in the Irish nationalist movement at the beginning of the century. The aim of my work is to examine the ideas and activities of Markievicz, pursuing "a dream of liberty" in Ireland between the years 1908–1927.

Born into a wealthy Anglo-Irish land-owning family, Constance Markievicz began her political career in her forties. In 1908 she became a follower of Sinn Fein and a year later she founded a youth organisation, Na Fianna Eireann. At about the same time, she joined a radical nationalist women's organisation, Inghinidhe na hEireann, and became associated with the socialist James Connolly. Markievicz served during the Easter Rising of 1916 as second-in-command of the St. Stephen's Green detachment in Dublin, for which she was sentenced to death. Because of her sex the sentence was commuted and in the British general election of 1918 she was returned for the St. Patrick's division of Dublin, thus being the first woman to be elected to the House of Commons. In the first Dáil Eireann established as a Shadow Government by the Sinn Feiners, she held a cabinet post as Minister for Labour. She opposed the Free State that came into existence in 1922 and supported the republicans in the Civil War thereafter. In 1926 she joined a new party, Fianna Fail, led by Eamon de Valera and was returned to the Free State parliament before her death in July 15 1927.

Markievicz aroused strong feelings in her time, particularly among her political opponents. Tall, confident in her manner, often dressed in a uniform or something else that separated her from the crowd, she was always news to the press. Many contemporaries found it difficult to take Markievicz seriously not just because of her background but because of her personality as well. Her friend, Helena Moloney, remarked that "..the greatest defect in her character

---

1   Markievicz, Constance, a typescript, Synge Papers, P 5482, mf, National Library of Ireland (NLI).

....was a childish love for the limelight. It never prevented her from doing good, hard, and unpleasant work....She could only express herself in terms of action and gesture and drama."[2] It has even been asserted that she abandoned any cause where the ordinary and the commonplace quenched the drama.[3] In addition to drawing attention to this "dramatic" feature impatience is often a term used by those attempting to describe her. For Yeats she was a "steam whistle".[4] According to the dramatist Sean O'Casey "...she pounced on Connolly and dazzled him with her flashy enthusiasm." Even her friend, the writer George Russell (AE) found her "a fine breathless character, straight as a lance, truthful, and as devoid of fear as any human being I have ever met - but in too much of a hurry, like a child who dibbles down flowers without a root...".[5] Her personal life has been criticised as well. Even before her involvement with politics, Markievicz left her daughter to be raised by her own mother and after her start of the political life her marriage broke up.[6]

A simplified picture of Markievicz is still often presented even today. Among the leading Irish figures of the first decades of the century, there is this one extremely militant woman, Constance Markievicz, steeped in her "bloodthirstiness", a person who "could not burn with an even light of steady endeavour, but flared out in a series of explosions..."[7] At the same time also the stories of her philanthropy and the respect and even love that people felt for her have also been constantly repeated as if in an attempt to balance her militant qualities by revealing a softer side. In this research the point of departure is to question the popular picture of her.

*   *   *

Constance Georgina Gore-Booth was born in London on February 4th 1868, the first child of a wealthy land-owning and Protestant family. Constance, born into the Victorian world and educated at home to fulfil the expectations society had of the Ascendancy girls – to learn music, poetry, sketching, languages and etiquette – spent most of her first 30 years in Lissadell, the great house of the Gore-Booths in Sligo, on the western coast of Ireland. Her ancestors on her father's side had come to Ireland at the end of the 16th century. Her mother was drawn from the English aristocracy.

---

2   O'Faolain, Sean, Constance Markievicz, London 1987 (1934), 78.
3   O'Faolain, 201-202.
4   Foster, R.F., W.B.Yeats: A Life. I. The Apprentice Mage 1865-1914, Oxford 1997, 384.
5   Mitchell, David, Women on the Warpath. The Story of the Women of the First World War, London 1966, 353-354.
6   In fact, Sean O'Faolain begins the foreword to his biography by comparing Markievicz's "ruinous personal relation with her own family, her husband and her only child, whom she virtually abandoned as a baby" to her declared love for all mankind in general. O'Faolain, Sean, Foreword to the 1967 edition, Constance Markievicz, 1987 (1934),7. In 1914 Casimir left for the Balkans as war correspondent and spent some time Kiev and Poland. He visited Dublin in summer 1924 and returned Dublin from Warsaw in 1927 to be by Constance's side in her death. About his activities at that time see MacWhite, Eoin, A Russian Pamphlet on Ireland by Count Markievicz, in *Irish University Review. A Journal of Irish Studies*, Vol. I, 1, Autumn 1970.
7   Mitchell, 349.

The Gore-Booths were known for their eccentricity [8] Otherwise, their way of living was no different from that of the usual Anglo-Irish upper class family. It consisted of visits to the Dublin Horse Show in the summer and in the winter season to the Viceregal Court. They lived in a fine Georgian house and indulged in shooting, fishing, riding and hunting, but rarely in reading.[9] In Markievicz's own words:

> "...Brought up in Ireland is an isolation that it is hard to understand to-day when bicycles and motor-cars annihilate even Irish miles. I met no people with ideas beyond our own happy little circle...Sport, art, and the doings of friends and relations were the interests of our elders, and consequently of our generation. An occasional visit to London - the centre of the Universe!-was the great excitement of our lives. To drive to Sligo, only 10 miles away, was an event..."[10]

Her closest relative was a younger sister, the poet Eva Gore-Booth (1870-1926), who at the turn of the century moved to Manchester to live and work together with Esther Roper for women's suffrage and to organise the women of the Labour movement. A hint of a boundary-breaking life was discernable in her youth. Not interested in marriage or studies, Markievicz strove to become an artist. In her diary there is an indication to find something to live and die for. At the same time, she was tormented with the fear of failure and feelings of having to choose between art and a more conventional life.[11] After finally getting her parents' permission, she studied first art in London and then in Paris from the year 1897 onwards. She wanted to become a great artist and wore a ring to demonstrate her marriage to her art.[12] In Paris, she met a Polish count, an artist and young widower, Casimir Dunin-Markievicz, whom she married in 1900.[13] Their only daughter Maeve was born in November 1901. A boy, Stanislaus Dunin-Markievicz, the child of Casimir's first marriage was also a member of the family. In 1903, Casimir, Constance and Stanislaus Markievicz moved to Dublin permanently.[14] From 1908 onwards, Constance's

---

8   About the Gore-Booths, see Farrell, Brian, Markievicz and the Women of the Revolution, in Martin, F.X. (ed.), Leaders and Men of the Easter Rising. Dublin 1916, London 1967, 230-231; Cowell, John, Sligo. Land of Yeats' Desire. It's history, literature, folklore and landscape, Dublin 1989; also Morrow, Ann, Picnic in a Foreign Land: The Eccentric Lives of the Anglo-Irish, London 1989. Constance's father was an amateur scientist and explorer of the Polar Cap, Van Voris, Jacqueline, Constance de Markievicz: In the Cause of Ireland, Vermont 1967, 20.

9   Lyons, F.S.L., Culture and Anarchy in Ireland 1890-1939, Oxford 1979,21.

10   Markievicz, Constance de, Memories -Mr.Arthur Griffith. The Sinn Fein Organisation, Eire,18.8.1923.

11   Markievicz, Count S., Memories of My Father, Irish Times, 9.1.21937 and 17.12 1937; extracts of her diaries in 1892-1893 in Marreco Anne, The Rebel Countess: The Life and Times of Countess Markievicz, London 1967, 41-54; Norman, Diana, Terrible Beauty. A Life of Constance Markievicz, Dublin 1987, 26-28; Haverty, 28; Hetmann, Frederik, Eine Schwierige Tochter, Köln 1987,46.

12   Marreco, 66; Ireland's Joan of Arc, The Literary Digest for July 15, 1916, New York.

13   As an artist he was more succesful than Constance, since he won a medal in Paris in 1905, O'Faolain, 38.

14   Van Voris, 50; Haverty, 55.

mother, then widowed, reared Maeve at Ardeevan in Sligo, where Constance occasionally visited.[15] In Dublin Markievicz couple joined the circles of the Irish cultural revivalists and there Constance Markievicz, then in her forties, discovered the cause of Ireland which became the focus of her life.

*   *   *

At the beginning of the century Ireland formed a part of the United Kingdom of Great Britain and Ireland. In 1801, Ireland had been joined to Britain by an Act of Union. Irish life and Irish history from the 1850s were transformed by the effects of the catastrophic Great Famine of 1845 to 1849, which was caused by the failure of the potato through blight. Around a million out of eight million people died and emigration on a very large scale followed. After the Famine the remaining population declined, leaving the rural landscape more and more characterised by deserted villages. Hand in hand with that development, the Irish language was driven out by the growth of the market economy, the transport revolution and by the Famine dislocations. Accompanying this process was the consolidation of the large or middle-sized farm. [16]

In political life, the British government attempted to find answers to "the Irish question" from the 1860s onwards with a series of political measures designed in large measure by Gladstone. In Ireland, Irish Catholic leaders blamed the Union for Ireland's economic difficulties, her poverty and famines. Between 1879 and 1882 there was a violent struggle between landlords and tenants led by the Land League, which was formed as a reaction to the worsening conditions experienced by the tenant-farmers during the agricultural depression of the late 1870s. The League started the process which eventually broke the power of the landed gentry in Irish social and economic life. Its President was Charles Stewart Parnell, whose Home Rule movement demanded Irish management of Irish affairs through an Irish parliament in Dublin and gained considerable electoral success in the 1880s. By the turn of the century, the Conservative Government's policy of killing Home Rule by kindness had produced the Local Government Act of 1898, and in 1903 a Land Purchase Act which allowed large-scale transfers of land ownership from landlord to tenant. However, problems and poverty remained and a large number of the transferred holdings proved uneconomic.[17]

Industrial development in Ireland occurred very unevenly. Ireland depended on the products that were exported to the British market which reinforced its industrial backwardness. Emigration continued to remove the surplus population. Dublin, the major administrative centre, was industrially relatively underdeveloped being concerned largely with processing the agricultural

---

15   After a visit form her mother, Maeve once said:"Well, that's over. She won't think of me for another year.", Coxhead, Elizabeth, Daughters of Erin, London 1965, 87.

16   See for instance Foster, R.F., Ascendancy and Union, in Foster, R.F. (ed.), The Oxford History of Ireland, Oxford 1989, 167-169.

17   Harkness, David, Ireland in the Twentieth Century. Divided Island, Houndmills 1996,7.

produce of its rural hinterland. Ulster, the northern province, had Ireland's highest average per capita income and produced the bulk of Ireland's manufactured goods. Belfast depended heavily upon three industries which were oriented towards the export trade: linen manufacture, engineering and shipbuilding.[18]

The political arena in Ireland at the beginning of the century was dominated by the moderately nationalist Irish Parliamentary Party (the IPP), which had grown out of the Home Rule League and which was led by John Redmond. At the turn of the century also the United Irish League, a new mass movement of the tenantry, which called for the redistribution of large estates, grew rapidly and became a part of the IPP. The victory of the Liberals who were for Home Rule, in the 1906 elections strengthened the position of the IPP in Parliament. Nonetheless, the road towards a greater autonomy was not without its problems. In spite of its continued alliance with the IPP the new government was far more concerned with other matters than with the Irish question and any new Home Rule Bill would most probably have been rejected in the Upper Chamber, the House of Lords. In addition to that, Northern Ireland Unionists strongly opposed the schemes for Home Rule. The party had problems of its own also. The IPP had at one and the same time to combine appearing reasonable in the British Parliament with satisfying its own voters in Ireland and maintaining its nationalist enthusiasm.[19]

The phase of Ireland's history during which Markievicz worked, was essentially dominated by the struggle for Home Rule and for independence and was always coloured with nationalism. Nationalism, as a political force, had been gaining ground in Europe from the 1870s, sustained by both social and political changes.[20] According to George Boyce, the chief charasteristics of nationalism in Ireland had been race, religion, and a strong sence of territorial unity and integrity; and in all its modes it had been profoundly influenced by the power and proximity of Britain. Roman Catholic Ireland constituted a self-conscious minority in the United Kingdom while Ireland in general had a tradition of separate parliamentary government, of her own constitution, of her own symbol of nationhood.[21]

---

18 Wardley, Peter, Edwardian Britain: Empire, Income and Political Discontent, in Johnson, Paul, 20th Century Britain. Economic, Social and Cultural Change, London 1994, 73.

19 Boyce , D.George, Nationalism in Ireland. (3rd edition), London 1995 (1982),269; Laffan, Michael, The Partition of Ireland 1911-1925, Dublin 1987, 14-15; Lyons, F.S.L., Ireland since the Famine, Glasgow 1973,260. The Irish Parliamentary Party had by then recovered from the split and confusion that had occured after the involvement of Charles Stewart Parnell (1846-1891), the charismatic leader of the party in a divorce case.

20 Hobsbawm, Eric, Nations and nationalism since 1780. Programme, myth, reality, 1991, 109-110. See also Gellner, who defines nationalism as a very distinctive species of patriotism, which becomes pervasive and dominant only under certain social conditions, conditions which in fact prevail only in the modern world, Gellner, Ernest, Nations and Nationalism, Oxford 1983, 138. Benedict Anderson lists the role of state, school-system, development of communications and the role of the intelligentsia as underlying factors influencing nationalism, Anderson, Benedict, Imagined Communities. reflections on the Origin and Spread of Nationalism. Rev. edition, London 1991 (1983), 140. He sees that in the background of nationalism lay "a new way of linking power and time meaningfully together" which entailed economic change, discoveries and improved communications, ibid., 36.

21 Boyce 1995,19,382-384.

At the beginning of the century, both the nationalist ideal – which required that a nation must have the right and the duty to improve its essential qualities including the national language, its folk-poetry, its folk-lore, national literature and national arts, the inherited judical institutions, ideas of education and old customs and manners – and the nationalist principle – according to which a nation must have the right to establish an independent state, if the nation in question has national consciousness and is mature enough –[22] were in a very lively way discussed in Ireland. In the Irish nationalist camp there were different opinions regarding independence; on the one hand there were the Home Rulers and on the other the absolute separatists, who were in the minority. Markievicz was active both in the period of transition, when she and her colleagues strove to spread national consciousness in order to achieve national autonomy and in the period when mass support was kindled, and when the differentiation between different political programmes deepened and became apparent[23], a development in which Markievicz played a major part.

Nationalism is one of the most ambiguous concepts in political thought. It has been quite correctly suggested that it would be more appropriate to speak of nationalisms in the plural than of nationalism in the singular, given that the term conceals within itself extreme opposites and contradictions, and has so many different variations in space and time.[24] In the Irish case, it has been pointed out that rather than representing nationalism as a "flat homogeneous whole" its varieties should be analysed.[25]

It is essential to recognise that nationalist ideas were not only discussed by and shaped the political parties but also influenced discussion in other movements such as the worker's and women's movements. In this work nationalism is not considered as a totally mechanical idea that was used either more or less consciously by the state authorities or as something that was

---

22 Kemiläinen, Aira, The Idea of Nationalism, *Scandinavian Journal of History* 1984, Vol. 9, No 1, 32-33.

23 In this the model of Miroslav Hroch, according to which nationalist movements in small European countries are analysed through three phases is followed. Hroch excluded Ireland from his treatment on Social Preconditions of National Revival in Europe, 1985, 194, n11. However, Alan O'Day has used his approach in his article. According to him, Ireland does not vitiate the model but suggests a less than neat picture, O'Day, Alan, Ireland's Catholics in the British State, 1850-1922, in Comparative Studies on Governments and Non-Dominant Ethnic Groups in Europe 1850-1940. Volume VI. Edited by Andreas Kappeler in collaboration with Fikret Adanir and Alan O'Day, Worcester 1992, 54. During the first phase, the activists showed a scholarly interest in the cultural, linguistic, social and sometimes historical characteristics of the non-dominant ethnic group, Brunn,Gerhard, Hroch, Miroslav, Kappeler, Andreas, Introduction, ibid, 7.

24 Alter, 2.; see also Kamenka, Eugene, Political Nationalism - The Evolution of the Idea, in Nationalism. The nature and evolution of an idea, Kamenka, Eugene (ed),London 1973, 3,18-20. Aira Kemiläinen has noted that the English word "nationalism" has often meant striving for an autonomous position or for an independent state and implies a struggle for national liberty, Kemiläinen 1984, 31. In her study, Liah Greenfeld suggests that apart from a national identity - an identity which derives from membership in a "people,"the fundamental characteristic of which is that it is defined as a "nation"- different nationalisms share little, Greenfeld, Liah, Nationalism. Five Roads to Modernity, Cambridge (MA)& London 1992, 7.

25 Maley, Willy, Varieties of Nationalism:Post-Revisionist Irish Studies, *Irish Studies Review*,no 15, 1996, 34-37.

somehow irrevocably due to different social and political factors[26], although the existence and impact of those factors as such is not questioned. Rather, nationalism is treated as an idea that was constructed and discussed among different people and groups and which linked on to other political ideas under discussion. Following the definition of Elie Kedourie, nationalism is taken to be a doctrine that holds that humanity is naturally divided into nations, that nations are known by certain characteristics that can be ascertained, and that the only legitimate type of government is national self-government.[27]

Previous research on Constance Markievicz

Historians, who have focused on Irish themes have in general regarded Markievicz as either a thoroughly studied subject – there is more than one biography of her – or as a person of minor importance, who does not need to be examined further. In the words of Sean O'Faolain written in the thirties, "Constance Markievicz, in her woman's way, had no intelligible ideas but many instincts."[28] That stereotyped picture of Markievicz has dominated the historiography. A rebellious and fascinating woman in the turmoil of Ireland's independence fight, she is constantly portrayed as an opportunist gunwoman, who changed her ideas according to whichever of male politicians she happened to become acquainted with. She has been described as a woman who brought "the spirit of the hunting-field" into Irish nationalist politics[29]; or as a "gallant creature" whatever her "fancies, follies and fanaticisms" were.[30] Not surprisingly, being a woman, she has been praised for her beauty in youth; yet political life and age turned her into "a haggard and witch-like creature"[31], a woman who looked older than she was.[32]

Her actions in public have been seen as mere play-acting. In the words of Sawyer, feminist militancy was to be immortalized in republican mythology by Countess Markievicz posing with her revolver.[33] Thus, it seems that her personality has in a way overshadowed her message and her doings. It has

---

26   As Stuart Woolf has observed, the interpretations in English-language historiography on nationalism has often been "reduced to an ideology of unusual efficacy, an instrument of political manipulation, increasingly associated with the Right", Woolf Stuart, Introduction in Woolf, Stuart (ed.), Nationalism in Europe. 1815 to the present. A reader, London 1996,6; also Ben-Israel, Hedva, From Ethnicity to Nationalism, in 18th International Congress of Historical Sciences from 27 August to 3 September. Proceedings, Montreal 1995,28.

27   Quoted in Hutchinson 1987, 10.

28   O'Faolain, 74.

29   "Her intellect was not great and her artistic talent was no better than second rate, but it was this spirit of the hunting-field, and a lonely wildness that endured beyond all the physical ravages of time, which she was to carry into Irish nationalist politics.", Kee, Robert, The Bold Fenian Men, London 1972, 161.

30   O'Faolain, 10.

31   According to the memoirs of Maurice Headlam, who described Markievicz "as having lost the looks which Yeats as a young man had so much admired..." White, Terence de Vere, Mahaffy, the Anglo-Irish Ascendancy, and the Vice-Regal Lodge, in Martin 1967, 23-24.

32   O'Faolain, 196.

33   Sawyer, Roger, 'We are but Women'. Women in Ireland's History, London 1993,72.

been argued that she was one of those who put into their love of Ireland obscure psychological motivations of their own.[34] Similar statements, blaming failure as an artist or unhappiness in private life, have also been made concerning many other agents in the national movement.[35]

However, it has been justly observed that nationalism, even for its critics, is clearly more than just cynical self-interest; that its advocates were also driven by a passion for social justice.[36] The cynical view is not as objective as it claims to be. Rather, it often relies on hindsight instead of an objective scrutinising of the reasons and ideas behind a person's policy.

The common picture of Markievicz as either a reckless and/or naive politician has also been a feature of the works of those historians who have sought to "demythologize" the Irish past during the period of independence struggle at the beginning of this century and who have criticised the nationalist historiography. [37] The revisionist trend in Irish historiography the aim of which is to explore the complexity and diversity of Irish society is understandable and correct. Yet it has not brought with it a balanced study of Markievicz and it will obviously have to wait its turn so long as the view of her assumes that before joining Fianna Fail Markievicz was simply a subscriber to the republican tradition which has caused the situation in Northern Ireland to deteriorate so alarmingly during the past two decades. It is quite obvious that not only her policy but also her sex have both been important factors in most assessments of her for female violence is often perceived as overpersonalized and vindicative.[38]

The first published biograpy of Markievicz by Sean O'Faolain was written in 1934. He had known her and uses many of the reminiscences of contemporaries.[39] In a quite patronising way O'Faolain presents Markievicz as a warm-hearted daydreamer, for whom political reality was a strange land,

---

34   Kee,160.
35   See arguments on Pearse etc. ; For a sociological explanation of nationalism as the creed of the displaced, frustrated sector of the native middle class, see Eagleton, Terry, Heathcliff and the Great Hunger: Studies in Irish Culture, London and New York 1995, 286. In 1960's Ernerst Gellner asserted that the national independence meant for intellectuals an immediate and enormous advantage, "jobs and very good jobs.", Gellner, Nationalism, in Thought and Change, London, 1964, in Hutchinson 1994, 63. Boyce has remarked that Anglo-Irish sought a role in Ireland that would guarantee them leadership of a Catholic nation, Boyce 1995,395.
36   Eagleton, 286.
37   About Irish historical revisionism see for instance Brady, Ciaran (ed.), Interpreting Irish History. The Debate on Historical Revisionism, Dublin 1994; Laffan Michael, Insular Attitudes: The Revisionists and Their Critics, in Mairin Ni Dhonnchadha and Theo Dorgan (eds.), Revising the Rising, Dublin 1991, 106-121; Nutt, Kathleen, Irish Identity and the Writing of History, Éire–Ireland, 3/1994, 160-172; Curtis, L.P., Jr., The Greening of Irish History, Éire–Ireland, 3/1994, 7-28.
38   See Bethke Elshtain, Joan, Women and War. With a New Epilogue, Chicago 1995 (1987), 169-170.
39   There is also a brief biography by Esther Roper , who knew her personally and whose reminiscences have provided subsequent biographers with plenty of material , in Prison Letters of Countess Markievicz. The book by German Friedrich Hetmann is a combination of fact and fiction. The works of Mary Moriarty and Catherine Sweeney, Markievicz : The Rebel Countess (Dublin 1991) and Eibhlin Ni Eireamnoin, Two Great Irishwomen: Maud Gonne and Constance Markievicz (Dublin 1972) were written for young readers .

and who took nationalist ideas too much in earnest. It took thirty years before the next two biographies by Jacqueline Van Voris and Anne Marreco appeared, probably inspired by the 50th anniversary of the Easter Rising. The work of Van Voris, which has used much of the available material has been a kind of a cornerstone for later writers. The second pair of biographies – those of Diana Norman and Anne Haverty – were published at almost the same time in the latter part of the 1980s. These works, albeit partly inspired by women's studies, do not stray far from the guidelines laid down by the preceding biographies. Norman, whose emphasis on the need to search for the "true character" of Markievicz is well taken, is, however, too bound up with her attempt to show that Markievicz was "one of the nicest human beings God ever made" and that "nearly all Constance's contemporaries loved her"[40] for her to concentrate on also analysing her ideas to the necessary extent. Furthermore, even though Norman rightly stresses that the political achievements of Markievicz have long been taken for granted[41], her own work – like that of Van Voris – starts by describing Markievicz " in action" in the Easter Rising,[42] implying that, after all, she is most interesting and important as a military figure.

Biographies of Markievicz are, surprisingnly, often centred around the same citations from the same sources and correspondingly exclude some aspects almost totally.[43] In the works relating to the women's movements at the beginning of the century Markievicz's action is examined almost exclusively in the context of those movements or contemporary women's life in general leaving her other spheres of action largely unexplored. [44] In a recent work concerning women in Irish history she is only briefly referred to and then examined in conjuction with another radical nationalist, Maud Gonne. [45] In addition to that, historians engaged in gender or women's history have been more interested in other questions rather than focusing on "one great woman" more closely. [46] Thus, in spite of being perhaps the first woman that comes to mind in relation to the independence struggle in Ireland, she is still left almost in a vacuum so far as research is concerned.[47]

---

40   Norman, 12, 13, 262.
41   Norman, 13 In the recent work dealing with the Irish socialist James Connolly Markievicz's election as an MP and as a minister are referred as personal achievements, Anderson, W.K., James Connolly and the Irish Left, Dublin 1994, 78.
42   See Norman, 15; Van Voris, 12.
43   One example: A sentence from Markievicz's "gardening notes" in *Bean na hEireann* 8/1909, in which she advices the good nationalist to " look upon slugs in the garden...as she looks on the English in Ireland and only regret that she cannot crush the Nation's enemies with the same ease that she can the garden's..." has been repeated from work to work. At the same time her other writings in *Bean na hEireann* have been given less attention., or left completely without analysis.
44   For instance Ward, Margaret, Unmanageable Revolutionaries, Dublin 1983; Cullen Owens, Rosemary, Smashing Times, Dublin 1990; the work of Liz Curtis, which pays attention to women, is not giving new aspects on Markievicz, see Curtis, Liz, The Cause of Ireland. From the Uniited Irishmen to Partition, Belfast 1994.
45   Sawyer, Roger, 'We are but Women'. Women in Ireland's History, London 1993.
46   See for instance Cullen 1985, "we need biographies which do not concentrate simply on women's contribution to male-defined movements and goals.", 192.
47   See Oikarinen, Sari, The Rebel Countess: Constance Markievicz, in Hannon, Philip & Gallagher, Jackie, Taking the Long View. 70 Years of Fianna Fail, Dublin 1996, 47-53.

The research task and sources

The purpose of this dissertation is to examine the ideas and activities of Markievicz within the context of Irish intellectual and political history during the first two decades of the century. As part of that task, the common image of Markievicz is also scrutinized. Markievicz's friend Hanna Sheehy- Skeffington described her as "...always interested in direct action of any sort against authority..."[48] . However, it is important to deal not only with the action but the thinking that lay behind it. What was her vision of the Irish past, present and future? And which methods did she think should be applied in order to achieve the independence of Ireland, that was her primary goal?

This research is not presented in the form of a traditional biography, and the focus will be on examining the political career of Markievicz, which shaped the last 20 years of her life. Only occasionally are her personal life and choices used to help demonstrate and illuminate her ideas concerning Irish politics. The methodological approach used is that of the history of ideas. As all human activity essentially contains thinking, to understand action entails understanding the thinking it encompasses. In this research, the method of question and answer has been employed. A text is seen as the answer of its writer to a problem that occupied his or her mind while he or she was writing the text.[49]

Markievicz incorporated different elements – from nationalism, feminism, socialism and the co-operative movement – into her ideas and action. She worked simultaneously in several organisations, whose means and ends in relation to the Irish question differed from those of each other. How did she understood the different ideas she adopted and worked with? Secondly, how did the different elements relate to each other? How did their importance vary in different situations and how did they develop in the course of time? An important part of the work will be concerned with asking how Markievicz understood the relationship and roles of the sexes not only in the struggle for independence, but also in the ideal society that was to be forthcoming. In that, gender is used as an analytical tool and is socially and politically defined.[50] The wide scope of Markievicz's activities offers also a means of exploring Irish political debate at that time. Through examining the problems and possibilities of an individual one not only studies the ideology of that person but also the discussions going on in society generally.

As Markievicz linked seemingly different aspects in her political agenda she was involved in the diverse problematics to be found within different sections

---

48   Hanna Sheehy Skeffington Papers, MS 24 189,NLI.

49   Hyrkkänen, Markku, Aatehistorian mieli, *Historiallinen Aikakauskirja* 4/1989,325,334. In the issue of question and answer he refers to the ideas of R.G.Collingwood and Hans-Georg Gadamer. See also Immonen, Kari, Metodikirja, Turku 1993 on Gadamer, 28.

50   Bethke Elshtain, Jean, Feminism and the Crisis of Contemporary Culture, in Melzer, Arthur M., Weinberger, Jerry and Zinman, M. Richard, History and the Idea of Progress, Ithaca and London 1995,197. Joan Scott has defined gender as an analytical category in the work of historian, see Scott, Joan W., Gender: A Useful Category of Historical Analysis. *The American Historical Review*, 5/1986, see also Scott, Joan W., Gender and the Politics of History, New York 1988, 42-46.

of Irish society regarding nationality, class and gender. The way in which she constructed her identity as an Irish person and as a woman, and also construed the British as "others", gives an insight into the complexities of Irish nationalism in that era. In the course of the research, an attempt was made to discern which were the elements that made Markievicz an "Irish Saint and Martyr."[51] In this context, her role and significance in the process of independence will be discussed.

Finally, even though Markievicz stoutly maintained that her ideas derived from ancient Irish past, she was undoubtedly a part of a European process. Therefore I will seek to indicate connections on a general European level in terms of the ideas of nationalism, feminism, socialism and the co-operative movement. In the case of feminism and socialism Markievicz was influenced by her sister, Eva Gore-Booth, who was much involved in the discussion of feminism and socialism among British intellectuals. Even though the close relationship between the two rebel sisters has been acknowledged in earlier works, the full significance of the impact of Eva Gore-Booth on Markievicz's political agenda has not yet been recognised. The connection with Britain, not only through her sister, but also on a wider scale, can be traced in other contexts also, for instance in discussions of female franchise. However, it is naturally important to study Markievicz's dialogue with and the thoughts of those individuals – mostly Irish – who pondered the same problems as she did. The most important of these was the socialist James Connolly, but one must also take into account the views of Arthur Griffith and Eamon de Valera, among others, in relation to those of Markievicz.

The structure of the thesis is chronological in a broad sense. However, to give a coherent picture of Markievicz's multifaceted activities, different themes are analysed in their own context, not in necessarily strict chronological order. The text is centred on situations which had an impact on Markievicz and which made her act and take a stand. The main sources are Markievicz's own writings, which include articles in newspapers and pamphlets. Her Prison Letters to her sister have been published and some of her letters are available in the National Library of Ireland as well as her prison notebooks in the National Museum of Ireland. The Dáil Eireann material, which consist of both printed proceedings and the files of Labour in the National Archives of Ireland, give information on her period as a Minister. In addition to that, Markievicz's speeches have been referred to in accounts in contemporary newspapers. The source material is quite diverse and contains only a small amount strictly personal material. Most of her own texts were written for public consumption and touch on current political questions.

---

51   Lily Yeats, sister of W.B. Yeats remarked in 1939 that "We are far more Irish than all the Saints and Martyrs -Parnell-Pearse-Madam Markiewicz-Maud Gonne -De Valera- and no-one ever thinks of speaking them as Anglo-Irish...", Foster 1997,5.

■ Markievicz joins the National Movement

The Irish Revival and the Gaelic League

When the Markievicz couple arrived in Dublin at the beginning of the century, the Irish Revival promoting Irish art, culture and language was flourishing in the city. According to a contemporary, everywhere little clubs were springing up for the study of the Irish language and of Irish history.[1] It was a time when Irishmen were "ceasing to be men and becoming movements."[2] In that respect, Irish revivalists were a part of a larger European discourse on cultural nationalism.[3]

The major movement channelling this enthusiasm was the Gaelic League, established in 1893. By 1904, there were some six hundred registered branches of the League throughout Ireland, and their efforts had ensured that the teaching of the native language was now ensconced in the national schools. As the first major urban-centred mass movement in the country, the League took an active interest in temperance, technical education and industrial reform. Moreover, it was to place its stamp on a whole future generation of political leaders.[4] The new movement was approved by many who did not want to participate in politics, although the ordinary people were more sceptical about its benefit to them.[5] The Gaelic League came out of a tradition of antiquarian research into Gaelic civilization, and was fundamentally similar to other nationalist movements in Europe dedicated to a rediscovery of the national past.[6]

The leader of the non-political Gaelic League was Douglas Hyde, who wanted to recreate a Gaelic speaking and de-anglicised Ireland. His opinion was that the Irish, once one of the most cultured nations in Europe were now one of the least so, and that this state of affairs had been brought about by anglicization. By giving up their native language and customs the Irish had thrown away the

---

1   Young, Ella, Flowering Dusk. New York 1945,70.
2   Gifford, Sydney, Countess de Markievicz, in Joy, Maurice (ed.), The Irish Rebellion of 1916 And Its martyrs: Erin's Tragic Easter, New York 1916, 345. These movements included for instance the Gaelic Athletic Association (established in 1884) which was formed for the preservation and cultivation of national pastimes, rapidly spreading throughout the country.
3   See e.g. Eagleton, 259-262; Hutchinson, John, The Dynamics of the Cultural Nationalism. The Gaelic Revival and the Creation of the Irish Nation State, London 1987, 197.
4   Mac Aodha, Brendan S., Was This a Social Revolution, in Ó Tuama, Sean (ed.), The Gaelic League Idea, Dublin 1972, 22; Eagleton, 263. By year 1913 it was a mass movement with 100, 000 members and 1000 branches, Garvin 1987, 79.
5   Ó Broin, Leon, Protestant Nationalists in Revolutionary Ireland: The Stopford Connection, Dublin 1985, 27-28.; Nowlan, Kevin B., The Gaelic League and Other National Movements, in Ó Tuama, Sean (ed.), 44.
6   Garvin 1987,79.

best claim they had upon the world's recognition as a separate nation. While they claimed to hate the English they imitated them in dress, literature, music, games and ideas. But at the bottom of the Irish heart lay the Gaelic past which prevented them from becoming citizens of the Empire. In order to de-anglicise themselves, the Irish would have to create a strong feeling against West-Britonism and arrest at once the decay of the language.[7]

The Irish revivalists had adopted the idea of language as a mark of nationality, deriving from the ideas of German romantic nationalism that had inspired Thomas Davis, one of the founders of the Young Ireland movement in the 1840s.[8] D.P. Moran, a colleague of Hyde, a journalist and Irish Revival activist, stressed the significance of the national language which separated Ireland from the rest of the world. However, Moran insisted that the Gaelic League was much more than a mere language or literary movement. In its propaganda it had a means of turning the mind of Ireland towards Ireland and making the people sober, moderate and masculine, thereby paving the way for industrial and economic reform. Moran designed a 'Buy Irish' campaign, which afforded voluntary protection to Irish industry. With him the Gaelic League created a great "do-it youself"-enthusiasm which urged the Irish to have self-respect and initiative, be self-criticial and self-reliant.[9] According to Moran, the Gaelic League would be the engine to remould the national character which "as much as an individual character, can be moulded and changed."[10]

Hence, Irish Irelandism fostered self-confidence and self-reliance and cultivated a pride in national distinctiveness. It was also the channel through which some of the cultural exclusiveness and determinism of the rest of Europe came to Ireland.[11] The writers and journalists in Dublin formed the new ideology through the cultivation of antithesis. They juxtaposed past and present, agrarian community and industrial collective, a small and moral state and a decadent imperium. For the man in the street the ideology became simply Ireland versus England.[12]

To present such a black and white picture of the situation was by no means uniquely Irish way of doing things. For instance in India, Indian nationalists argued in the late 19th century that in the spiritual domain the East was superior

---

7   McCartney, Donal, Hyde, D.P.Moran and Irish Ireland, in Martin 1967, 44. See also Ó Cuiv, Brian, The Gaelic Cultural Movements and the New Nationalism, in Nowlan, Kevin B., (ed.),The Making of 1916: Studies in the History of the Rising, Dublin 1969, 11. Whereas in the year 1845 half of the population spoke Gaelic, only six years later the percentage was 23 % of which only 5 % spoke only Irish, Lyons 1979, 8.
8   Boyce 1995, 155.
9   McCartney, 47-49.
10 Moran in Irish Ireland, 76-77, quoted in O'Callaghan, Margaret, Denis Patrick Moran and 'the Irish colonial condition', 1891-1921, in Boyce, D.George, Eccleshall, Robert and Geoghegan, Vincent (eds.), Political Thought in Ireland Since the Seventeenth Century, London and New York 1993,152-153.
11 McCartney, 52.
12 Thompson, William Irwin, The Imagination of an Insurrection: Dublin, Easter 1916, Massachusetts 1982 (1967), 58-59. See also Brunn, Gerhard, Historical Consciousness and Historical Myths, in Comparative Studies on Governments and Non-Dominant Ethnic Groups in Europe 1850-1940,335. About presenting alien culture as immoral, evil and dangerous, see Mosse, George L., Nationalism and Sexuality: Middle-Class Morality and Sexual Norms in Modern Europe, Wisconsin 1985.

to the West. European power had failed to colonize the inner, essential identity of the East which lay in its distinctive, and superior, spiritual culture.[13] The writers of the Gaelic Revival had a vision of a completely new Ireland, one that would reject the materialism of England, the commercial aspirations of a decadent empire, and cling instead to its spiritual past, to its small, integrated, agrarian communities and to its own language. According to the poet W.B. Yeats, one of the most prominent figures in the Irish revivial, Ireland would always be a country "where men plow and sow and reap, not a place where there are great wheels turning and great chimneys vomiting smoke." Its people would keep alive "the ideals of a great time when men sang the heroic life with drawn swords in their hands."[14]

Although the Gaelic League wanted to maintain its non-political image[15], its ideology encompassed significant potential political impact. Emphasizing a unique culture was a way to back up the political demands for greater autonomy, and ultimately for an independent nation-state. Moran declared that Ireland would be nothing until she was a nation, until she fell back upon her own language and traditions, recovered there her old pride, self-respect, and initiative, and developed and marched forward.[16] To march forward politically meant, for the mainstream of nationalists, self-determination. For some of the nationalists, it meant creating an independent nation-state.

Markievicz cherishes Irish Culture

Markievicz had been introduced to the Irish revival long before she moved to Dublin. She and her family had first beome acquainted with the young poet W.B. Yeats in 1892. After that, he visited Lissadell twice in 1894-1895. Later he sent Constance some books, one by Standish O'Grady,[17] whose History of Ireland retold the Irish heroic tales. Both sisters were excited by folklore and Yeats saw their enthusiasm as representative of a "nationalizing" of the "more thoughtful Unionists."[18] The Gore-Booth sisters and Yeats also shared an interest

---

13 Chatterjee, Partha, Colonialism, nationalism, and colonized women: the contest in India, *American Ethnologist* 1989, 622-633.

14 Kiberd, Declan, Inventing Irelands, *The Crane Bag*. Ireland:Dependence & Independence. Vol 8,no 1. Dublin 1984,11; Foster R.F., Paddy and Mr Punch. Connections in Irish and English History, London 1993, 29; O'Callaghan, 148, Yeats in 1904, quoted in Hall, Wayne E., Shadowy Heroes. Irish Literature of the 1890's. Syracuse 1980, 44; Yeats attacking English commercialism and vulgarity, Foster 1997, for instance 220,235. In the 1840, the Young Irelanders Thomas Davis described the Irish people as "pious, hospitable, and brave, faithful observers of family ties, cultivators of learning, music and poetry" - values jeopardized by materialist English values, Daly, Mary E., The Economic Ideals of Irish Nationalism: Frugal Comfort of Lavish Austerity?, *Éire-Ireland* 4/1994, 78.

15 Moran asserted that it was a great error to assume that nationality is politics and accused both constititutional leaders and the physical force men of hoodwinking the Irish people, Moran, D.P., The Battle of Two Civilizations, in Lady Gregory (ed.). The Ideals in Ireland, London 1901, 30-39.

16 Moran 1901, 30-39.

17 Kelly, John (ed.), The Collected Letters of W.B. Yeats. Volume One 1865-1895, Oxford 1986, 461; Foster 1997, 129, 144.

18 Foster 1997, 144.

in mysticism and spiritualism: in London Yeats had been taken to a spiritualist sèance by Constance, and he had arranged fortune-telling sessions for the sisters.[19] In 1916 he wrote to Eva: "Your sister [Constance] and yourself, two beautiful figures among the great trees of Lissadell, are among the dear memories of my youth."[20]

The writer, journalist and artist George Russell (AE) who was to be a friend of Constance Markievicz through all her Dublin years, was also an enthusiastic promoter of the Irish Revival. On the couple's arrival, he wrote: "...as they are both clever it will help to create an art atmosphere. We might get the material for a revolt, a new Irish Art Club."[21] The couple were indeed interested in creating "an art atmosphere." They established and later taught with AE and Yeats in the Dublin United Arts Club, which has been described as the meeting-place for the city's respectable bohemians.[22] In addition to painting, the couple were also interested in drama. Casimir wrote and directed plays in which Constance usually played the leading part and the couple was involved with the Theatre of Ireland, an explicitly nationalist company.[23] According to a contemporary, plays were the order of the day and everyone was trying to write them, because, as the historian Standish O'Grady declared, the drama could be a great agent of nationalist regeneration.[24]

Markievicz had chosen to contribute to the Irish Revival instead of favouring the high art of Europe. However, cherishing Irish culture in Dublin's artistic circles was not enough for Countess Markievicz. On the other hand, her involvement with nationalist politics started quite by chance. According to her own reminiscences she came across a bundle of nationalist-minded newspapers *The Peasant* and *Sinn Fein*. While reading about the speeches and death of Robert Emmet – whose face was familiar to her from cottage walls, and whom she had vaguely thought to have been a Fenian[25] – and about what a small group of people were now trying to do, she "like a flash" made up her mind to join them.[26] Reading Emmet seems to have affected Markievicz quite strongly;

---

19   Murphy, Daniel J. (ed.), Lady Gregory's Journals. Volume One. Books One to Twenty-Nine. New York 1978, 3.11.1924, 601; Foster 1997, 152. About the Anglo-Irish interest in occultism, Foster 1993, 220-222.

20   Roper, Esther, Biographical Introduction, in Poems of Eva Gore-Booth. Complete edition with The Inner Life of a Child and Letters, London 1929, 7.

21   AE to Sarah Purser 5.3. 1902, Danson, Alan (ed.), Letters from AE., London 1961, 39.

22   Dickinson, 67; Czira, Sydney, The Years Flew By, Dublin 1974, 15; Foster 1997, 383.

23   The Gore-Booth family had a tradition of play-acting, Van Voris, 27; Foster 1997, 344, 404. In August 1909 Constance was elected a vice-president of the Theatre of Ireland, Van Voris, 66.

24   Young 1945, 72.

25   Markievicz, Constance de, Memories -Mr. Arthur Griffith. The Sinn Fein Organisation, *Eire*, 18.8.1923. Robert Emmet has always had an importance in the Irish imagination far in excess of his actual contribution to Irish history. He was so popular with the people that at the time Markievicz started her political career a typical Irish home of would be furnished with pictures of Robert Emmet and Pius X on the walls, Hawkins, Maureen S.G., The Dramatic Treatment of Robert Emmet and Sarah Curran, in Gallagher, S.F., 1983, 125. Robert Emmet (1778–1803) was known from his abortive rebellion against the British in 1803. His speech from the dock was an inspiration to later nationalists. On another occasion Markievicz also notes the part played by getting to know people in Dublin as to her 'awakening', see her speech in Sligo 24.7.1917, Van Voris, 236.

26   Markievicz, Constance de, Memories -Mr. Arthur Griffith. The Sinn Fein Organisation, *Eire*, 18.8.1923.

later she recalled the first time she had read his famous speech from the dock.[27] Her sudden conversion resembled the way in which Standish O'Grady describes the awakening of his own interests; how he on a rainy day happened to pick up a book in which he first came across the heroes of Irish history.[28] However, to portray her decision to join Sinn Fein as a sudden and dramatic act may simply be a way of romanticising her involvement with the nationalist movement. At that point Markievicz, who had spent her childhood in West of Ireland, was already familiar with the Irish history and legends, that were now on everybody's lips. Since her earliest days, she had listened to the story of how the Irish people had been persecuted.[29] In Dublin, she was constantly with people who strove to recreate the Irish national culture and her friends were among the central figures of the Irish Revival and the Gaelic League. That background, together with her courage in trying new things, had prepared her to take one further step and to forsake her previous life for a new one.

Markievicz and Sinn Fein

One night at AE's house Markievicz expressed her interest in being involved to Arthur Griffith, the leader of a small new separatist party Sinn Fein. She did not get a warm reception, possibly because Griffith assumed that she was an English agent spying on his organisation. Other separatist activists also shared his suspicions. However, a meeting with Bulmer Hobson, who was on the Executive of Sinn Fein at the time and, according to Markievicz, "the leader of the opposition", proved more fruitful. Hobson launched Markievicz as a member of the Sinn Fein organisation.[30] In March 1908 she is mentioned as being among the members of Sinn Fein at a nationalist rally in Dublin.[31] The next year Hobson arranged for Markievicz to become a member of the Drumcondra branch of the party.[32] She took the task of spreading the ideas of Sinn Fein seriously and was soon known for her radical speeches and enthusiasm.[33] In the summer of 1909 she began to campaign actively[34] and at the annual meeting of the party she rose from the rank and file to become a decisionmaker when she was elected to the Sinn Fein Executive, "much to the annoyance of Mr.Griffith."[35]

27 Markievicz, Dáil Eireann. Dáil Eireann. Debate on the Treaty between Great Britain and Ireland signed in London on 6th December 1921, Dublin 1922, 185.

28 Foster, Roy, A.M.Sullivan- The Story of Ireland, *Times Literary Supplement*, 16.12.1994.

29 Markievicz, Constance, typescript, P 5482, NLI; Markievicz, Constance de, Memories, Mr. Griffith, *Eire*, 25.8.1923.

30 Markievicz, Constance de,Memories -Mr.Arthur Griffith. The Sinn Fein Organisation, *Eire*, 18.8.1923. O'Faolain mentions that Griffith had advised Markievicz to join the Gaelic League, O'Faolain, 78. However, she does not mention that herself nor are there any indications of her active participation in the work of the Gaelic League.

31 *Sinn Fein*, 28.3.1908.

32 Markievicz, Constance de,Memories -Mr.Arthur Griffith. The Sinn Fein Organisation, *Eire*, 18.8.1923.

33 Cronin, Sean, McGarrity Papers, Tralee 1972,25-26; Ryan, 81-82.

34 She gave speeches under the auspices of Sinn Fein; *Sinn Fein*, 19.6.; 24.7.; 31.7.1909.

35 *Sinn Fein*, 3.9.1909; Markievicz, Constance de,Memories -Mr.Arthur Griffith. The Sinn Fein Organisation, *Eire*, 18.8.1923.

Sinn Fein embraced the idea of a modern nation: each national group should be master of its own destiny and its public life should express its unique culture.[36] The primary principle of Sinn Fein upheld the ideal of the Gaelic League of forging the future by personal action, of achieving by doing.[37] Arthur Griffith emphasized the Gaelic cultural tradition because it was part of a wider idea of self-sufficiency, a barrier to anglicization, a defence against a physically stronger neighbour and a guarantee of Ireland's place in the world. However, the significance of the ideas behind Sinn Fein did not lie in their political aspirations, but in their attempt to give substance to Irish nationalism, to supply it with a cultural and economic programme, and give it a purpose and a meaning for the time when freedom was finally achieved. Griffith, valuing the protectionist ideas of the German Friedrich List, did not dream of Ireland as a kind of rural arcadia in a modern industrial world; for, he believed, not only Irish literature and language, but also Irish industries must be protected and secured if the nation were to be saved. A merely agricultural country could not develop the commerce necessary for the nation's well-being, and tariff barriers and protection and prosperous home industries were as much part of the nation's needs as art and literature.[38] Economic independence was for him the most important form of national independence.[39]

Instead of seeking the Home Rule that was striven for by the Irish Parliamentry Party, Griffith upheld the idea of an independent Irish parliament as part of a Union linked under one King, an idea which in Irish history had most closely been achieved during the time of the independence of the Irish Parliament, the "Grattan parliament" of 1782-1800. As an alternative to both the politics of the Irish Parlimentary Party and of revolutionary politics, Griffith presented the "Hungarian policy"[40] which in the Irish case meant that the Irish should withdraw from Westminster and create their own national parliament.[41]

When Markievicz joined Sinn Fein in 1908 the goal of the party was to create "a prosperous, virile and independent nation."[42] Its practical objectives included among others

-protection for industry and commerce
-the establishment of a national bank, a national stock exchange, and a national system of insurance
-the setting up of national arbitration courts and of a national civil service
-the institution of national control over transport, waste lands and fisheries
-the reform of education and of the poor laws

---

36   Hutchinson 1987, 3.
37   About Sinn Fein, see Mitchell 1995, 341.
38   Boyce 1995, 295-296; Lyons 1973, 253-254.
39   MacDonagh, Oliver, States of Mind: A Study of Anglo-Irish conflict 1780-1980, London etc. 1984, 64; Boyce, 296. Ireland was undoubtedly dependent on England economically, for instance Eagleton, 65.
40   Lyons 1973, 251-252; Davis, Richard P., Arthur Griffith and Non-Violent Sinn Fein, Tralee 1974, 32.
41   In the year 1867 the Hungarians had won autonomy through passive resistance, by rejecting all parliamentarian and other co-operation with Austria, Davis, 23.
42   Davis, 35.

-the prosecution of a policy of non-cunsumption of articles paying duty to
the British Exchequer
-the withdrawal of all voluntary support for the British armed forces
-the non-recognition of the British parliament

In the short term, to bring about these goals, locally elected bodies and especially
the county councils had a leading part to play.[43]

In terms of economic policies the views of the two leaders of Sinn Fein, the
more radical Hobson and more moderate Griffith were similar: boycotting
British manufactures would strengthen Irish industries and shake the British
dominance in that respect. According to Hobson, "defensive warfare" preceded
every real independence movement. It aimed at making the British government
impossible by ceasing to send men to Westminster, ceasing to use British
manufactures, ceasing to invest money in British commerce, or ceasing to pay
those taxes which were paid voluntarily.[44]

Markievicz accepted the Sinn Fein policy of passive resistance. She remarked
that if Irish people were united in their determination not to obey English-
made laws or pay English imported taxes, and to make Ireland a great country
as well as in their determination to govern their own country, then nothing
could stop them.[45] Sharing the perception of the Irish revivalists, Markievicz
feared that the national distinctiveness which made the Irish nation unique in
the world, was now threatened because of British influence, an influence
responsible for all the hardships Ireland had faced in the past from overtaxation
to the killing of the Irish language and from famine to emigration. By portraying
modern inventions – trains, the penny post, the telegraph system, the daily
papers – as helpers in giving Britain more power over the Irish,[46] Markievicz
defined the nationalist struggle as a struggle between the modern and the
traditional.

Saving the soul of the nation

To Markievicz's way of thinking, a nationalist agenda was needed because
Ireland was not free, but enslaved. Markievicz highlighted her view by quoting
her sister Eva in her first published article in January 1909: "I know that Liberty
is best, and no man sadder than a slave."[47] According to Markievicz, Ireland's
soul had been born free, and her body must be freed too.[48]

Markievicz shared the romantic nationalist vision of the national soul; she
wrote that "each one of us has a soul, an Irish soul, a tiny atom of the great

43 Lyons 1973, 256-257; See MacDonagh 1983, 62.
44 Hobson, Bulmer, Defensive Warfare, Belfast 1909, 16-19.
45 Maca, Free Woman in a Free Nation, *Bean na hEireann*, January 1909.
46 Markievicz 1909, 2,7,12.
47 Maca, Free Woman in a Free Nation, *Bean na hEireann*, January 1909.
48 Markievicz 1909, 15.

national soul of Ireland"[49] , mirroring Ernst Renan's conception of nation as a "soul, a spiritual principle."[50] She embraced the idea of cultural nationalism, where a nation was not founded merely on consent or law but on the passions implanted by nature and history.[51] Following the ideas expressed by Rousseau and Herder, who argued that climate had a constitutive impact on culture and character[52] , Markievicz articulated the intertwining of Irish nature, history and soul in a romantic vein:

> "somehow, in the hour of twilight the dividing lines that one imagines between oneself and Nature seem to melt away. One feels one with -or rather an indissoluble atom of Nature - of Life and Death. Barriers slip away, and as a breath of blue air is to eternity so one's soul seems to be the great soul of the universe...We have but scanty records of the brave deaths men have died for Ireland, but this we know: every hillside, every valley, each cornfield, and grazing ranch, every potato patch, bog, town, or lonely cottage has its own story to tell us, a story of oppression and murder, tyranny and starvation, met with self-sacrifice and martyrdom, and what our July garden with its roses should remind us of is that it is we who must live so that our martyrs' blood shall not have been shed in vain..."[53]

Her language was not exceptional in terms of Irish nationalist rhetoric, which sought to find justification for their political behaviour in Ireland's past. Only very rarely were fundamental or abstract rights emphasized; it has been argued that "nationalism in Ireland has been reared less on the rights of men than on historical wrongs."[54]

Behind Markievicz's message adopts the view of Irish history as a passage through sorrows and triumphs, then being presented by the nationalist-minded historians. The nationalist lesson of Irish history exposed English vices and Irish virtues.[55] The English vices brought up the subject of Irish martyrs: Irish historian Alice Stopford Green dedicated her book on Irish Nationality in 1911, "In memory of the Irish Dead."[56] On the other hand, history also offered a chance to be proud of one's Irishness. Historian and Gaelic League activist Eoin MacNeill described Ireland as an ultimately democractic nation, whose Middle Age was a Golden Age of the past.[57] For Stopford Green pre-invasion

---

49   Markievicz 1909, 15. Also Arthur Griffith pointed out that every Irish man or woman's own self was the Irish nation, in R.U. Floinn, The Ethics of Sinn Fein, Pamphlet, n.d., 4 .
50   Renan, Ernest, Qu'est-ce qu'une nation?, in Hutchinson, John and Smith, Anthony D. (eds.), Nationalism, Oxford 1994, 17.
51   Hutchinson 1987, 13.
52   Anderson, Benedict, Creole Pioneers of Nationalism, in Hutchinson 1994, 202.
53   Armid, The Woman with a Garden, Bean na hEireann, 9/1909; See also Love of Country. Extracts from a lecture by Constance de Markievicz, Bean na hEireann, 20/1910 (July).
54   Boyce 1995, 20. The essence of Irish nationalism reminds one of Ernest Renan's explanation that national sorrows are more significant than triumphs because they impose obligations and demand a common effort; and that a nation is a grand solidarity constituted by the sentiment of sacrifices which one has made and those that one is disposed to make again. Renan, Ernest, Qu'est-ce qu'une nation?, in Hutchinson 1994, 17.
55   Like A.M.Sullivan in his popular The Story of Ireland, first published in 1867, Boyce 1995, 246-247.
56   Green, Alice Stopford, Irish Nationality, London and New York, 1911.
57   Hutchinson 1987, 123-125. About the universality of the vision of a past Golden Age, Garvin 1987, 162. About the democratic nature of Irish history, see also Green 1911, 28

Ireland was a classless, egalitarian "commonwealth", where "the earliest and the most passionate conception of 'nationality' flourished."[58] According to her, Irish history could only be understood by realising "this intense national life with its sure basis in the broad self-government of the people."[59]

For Gaelic Leaguers the past also gave a vision of the future: Moran and Hyde insisted that the only true basis of the nation was the remote Gaelic past. [60] AE explained that the Irish were asking for the liberty to reshape the social order in Ireland so as to reflect "our own ideals, and to embody that national soul which has been slowly incarnating in our race from its cloudy dawn." The form of government might be a good one, but that was irrelevant, because it was not the expression of Irish national life and ideas.[61]

Looking for inspiration from the remote past of the nation equally inspired nationalists outside Ireland. The "golden age" was not usually in the disagreeable recent past, but in a more remote period, and it could be recovered only by historical research and interpretation.[62] For instance, in the nineteenth century, the nationalist movement in Finland strove to construct a Finnish identity through national myths and even fiction based on the glorious past of an ancient society consisting of tribes.[63] The Czech historian and nationalist Palacky saw Czech history as a centuries-long conflict with the Germans. He recovered the Czech past virtually single-handed and hoped that his history would help restore a keen sense of national identity which was, in turn, a necessary condition for the reassertion of Czech rights.[64] Thus, consciousness of history was an important part in building up ethnic identity.[65]

However, demanding national rights was not so simple at a time when the people had still not all awoken to the importance of a united nationalist struggle. Markievicz accused England of conceding rights in a way that had helped to split the Irish into divisions and sub-divisions; the schools had concentrated on developing strong sectarian feelings in the children, instead of the broader creed of nationalism.[66] In this respect she clearly echoed the themes and aims of Irish nationalist Wolfe Tone: Ireland should be unified; the divisions between the Catholic masses, the Anglo-Irish or the Ulster Unionists were ultimately irrelevant. What in her opinion mattered was that everyone should join the movement and find the position their capabilities entailed; their "place in the nation", whether as "leader or a humble follower."[67] With some concern

---

58   Green in her A History of the Irish State to 1014, chapter 6, quoted in Foster 1993, 14.
59   Green 1911, 15.
60   McCartney,49.
61   AE, Nationality and Imperialism, in Lady Gregory (ed.), Ideals in Ireland, London 190, 17-18.
62   Matossian, Mary, Ideologies of Delayed Development, in Huthcinson 1994, 221-222.
63   See for instance Sihvo, Hannes, Suomalaisuuden pyhä tuli, in Tommila, Päiviö, Herää Suomi. Suomalaisuuliikkeen historia, Jyväskylä 1989, 351-352.
64   Breuilly, 107, Brunn, 334; Tosh, John, The Pursuit of History. Aims, Methods & New Directions in the Study of Modern History (2nd edition), London & New York, 1991 (1984), 3.
65   Brunn, 327; Hutchinson 1987, 29.
66   Markievicz 1909, 7.
67   Markievicz 1909,12. Theobald Wolfe Tone (1763–1798) is the recognised founder of Irish republican nationalism.

Markievicz noted that in history one learned that at the most important moments Irish patriots had allowed themselves to be drawn into faction fights to the derriment of the great national struggle. She maintained that affiliation with English Trade Unions or political parties caused "us to forget the hatred we should feel towards our country's enemies."[68] Instead, she advised Irish women to join those clubs which everyone in spite of their religious, class or political differences could join: Sinn Fein and the Irish Industrial Development Associations.[69] The historian Alice Stopford Green gave similar advice: now, as ever, the traditions of the national life could provide a link of fellowship between all classes, races and religions.[70]

The ideal of national unity had become particularly important in Ireland during the latter part of the 1890's after the death of Parnell whose fare had led to divisions within the IPP.[71] But the need for unity was not perceived only because of that; as George Boyce has remarked, Irish nationalists were obliged to search for a common denominator, a unifying principle or set of principles.[72] The Young Irelander Thomas Davis sought for the brotherhood of all Irishmen in the common cause, nationalism. To reconcile his own English-speaking Protestant background with his aims, he evolved the idea of the essential unity of all Irishmen, of whatever creed, race or class they might be. Davis arrived at the conclusion that Irishness was the product, not of race, but of environment; and that only by accepting that uniqueness of the Irishman was the product of the uniqueness of Ireland herself could a truly united nation be created.[73] In a similar way, the historian Alice Stopford Green noted that the real significance of Irish history lay the idea of a society bound together in a spiritual union. [74] In the same way, Markievicz aimed at nation-building; she urged the people to integrate and harmonise divided sections of the people. [75]

Forward to the armed rebellion

The idea of passive resistance was accepted by radicals and moderates in Sinn Fein, but their views differed on the question of what would happen after the British government had been demoralized. Radicals supported the establishment of a republic by violent uprising; while moderates sought autonomy achieved through negotiation.[76] Many republicans felt that the Sinn Fein policies were

---

68   Maca, Free Woman in a Free Nation, *Bean na hEireann*, January 1909.
69   Markievicz 1909, 9.
70   Green 1911, 254.
71   Hall, 28-29, 40.
72   Boyce 1995, 21.
73   Boyce 1995, 155-158. Davis had called all to respond to "a Nationality of the spirit as well as the letter...which may ambrace Protestant, Catholic and Dissenter - Milesian and Cromwellian - the Irishman of a hundred generations and the stranger who is within our gates...", C Gavan Duffy, Thomas Davis:A Memoir, London 1895,66, quoted in Harkness 1996, 13.
74   Green 1911, 20.
75   About the aim of nation-building, Alter, 14.
76   Davis, 149.

not advanced enough.[77] In Sinn Fein the division between moderate and extreme nationalists caused tension. In private discussions Griffith pointed out that the majority of the Irish people were not separatist and would not support any policy striving for separation.[78] Also, even though Griffith did not oppose force in principle, he preferred civil disobedience and non-violence.[79]

Markievicz usually supported suggestions put forward by Hobson which were "much more revolutionary than those advocated by Mr. Griffith." Obviously Hobson evaluated Markievicz as a potentially important ally, because he, together with his friends Patrick MacCartan and Sean McGarry, took Markievicz under their wing and educated her, "giving me books on Ireland to read, and explaining to me all the intricacies of such simple things as organisations and committees."[80]

The guidance that Markievicz got from these radical young men, was essentially that of republican nationalism. She had grasped the idea of a national struggle from the writings of Wolfe Tone, Mitchel, and Lalor; they "were the gospel ...it was they who made me realise at the beginning of my work that the only freedom worth having was the freedom to root out the foreign civilisation with all its cruel and material ideals, and to build up a noble civilisation on Gaelic lines." What most significantly separated Griffith from Hobson in the view of Markievicz was that "his policy did not include the use of physical force."[81] Hobson, the mentor of Markievicz, cherished the ideas of Wolfe Tone and Lalor and his guiding line was a celebrated passage from the former:

> "To subvert the tyranny of our execrable government, to break the connection with England, the never failing source of all our political evils, and to assert the independence of my country. These were my objects. To unite the whole people of Ireland. To abolish the memory of all past dissensions and to substitute the common name of Irishman in place of the denomination as Protestant, Catholic and Dissenter -these were my means."[82]

Wolfe Tone, Mitchel and Lalor were all the apostles of extreme nationalism whose importance for their followers lay first and foremost in their attempts at a rising to separate Ireland from Britain. The idea of an armed uprising was at the core of the Irish Republican Brotherhood (IRB), a nationalist secret society whose aim was to establish a Republic of Ireland and whose members included the most influential radicals of the Gaelic League and Sinn Fein.[83] To put it simply, in Ireland republicanism meant that only physical force could change the minds of the British so far as the Irish question was concerned. [84] This

---

77   Nowlan, Kevin B., Tom Clarke, MacDermott, and the I.R.B., in Martin 1967,113.
78   Davis, 31.
79   Boyce 1995, 298.
80   Markievicz, Constance de,Memories -Mr.Arthur Griffith. The Sinn Fein Organisation, *Eire*, 18.8.1923.
81   Markievicz, Constance de, Memories, Mr. Griffith, *Eire*, 25.8.1923.
82   Hobson, Bulmer, Ireland Yesterday and Tomorrow, Tralee 1968, 2-3.
83   Ó Cuiv, 24.
84   Cronin, Sean, Irish Nationalism. A History of Its Roots and Ideology, Dublin 1980,1.

physical force tradition acquired once more a kind of hidden strength in the early part of the twentieth century. This was partly because a group of young members of the IRB – among them Hobson – came to the fore alongside a representative of an older generation, Thomas Clarke, a Fenian who had been a prisoner for 15 years and who had now returned from America.[85] For Markievicz a meeting with Clarke was a memorable event; he was the "link and the living inspiration" between the dead Fenians and the young."[86]

Markievicz had chosen the side that ultimately supported the idea of an armed insurrection. She embraced the 19th century nationalist view of war as an essential in the building of a nation. From the very beginning the principle of nationalism was almost indissolubly linked, both in theory and practice, with this idea of war. It was assumed that mere existence did not entitle a people to political independence; only the use of force to assert itself as a state among equals.[87] According to Hegel, just as the individual emerged to self-conscious identity only through a struggle, so each state must struggle to attain recognition. That state was free which could defend itself, gain the recognition of others, and share an acknowledged identity. It was in war that the strength of the state was tested, and only through that test could it be shown whether individuals were capable of overcoming selfishness and were prepared to work for the whole nation and to sacrifice themselves in the service of the most inclusive good.[88] Nineteenth-and twentieth-century national revolutions often turned to the cult of human sacrifice; the nation, it was believed, could not be born without blood and suffering.[89]

This belief that rebellion and revolution finally meant sacrifice, was evident in Markievicz's writings from the very beginning. In March 1909 she pointed out that "as the death of Christ brought a new hope and a new life to an old world, so the blood of each martyr shed in the cause of liberty will give a new impetus to the comrades who are left behind to continue the work." She maintained that Christianity and other religions which had succeeded, had done so through their ideals, for which men and women were not afraid to die. No physical force could bind forever a free-souled and steadfast people.[90] For Markievicz, the essential characteristics of Ireland, known through the world, were to be found in the great legacy of her martyrs, in tales of noble deeds, of fearless deaths, of lives of self-denial and renunciation.[91] Markievicz remarked that in every action in life it was the idea behind it that counted. The ideal, the

---

85   Coogan 1994, 43; The young men, organised in Dungannon clubs, strove to prevent their countrymen from joining the British Army and printed separatist literature, Hobson 1968, 22-23. They urged people to organise and prepare for a new, equal and independent Ireland, see Hobson, Bulmer, To the Whole People of Ireland: The Manifesto of the Dungannon Club, Belfast 1905, NLI.

86   Markievicz, Constance de, Tom Clarke and the First Day of the Republic: A Memory, *Eire*, 26.5.1923.

87   Howard, Michael, War and Nations, in Hutchinson 1994, 254-255.

88   Bethke Elshtain 1995, 75.

89   O'Neil, Daniel, The Cult of Self-Sacrifice: The Irish Experience, *Èire-Ireland*, Winter 1989, 92-93.

90   Markievicz 1909, 2, 15.

91   Markievicz 1909, 16, see also her Irishwomen and the Suffrage, *Sinn Fein*, 27.3.1909.

spirit of self-sacrifice and love of country, had to lie behind any striving for commercial prosperity, sex emancipation, and other practical reforms.[92] Her description of the Irish national heroes as "our martyrs and saints" [93] gave evidence of her commitment to the Irish nationalist idea. For Markievicz, that commitment meant turning her back on her own class.

The problems and possibilites of an Anglo-Irish background

Remembering her childhood and youth in Sligo, Markievicz criticised her family for their ignorance concerning politics and history. She declared that she had been brought up in isolation, meeting no people with ideas:

> "...no one was interested in politics or economics... Every one accepted the Status quo... it was absurd to try and to alter it, for that led nowhere and only made trouble. It was unlucky that landlords had been so bad, for if only they had done what they ought, everything would have been all right now...Irish history was also taboo, for "what is the good of brooding over past grievances?"...Growing children take their ideas from the people around them...hence... [o]ne took the conquest as a *fait accompli* and as irrevocable and believed that "things weren't too bad nowadays." One knew no history, one realised none of the resposibilities that one had inherited. Thus it was with me..."[94]

In fact the influence of her background on her later political career was not as irrelevant as she wished to pretend. In fact her family had a good reputation as enlightened landlords, who helped their tenants during the famine of 1879.[95] Yeats described her family as "ever ready to take up new ideas and new things."[96] Markievicz's eldest brother Josslyn Gore-Booth introduced co-operative pracitices to Sligo and became the first landlord in Ireland to sell his estate to his tenants after the 1903 Land Act as an act of principle.[97] As a child, together with her sister Eva, Markievicz grew up on terms of intimacy and friendliness with the country people.[98] That her parents believed "in the mission of the aristocrat...(and) saw themselves as leaders, builders, reformers", has been interpreted as having a marked effect on the life of Markievicz.[99]

---

92   Markievicz 1909, 15.
93   Irishwomen and the Suffrage, *Sinn Fein*, 27.3.1909.
94   Markievicz, Constance de,Memories -Mr.Arthur Griffith. The Sinn Fein Organisation, *Eire*, 18.8.1923.
95   See Roper, Biographical Sketch, in Prison Letters, 1; Sawyer, 29-30; Van Voris, 23; Haverty, 15.
96   Foster 1997, 144.
97   Lewis, 10. Markievicz, Constance de, Memories. Mr. Griffith, *Eire,* 25.8.1923.
98   Stories about her childhood and youth; how she during the land troubles had advised tenants to refuse payment to her own father or how she and Eva had secretly ridden to listen to Parnell, in Ireland's Joan of Arc, *The Literary Digest for July 15*, 1916,148; Roper 1934, 1,3.
99   Gifford, 343.

Thus, Markievicz was in her own way carrying on an enlightened landlord tradition, albeit more radically. Moreover, that no-one of her background knew Irish history, was not a completely correct statement. To a woman who had spent her childhood in the West of Ireland — quite near to where the stories placed the burial-place of the ancient High Queen Maeve[100]— Irish history and legends were certainly familiar. However, it is true that a large proportion of the Anglo-Irish gentry in the nineteenth century lived in a sealed, satisfied world. [101] The Anglo-Irish in Sligo were not too enthusiastic about cherishing the Irish heritage[102] and the Gore-Booth family seem to have been no exception to this. However, with the rise of nationalism in the nineteenth century, the Anglo-Irish found themselves shut out from what might otherwise have seemed their natural role in Irish politics.[103]

As a child Markievicz had wanted to revolt against home discipline.[104] To pursue the career of an artist was in a way a rejection of an upper-class lifestyle. Nevertheless, in Dublin the Markievicz couple had remained part of the viceregal Castle society, which consisted of land-owning officials and military.[105] Artistic aspirations and friendships had not jeopardised her involvement with "high society". However, joining Sinn Fein now meant the end of that life. Her personal choice, particularly because of its uncompromising nature, was a clear statement of opposition to the ignorance and policies of her own class, who were often seen in a very negative light by nationalists.[106] She claimed that her activities were "only a small atonement for her ancestors' sins in plundering the Irish people."[107] Apparently Markievicz regarded her development with pride: later she wrote that people, with only rare exceptions, discarded their earlier ideas or beliefs, once they had reached maturity.[108]

Markievicz's transformation from a high society lady and a bohemian painter to a politician was, looked at from the outside, quite swift and complete. In her speeches Markievicz portrayed herself from the very beginning as one of the Irish, who opposed the conqueror. How great a change this was, is partly seen in the reaction of Griffith and others, who were at first suspicious of her new stance. For Desmond Ryan, a contemporary nationalist, she seemed to be unconvincing in her "blood-thirsty sentiments", even though he admitted that

---

100   Roper 1929, 5.
101   Lewis, 15.
102   According to Yeats, everyone he knew well in Sligo despised nationalism and catholics, but, on the other hand, all disliked England with a prejudice that had come down perhaps from the days of the Irish Parliament. Also his nurses never spoke well of any Englishman, Yeats, William Butler, The Autobiography. Consisting of Reveries Over Childhood and Youth . The Trembling of the Veil and Dramatic Personae, New York 1953, 20-21.
103   Lyons 1979, 21.
104   Comerford, Maire, Women in the Irish Struggle, *The Irish Democrat*, May 1968, Maire Comerford Papers, MS. 24 896, NLI.
105   Cullen 1968, 170; O'Faolain, 48.
106   For instance Standish O'Grady damned the landlords for squandering their wealth, power, prestige and traditional heritage and claimed that in their "cowardly dependence on England, they had turned weak, selfish, and downright rotten."Hall, 30; about O'Grady's criticism, also Eagleton, 101-102.
107   Ryan, Desmond, Remembering Sion. A Chronicle of Storm and Quiet, Edinburgh 1934, 82.
108   C.De M, A Few Memories. II. The Fianna, *Eire*, 9.6.1923.

Markievicz was a courageous woman, for she had broken with all her friends and immediate circle to champion "an obscure movement." [109] Her family found it hard to accept her choice and even harder when she later went to prison and became known throughout Ireland. Her own view was that her sister Eva was the only relation she had left.[110]

In considering the conversion of Markievicz – and on a larger scale, the conversion of other Anglo-Irish, who often became more Irish than the Irish themselves – the idea of imagined communities of Benedict Anderson offers a valuable standpoint. According to him, the imagined community is not built on concrete ties, but on a set of shared ideas. Markievicz's identification with the Irish came through understanding and adopting the idea of national uniqueness, which did not entail being born into among the common people of Ireland. According to Markievicz, in those days "nobody minded" one's background, because "everyone realised that Robert Emmet, Wolf Tone, and many another Gael, whose lives had been given for Ireland, were of foreign origin."[111] Embracing the idea of the importance of national unity also legitimized her role in the movement. In her own words she had become part of the children of Ireland.[112]

The Gaelic past and culture of Ireland, which enchanted Markievicz, offered the Anglo-Irish a respite from the religious and cultural differences and antagonisms that unsettled Irish visions of unity.[113] It has been noted that the struggle for identity was not only national but personal; many prominent figures in the rising were drawn from a mixed political, racial or religious background.[114] In the passing of the years, the Anglo-Irish developed their own sense of national identity.[115] However, their tragedy was that, hesitating as they did between two worlds, they could never be fully accepted by either.[116]

Markievicz had embraced the ideas of Irish Irelandism, but was not a typical representative of the movement, which drew its support mainly from among young middle-class Catholics. [117] Nor was revival of the language which was

---

109 Ryan, 82.
110 Constance Markievicz to Stanislaus Markievicz, 14.1.1926, MS 13 778, NLI; Cowell, 59
111 Markievicz, Constance de, Memories, Mr. Griffith ,Eire, 25.8.1923.
112 "Have we the children of Dark Rosaleen proved true to our Mother?", Markievicz, Constance, a typescript, Synge Papers, P 5482, mf, NLI.
113 Hall, 40,46; Martin, F.X., 1916- Revolution of Evolution: Leaders and Men of the Easter Rising, in Martin, F.X. (ed.), Leaders and Men of the Easter Rising, London 1967, 250; Eagleton, 245.
114 Martin 1967, 250.
115 Julian Moynahan, who has studied the the Anglo-Irish literature, opposes the notion of Edward W.Said, who assumes that colonials, except for rare individuals, are everlasting tools of the power that sent them over to occupy, settle and dominate. Moynahan assumes that an entire colony gets cut off from its extraterritorial roots, becoming as Irish as everybody else, though the cultural contribution it makes remains distinctive as long as there are enough self-identified Anglo-Irish people on Irish ground. Moynahan, Julian, Anglo-Irish:The Literary Imagination in a Hyphenated Culture, Princeton 1995, Preface, xi.
116 Lyons 1979, 22.
117 Conor Cruise O'Brien has defined the characteristics of an Irish Irelander as preferably Catholic, if not, then thoroughly deferential to Catholic-nationalists, either constitutional-nationalist of Republican, enthustistic about the Irish language, passionately opposed to all forms of English influence in Ireland, and rigidly chaste, O'Brien 1995, 33. About the support for the movement,

at the very centre of the movement her primary concern. She began to study Gaelic only later in prison, though that was not exceptional; most Irish Irelanders never learnt Irish properly.[118] In that respect Markievicz was more connected with the Yeatsian literary revival which sought to create a specifically Anglo-Irish nation within the English-language civilization.[119] Much in the same way as Maud Gonne —another prominent nationalist woman—who declared that she was too busy trying to spread revolutionary thoughts and acts to sit down and learn the language[120], Markievicz focused herself first and foremost on political goals. As has been remarked, focusing on the national language was in one sense a paradox for political nationalists, because languages change only slowly, while in contrast, radical politics emphasize an exercise of will, swift action and revolutionary change.[121]

Like many of her fellow nationalists, Markievicz did not ponder the question of the racial origins of Irish nation. In her view, the island of Ireland contained a distinctive Irish race that had to regain the lost independence of the nation. At that time, the nationalist idea presupposed that a nation lived within a natural island border, and an immemorial sense of nationhood reinforced by 800 years of struggle against the oppressor.[122] There were problems, though. First, there was the question of the relationship between religion and nationalism. The Gaelic League had initially enabled Protestants to be Irish without being Catholic or separatist.[123] However, an important part of the emerging nationalist thinking was to identify Irish Catholicism with Irish nationalism.[124] Griffith, together with other nationalist ideologues, defined 'Irish' in a way that implied its meaning involved being 'Gaelic' and 'Catholic.' It was an identification which contradicted the official spirit of Young Ireland, but which had achieved dominance in the late nineteenth century.[125] Thus, while the nationalists on the one hand believed in an Irish race which they assumed was the Catholic and Celtic people of Ireland, they, at the same time, also accepted the idea of an Irish nation, which included the Irish Protestants.[126] On the other hand, there was a contradiction regarding the concepts of nation and race. For Griffith, as for many nationalists, the two concepts were confused.[127] That was not a problem in Ireland only. As was the fashion at that time, 'race' and 'nation' were used as virtual synonyms. [128]

---

    ibid., 44. Moran's particular aim was to bring the upper middle-class into life with nationalism. Thompson, 64,118; O'Brien 1995, 86.

119   Hutchinson 1987, 215, 217.
120   Ward, Margaret, Maud Gonne. Ireland's Joan of Arc. London 1990,21.
121   Eagleton, 264.
122   Foster 1993,87.
123   Foster 1993,34.
124   Conor Cruise O'Brien has remarked that even though official nationalism during that period separated religion from politics, the Catholic nationalism of the Christian Brothers and *The Leader*,edited by D.P.Moran, were much nearer the truth, O'Brien, 43.
125   Foster 1993, 13,89.
126   Boyce 1995, 251.
127   Boyce 1995, 296.
128   Hobsbawm 1991, 108.

"Live really Irish lives"

Most of the young men and women who brought militancy back into Irish politics had begun their apprenticeship inside the Gaelic League.[129] Also Markievicz was from the very beginning inspired by the Irish cultural legacy. Was the cultural revival, then, necessary in order to create political nationalism, or was it a product of it? According to Terry Eagleton, culture in Ireland was a continuation of politics by other means; it was always already political. [130] Surely, without the development of national consciousness, a national movement would be doomed to failure.[131] However, to see the Irish revival as a kind of a inevitable precondition for the future radicalisation of politics that brought support for sovereignty instead of mere Home Rule, is perhaps looking at things with hindsight and in a quite determinist way.

The distinction between the cultural nation and the political nation was first made by German historian Friedrich Meinecke at the beginning of this century. Movements for national unity regarded the nation as an entity preceding the state and resting upon common historical or cultural values or social ties.[132] It seems fair to assume that a nationalist ideology and movement can incorporate political and cultural dimensions. For the founding fathers of nationalism, the movement brought together the vital aspirations of the modern world: for autonomy and self-government, for unity and autarchy, and for authentic identity.[133]

John Hutchinson argues that in Ireland the followers of cultural nationalism rather than political nationalism constructed the modern nation-state.[134] According to him, cultural nationalism is a political movement[135], a distinctive form of nationalism which has shaped the modern political community. Hutchinson argues that cultural and political nationalism articulate different, even competing conceptions of the nation, form their own distinctive organizations, and have sharply diverging political strategies. Whereas political nationalists may be driven to adopt ethnic-historical identities, their objectives are essentially modernist: to secure a representative state for their community so that it might participate as an equal in the developing cosmopolitan, rationalist civilization. The aim of cultural nationalists is rather the re-creation of their distinctive national civilization. They want to inspire spontaneuous love of community in its different members by educating them to their common heritage of splendour and suffering. [136] For them history shows that social progress

---

129   Lyons 1979, 43.
130   Eagleton, 232, 254.
131   Alter, 12.
132   Alter, 9.
133   Introduction in Hutchinson 1994, quotes Kemiläinen, Aira, Nationalism. Problems concerning the word, the concept and classification. *Studia Historica Jyväskyläensia III*, Jyväskylä 1964.
134   Hutchinson 1987, 2.
135   ibid, 35.
136   Hutchinson 1987., 2,12, 16.

comes not from the imposition of alien norms on the community but from the inner reformation of the traditional order.[137]

Joining Sinn Fein and taking sides with the radical rebel tradition gave evidence that in Markievicz's view a flourishing Irish culture was not in itself a sufficient goal for the immediate future. Ireland, rediscovering her past and language, needed political sovereignty in order to be capable of establishing a distinctively Irish nation-state. In Markievicz's view, the cultural revival served as both a means and an end. She adopted its vision of Ireland as that of a unique nation, now in danger of losing its identity. The consciousness of a national culture and a national history offered material and a framework for Irish society of the future.

In Sinn Fein Markievicz was a member of a small, separatist political party which at that time was by no means a competitor to the IPP, even though it had to some extent grown and been strengthened before Markievicz joined it.[138] Also, Sinn Fein was not a party in the same sense as the IPP was; a contemporary has correctly described it as a spirit rather than a party.[139] Because of Sinn Fein's nature as a loose coalition it was possible within Sinn Fein to promote or bring forward various, even contradicting issues. So far as Markievicz was concerned, it suited her well to join a political movement that was not open to many opinions and needed commitment from its small group of members. Beforehand Markievicz had not been a traditional wife and mother; she had arranged her time to pursue artistic interests with all her vigour. Now her main concern moved towards a politics which entailed sacrifice.

In March of 1909 the agenda that Markievicz believed every Irishman and Irishwoman should follow was clear. She urged Irishwomen in particular to organise themselves, to join in the nationalist fight and "live really Irish lives"; which in practice meant buying Irish goods, dressing in Irish clothes and feeding on Irish food. They should arm themselves with weapons to fight their nation's cause, arm their soul with noble and free ideas, arm their minds with the histories and memories of their country and her martyrs, her language, and a knowledge of her arts and her industries. And they should not shirk the call to take up arms, should the call come. [140] Urging women to live Irish lives fitted well with the cultural nationalist notion of the nation not just as a political unit but as an organic being, a living personality, whose individuality must be cherished by its members in all manifestations.[141] The advice Markievicz gave them followed the line of passive resistance advocated by Sinn Fein as well as the cultural nationalist and self-reliance promoting programme of the Gaelic

---

137 ibid.,34.
138 About Sinn Fein, O Ceallaigh, Sean, Arthur Griffith, *Capuchin Annual* 1966, 137.
139 Joy, Maurice, Introduction, in Joy, Maurice (ed.), The Irish Rebellion of 1916 and Its Martyrs: Erin´s Tragic Easter, New York 1916,9.
140 Markievicz 1909, 11-16.
141 Hutchinson 1987, 12. About nations as organismus of which the individual was a subordinate part, see Kamenka, 11.

League. However, her words were pointed to the future; to the possibility of an armed rebellion. Even though Markievicz promoted Irish industry, the road for independence through passive resistance focusing on the economy and culture was for her a slow one compared to the road of sacrifice which was attainable by everyone. Markievicz's conversion to national politics came through a reading of Emmet, whose rebellion has been described as " a demonstration in arms."[142] Soon, that would be the thing that Markievicz herself was driving at.

---

142   Cronin, 27.

■ Independent Women to Independent Ireland — between Nationalism and Feminism

Markievicz – Edwardian Feminist

Before Markievicz joined Sinn Fein, she had already taken her first steps on the political path. While living at home in Sligo she had, together with her sisters Eva and Mabel, founded the Sligo branch of the Irish Women's Suffrage and Local Government Association (IWSLGA) in 1896. She was elected President of the branch at its first meeting.[1] The Sligo Branch was only the third in Ireland. Its objectives were to awaken Irishwomen and to encourage them in every way to take up their responsibilities. Their goal was to extend the female suffrage so that it was the same as that granted on men at parliamentary elections.[2] IWSLGA worked by constitutional methods by appeals, lectures and newspapers. It focused on demanding more educational opportunities for women and stressed the importance of the educative role of women's involvement in public affairs.[3]

Markievicz gave her first public speech at a meeting of the Sligo Branch in Drumcliffe. She urged her audience to support the demand for female suffrage and remarked that the first step was to form societies to agitate and

> ".. force the government to realise that a very large class have a grievance, and will never stop making themselves disagreeable till it is righted...John Stuart Mill said thirty years ago that the only forcible argument against giving women the suffrage was, 'that they did not demand it with sufficient force and noise'... not having done so, seems hardly a good enough reason for refusing us the franchise..."

After discussion the resolution demanding the franchise was accepted.[4] Despite this victorious start the Sligo Branch was not succesful.[5] The central figures in it moved away; Eva to Manchester, Constance to Paris. After coming back from Paris Markievicz did not appear to have been actively involved in any

---

1   About IWSLGA see Cullen Owens, 25.There were about 50 members of IWSLGA throughout the last quarter of the nineteenth century, Ryan, Louise, Women Without Votes:The Political Strategies of the Irish Suffrage Movement, *Irish Political Studies*, 9, 1994, 122.
2   Van Voris, 42.
3   Cullen Owens, 25.
4   Amusing Proceedings, *The Sligo Champion*, 26. 12. 1896.
5   Van Voris, 43.

kind of feminist or suffragist activities at an organisational level. In some studies these earlier activities have been totally ignored.[6] Considering her later career so few meetings do not represent a strong involvement, but believing in the necessity of women's emancipation was an important part of Markievicz's ideas, as well as the idea that one should promote one's goals with sufficient persistence and noise. Later she claimed to have grasped her first realisation of tyranny – and of freedom – in relation to the question of woman's suffrage; the fact that women were prevented from voicing their opinion publicly.[7] At the public meeting Eva Gore-Booth expressed the view which was to become the dominant line of the two sisters; that both men and women had duties to their neighbours, to their country and to society at large[8], just as liberals, who emphasized the importance of women taking part in politics, claiming that women had a double duty, first to their family, and secondly to the wider family, the whole world of human beings.[9]

At that time there were not many organised suffragists in Ireland, even though middle and upper class women had by the beginning of the 20th century become a recognized element in public life. The Irish situation was different from that in Britain, where various organisations had gathered many women into their ranks. There, the women's suffrage movement enjoyed mass support from thousands of adherents whose views ranged across the political spectrum.[10] Overall the sphere of action of the Irish suffragists was similar to that of their European sisters. Their first arena was the philanthropic societies. Furthermore, they organised women in co-operatives and sat on local councils. In 1898 they had been given a local government vote based on certain property qualifications.[11] However, for the majority of women the question of the suffrage was not of primary importance. Markievicz was able to focus on that question because of her privileged background. It seems that she was inspired by the new idea, but did not yet ponder it seriously.

Markievicz was clearly a woman who did not accept the traditional role reserved for wives and mothers in British society at that time. Choosing the career of an artist had become easier for women by the time she went to Paris,[12]

---

6   For instance O'Faolain, who has used contemporary reminiscenses from Sligo, does not mention them at all; nor does Margaret Ward in her more recent study Unmanageable Revolutionaries (1983). According to Rosemary Cullen Owens Markievicz would only have ceased her activities in the year 1907, 104. However, after she moved to Paris, there is no evidence of her continuing activities with the IWSLGA.

7   Markievicz speaking in Dàil Eireann, 2.3.1922, Dàil Eireann. Official Report. For Periods 16th August 1921 to 26th August 1921 and 28th February 1922 to 8th June 1922, with Index, Dublin 1922, 206.

8   Amusing Proceedings, The Sligo Champion, 26. 12. 1896.

9   Liberal Women and the Primrose League, in Rendall, Jane (ed.), Equal of Different. Women's Politics 1800-1914, London 1987, 174.

10   Garner, Les, Stepping Stones to Women's Liberty. Feminist ideas in the women's suffrage movement 1900-1918, Rutherford 1984,5

11   Murphy, Cliona, The Women's Suffrage Movement and Irish Society in the Early Twentieth Century. Brighton 1989,14; Cullen , Mary, How Radical Was Irish Feminism between 1860 and 1920, in Corish, Patrick J. (ed.), Radicals, Rebels & Establishments. Historical Studies XV. Belfast 1985, 185-201;Cullen Owens 1984, 30.

12   See Anderson, Bonnie S & Zinsser, Judith P., History of Their Own. Women in Europe from Prehistory to the Present, Vol. II, New York 1988, 173-175.

yet to enter it was still an unusual step for a upper-class woman. After moving to Dublin she was more interested in the arts than joining the committees of philanthrophic societies.[13] Also, when Markievicz got married, she ignored the word 'obey' in her wedding vows[14] – an expression of emancipation many Edwardian feminists used. In Paris, she was known for her unconventional lifestyle.[15]

Thus, Markievicz had in many ways abandoned the traditional role for women quite apart from demanding for them the right to vote. The rights of women were – again – among the first things she campaigned for after becoming active in politics. In forsaking the lifestyle of an Anglo-Irish upper class woman, Markievicz was not the first of her Gore-Booth siblings to do so. Her sister Eva, after making friends with a Manchester suffragist and Trade Union activist Esther Roper, had chosen to move to Manchester to help Roper in her work, because it was thought that she, Eva, was dying of consumption. By the time Markievicz started her career in politics, her sister had for nearly ten years struggled for the rights of working women. Through her Markievicz had most obviously got information concerning the women's question as it was perceived in Britain. Eva Gore-Booth worked within the National Union of Women's Suffrage Societies (NUWSS) which was non-militant and legal in its methods. She shared her sister's talent for art as well: she was a poet and at the same time as Markievicz was actively involved with the Irish theatre, Eva organised factory workers to play Shakespeare.[16] In April 1908 Markievicz travelled to Manchester to help her sister and Esther Roper in a dispute about the rights of women to work in the evening[17] and in June 1908 she spoke on behalf of the barmaids of London at a great demonstration.[18] Next year in Ireland she urged women to work in a very different arena.

---

13   O'Faolain, 49-50. About women and charity in general, see Anderson, Bonnie S., 176-184; Luddy, Maria, Women and Charitable Organisations in Nineteenth Century Ireland, *Women's Studies International Forum*, Vol. 11, No 4, pp 301-305, 1988.
14   Markievicz, Count S., Memories of My Father, *Irish Times*, 6.1.1938
15   Ireland's Joan of Arc, *The Literary Digest*, July 15, 1916.
16   About her activities see for instance Manchester & Salford Women's Trades and Labour Council Reports from years 1908, 1907; about her speeches on the reports of the Womens' Trade Union Council in 1902, 1903 and 1904 in Eva Gore-Booth Collection at Penn State University, Box 3, File 8; Lewis, 64-65; Pankhurst, E. Sylvia, The Suffrage Movement. An Intimate Account of Persons and Ideals, London 1931, 164; see also Roper, Esther, Biographical Introduction, in Poems of Eva Gore-Booth. Complete edition with The Inner Life of a Child and Letters. London 1929.
17   Liddington, Jill & Norris, Jill, One Hand Tied Behind Us: The Rise of the Women's Suffrage Movement, London 1978, 239-240; "The most spectacular piece of propaganda was the Manchester to Sheffield pleasure coach -the Atlanta- decked out with yellow ribbons and driven by Eva Gore-Booth and her older sister, Countess Markievicz, on behalf of the 'Barmaids.' The coachman in a white beaver hat sat behind them blowing the yard-long coach-horn, as the passengers showered literature from the roof at every corner. Whenever they stopped, the Countess and her sister announced to the crowd that they were not themselves barmaids, but would rather, far rather, be barmaids than 'sew,sew,sew, twelve hours a day for five shillings a week'", Raeburn, Anthonia, The Militant Suffragettes. Introduction by J.B. Prestley, London 1973, 54-55.
18   Lewis, 106.

Daughters of Erin and Markievicz

Soon after her involvement with Sinn Fein Markievicz joined the radical Irishwomen's organisation Inghinidhe na hEireann (Daughters of Ireland) after Hobson had introduced her to Helena Moloney, [19] the secretary of the group, a militant nationalist, feminist and actress at the Abbey Theatre. That, together with her friendship with Hobson and others who were more extreme than the majority of Irish nationalists, clearly showed the direction her politics were taking.

In joining Inghinidhe na hEireann, Markievicz was partly forsaking the role that both the Gaelic League and Sinn Fein allotted to women members. According to a nationalist politician, Jenny Wyse-Power, the Gaelic League

> "..rejected the false sex and class distinctions which were the result of English influence....The work was of such a nature that women's help was essential. The study of the Irish language was for all; the social side was almost wholly in the hands of the women members, who by absorbing the Irish tradition, and themselves giving expression to Gaelic ideals and culture, influenced in no small degree the growing effort to wean the people from an Anglicisation which had gone all too far. We were asked to support Irish manufactures, and here women naturally played a prominent part, both in private and public, many of them being now members of the elected Boards throughout the country."[20]

The part designated to women in economic warfare was not a new thing in itself. Already during the 1760s and 1770s in America the importance of women both as purchasers for their households and as producers for their households in the successive boycotts of goods from Britain had been stressed.[21]

However, even though Markievicz urged young Irishwomen to support everything Irish in much the same way that the programme of the Gaelic League proposed[22], she preferred Inghinidhe na hEireann, which in her words was "always in favour of the most extreme action possible."[23]

Inghinidhe na hEireann was founded on 1900. It was a channel for the most uncompromising nationalists who were also concerned with opportunities for

---

19   Markievicz, Constance de, Memories -Mr.Arthur Griffith. The Sinn Fein Organisation, *Eire*, 18.8.1923.
20   The Women of Ireland, *Poblacht na hEireann* 17.1.1922; A Woman's Thoughts, ibid; M.V., The Weaker Sex, *Poblacht na hEireann* 21.2.1922; *The Women of Ireland*, The Republican War Bulletin 5.10.1922.
20   Wyse-Power, Jenny, The Political Influence of Women in Modern Ireland, in Fitzgerald, W. G. (ed.), The Voice of Ireland: A Survey of the Race and Nation from All Angles, by the Foremost Leaders at Home and Abroad, Dublin 1922, 159-160. However, before that women had been excluded from nationalist-minded organisations, e.g. from the Celtic Literary Society, see memoirs of Maud Gonne MacBride in Ward 1995, 4; also Professor Mary Macken, Yeats, O'Leary and the Contemporary Club, in *Studies (Ireland)*, 1939, 137;139, in Ward 1995, 6.
21   Rendall, 35.
22   See her speech in Chapter II; Women's role in sustaining Gaelic culture, 1901, in O'Day, Alan and Stevenson, John (eds.), Irish Historical Documents Since 1800, Dublin 1992, 133.
23   Markievicz, Constance de, The King's Visit, *Eire*, 14.7.1923.

women. Its founder was undoubtedly the most famous nationalist Irish woman at that time, Maud Gonne.[24] Maud Gonne and Constance Markievicz have often been compared to each other, with the result that the image ot their experiences and politics has become virtually identical.[25] While it is true that both women were unyielding, radical nationalists and women of action, who were always in focus when in public, there were differences in their ideas and their sphere of action: Gonne was never a party politician like Markievicz, and in the years before 1916 she spent most of her time abroad, at a time when Markievicz was actively involved in Irish politics.

Inghinidhe na hEireann aimed at the re-establishment of the complete independence of Ireland. It encouraged the study of Gaelic, of Irish literature, History, Music and Art, especially among the young. It supported and popularised Irish manufacture and discouraged the reading and circulation of low "English" literature and the singing of "English" songs, attending vulgar "English" entertainments in theatres and music halls, and in every way combated "English" influence.[26] According to the rules of the organisation, each member had to adopt a Gaelic name. The members were committed to extending and popularising Gaelic as a spoken language and supporting Irish manufacture by using as far as possible Irish-made goods.[27] The members of Inghinidhe were mostly young women in Dublin, who worked in shops and offices.[28] After its first year Inghinidhe na hEireann's reason d'etre was described in a bold way:

> "...Woman rushes in where man fears to tread, and makes him foolish and fall back on the apple story to save himself...I am weary living in a world ruled by men with mouse-hearts and monkey brains and I want a change."[29]

When Markievicz joined Inghinidhe na hEireann in 1909, it was a part of Sinn Fein. It had achieved a reputation as a radical organisation, whose work with children and action against conscription were perhaps best known. It had spread outside Dublin, but otherwise it remained quite small.[30] Although Markievicz,

---

24 Maud Gonne (1866–1953) was a passionate nationalist and suffragette. She divided her early life between Dublin, London and Paris. During the famine of the 1890s in Donegal and Mayo she led peasant agitation over the land question. She also organised counter-attractions to loyalist celebrations for the jubliee of Queen Victoria and during visit to Dublin. She was a friend of Arthur Griffith and James Connolly. Her writings advocated physical force as a method of achieving Irish independence. She is famous for the love W.B.Yeats bore for her for years.

25 According to Sawyer, both women had experiences in common and shared attitudes to life. Furthermore, both faced a constant conflict of interest between political commitment and personal, especially maternal obligations. Again, both advocated using violence for just causes and both were 'women of action.' Sawyer, 55-57.

26 The objects of Inghinidhe na h'Eireann, *United Irishman*, 13 October 1900, quoted in Ward 1995, 19. The organisation was enthusiastically using theatre in order to activate children and to promote nationalist cause, see Young, 70-71.

27 Rules of Inghinidhe, on a leaflet of The Gaelic League, April 1902, Ella Young Papers, Library of Congress, Washington d.c., USA.

28 Young, 70.

29 In *United Irishmen*, quoted in Farrell, 230.

30 Ward 1983, 57-67. In year 1902 Inghinidhe had voted in favour of joining Cumann na nGaedheal, the precursor of Sinn Fein.

due to her background and society connections, faced suspicions at the first meeting she attended,[31] she became a member of a committee which was preparing to provide the organisation with its own journal. The first number of *Bean na hEireann* came out in November 1908. Among others the co-editors included Arthur Griffith, AE and the socialist James Connolly. According to Helena Moloney the reason for its foundation was that *The United Irishman*, edited by Griffith, which had started as a physical force, separatist journal, "had gradually changed its policy to one of reactionary social and dual-Hungarian policy. We wanted to start a paper to counteract this. We wanted it to be a woman's paper, advocating militancy, separatism and feminism."[32] Moreover, Sinn Fein was not acceptable to all nationalist women because of its idea of a dual monarchy.[33]

Bean na hEireann not only commented on politics, but also contained recipes, tips for furnishing the home, book reviews, labour notes and a children's column, stories and poems. The paper advocated uncompromising nationalism and was proud to describe itself as a radical women's journal which all young men read.[34] It urged Irishwomen to work instead of talking:

> "We believe there is in Ireland too much preaching and too little practice. The chief fault we find with men is that they talk very big and do very little, and we would like to foster amongst Irishwomen a desire to work, rather than talk about it in the columns of newspapers..."[35]

The demands of Inghinidhe stem from the old republican and Rousseauian model, which defined women as mothers and civic cheerleaders, who urged men to behave like men, who praised the heroes and condemned the cowardly.[36] In Ireland, the national movement valued women as moral guardians. The famous play of W.B.Yeats, Cathleen ni Houlihan, portrays Ireland as an old woman who is looking for men to fight for her and who demands the ultimate sacrifice: "If someone would help me, he should give me himself, give me all."[37]

That image, which held men responsible for action, was supported by the image of the true nationalist woman as an educator ready for sacrifices. Women

---

31   Czira, 48.
32   Fox 1935, 66.
33   Norman, 60; for instance republican politician Mary MacSwiney did not support it, Fallon, Charlotte H., Soul of Fire: A Biography of Mary MacSwiney, Dublin 1986, 24.
34   About men reading the paper, see Czira , 50.
35   To Our Sisters, *Bean na hEireann*, January 1909. Before the paper there had been another edited by women, which also strove to enflame the rebellious spirit, *Shan Van Vocht* , see Ward 1995, 8-11.
36   Bethke Elshtain 1995, 121; Curtin, Nancy J., Women and Eighteenth-Century Irish Republicanism. In Margaret MacCurtain and Mary O'Dowd (eds.), Women in Early Modern Ireland, Edinburgh 1991, 136-137. About women participating in violent protests in the history of Europe, see Anderson, Bonnie S., 278-284; Godineau, Dominique, Daughters of Liberty and Revolutionary Citizens, in Fraisse & Perrot (eds.) 1995, 16-17.
37   Yeats, W.B., Cathleen Ni Houlihan, Collected Plays. London 1982, 84. Lady Augusta Gregory, a playwright and folklorist, also participated in writing this play. Drawing on evidence from the notes it has been claimed that she wrote the main part of it, see Innes, C.L., Woman and Nation in Irish Literature and Society, 1880-1935, London 1993, 45.

were trusted also because they were perceived as exemplary in their moral purity.[38] Many nationalist women lent their support to the adoption of this role by emphasizing their moral force: they were taking the tradition of independence forward from one generation to another. They put honour in first place, unlike men, for whom economic factors were of primary importance. Because of their instinct women were seen capable of separating morally good things from bad.[39] This division of labour in the nationalist movement did not in itself differ from the ideas of most other countries engaging in nationalist activity at that time.[40]

Markievicz's pen-names in the journal were Macha and Armid, and she wrote gardening notes under the title "A Woman With a Garden."[41] Those notes have interested the biographers to a greater extent than her other writings in *Bean na hEireann*. Somewhat one-sidedly, a quotation in which Markievicz compares killing the "English" with killing snails, has been cited again and again.[42] For Van Voris and Ward her notes represented a bloodthirsty, if humorous parody of nationalist propaganda.[43] However, it does not seem plausible that Markievicz would have consciously made fun of the issue she was fighting for; rather, she did not ponder her style but chose the most colourful comparisons she could find.

In addition to contributing to the new journal, Markievicz, following the stand of Inghinidhe and Sinn Fein, urged Irishwomen to boycott British soldiers and to make Irish public opinion so strong that Irishmen would not join the army.[44] She was also involved in another of the major activities of Inghinidhe, its work with children and she participated in giving food to school children.[45] She became the vice president of the organisation in 1910.[46]

Markievicz agreed with the women of Inghinidhe, who were convinced of the need for physical force; it was only because this had been avoided that Ireland was in the plight.[47] She wanted Irishwomen to join with the men who believed in liberty, so that they could "fan the flame of Rebellion and Revolution."[48] She wrote of the rebel John Mitchel , who would not have cringed

---

38   See for instance words of Arthur Griffith in 1903, Curtis, 189.
39   See for instance The Women of Ireland, *Poblacht na hEireann* 17.1.1922; A Woman's Thoughts, ibid; M.V., The Weaker Sex, *Poblacht na hEireann* 21.2.1922; The Women of Ireland, *The Republican War Bulletin* 5.10.1922.
40   See for instance McClintock, Anne, Family Feuds:Gender, Nationalism and the Family, *Feminist Review* No 44, Nationalisms and National Identities, Summer 1993, 63,66; Blom, Ida, Nation-Class-Gender. Scandinavia at the Turn of the Century, *Scandinavian Journal of History*, 1/1996,4.
41   Czira, in Ward 1995, 26-27.
42   Armid, A Woman with a Garden, *Bean na hEireann*, 8/1909. According to Helena Molony the garden notes was first written by Maud Gonne, Fox 1935, 66, but Margaret Ward contradicts her in her recent study of Maud Gonne, Ward 1990, 96; of biographers Norman uses only this citation when referring to Markievicz's writings in Bean, see also Van Voris, 63, Marreco, 111; Haverty, 78; Curtis, 193.
43   Ward 1983, 69, Ward 1990, 96.; Van Voris, 69.
44   Markievicz 1909, 13 ; Appendix II, Cronin, 311
45   Czira, 53.
46   *Bean na hEireann*, 22/1910.
47   Physical Force, *Bean na hEireann*, September 1909.
48   Irishwomen and the Suffrage, *Sinn Fein*, 27.3.1909.

or begged for his freedom or his rights in the face of the British Government. Markievicz also asked women to stay away from societies which worked in both England and in Ireland as pursuing mutual causes served only to bind the Irish more clearly to the English, and caused them to "forget the hatred we should feel towards our country's enemies." By remarking that violence – destruction of property, civil war, and bloody revolution – was considered justifiable by men who were fighting for their rights,[49] Markievicz not only implied that violent methods were acceptable but was taking sides with the militant suffragettes who had began their campaign in Britain. However, the question of the relationship between nationalism and feminism still needed further consideration.

Markievicz and the question of nationalism and feminism

The nationalist movement, in its attempts to recruit women to its ranks, had to compete with the suffrage movements. As elsewhere in Europe and other parts of the world, many Irish women put getting the vote in first place. Furthermore, broadening the educational possibilities for women, while stressing the educating role of being active in public life, was also on their agenda. The objectives of Irish suffragists were hampered by the negative attitude of John Redmond, leader of the IPP. The suffrage movement in Ireland was, however, proportionally larger than the movement in England.[50] It gained support mainly from the cities, even though attempts were made to spread information on their work all over Ireland. In May 1912 it was reported that there were over 3000 suffragists in different groups.[51] They wanted to remove all social, economic and political obstacles in the way of women.[52] However, the suffrage movement was not a single -issue lobby group. They also challenged the view of their opponents, that men could represent women's interests within the public domain, and that women were not interested in politics and concerned only with the private world of domesticity.[53]

Both nationalist women and suffragists shared a view of history that stressed the importance of women and which gave basis for their demands.[54] Yet that did not form a strong foundation for united action. Rather, both sides regarded each other with suspicion. Many nationalists thought, like Markievicz, that the question of the vote was leading women down a sidetrack when it came to the bigger question, of national freedom.[55] On the other hand Hanna Sheehy

---

49 Maca, Free Women in a free Nation, *Bean na hEireann*,January 1909.
50 Murphy 1989, 7-8.
51 A Year's Progress, *Irish Citizen,* 30.5.1914.
52 *Irish Citizen*, October 1919.
53 Ryan 1994, 120, 137; Ryan, Louise, Traditions and Double Moral Standards: the Irish suffragists' critique of nationalism, *Women's History Review*, Volume 4, Number 4, 1995, 498.
54 About suffragists in this respect, see for instance Dora Mellone, Women in Ancient Ireland, *Irish Citizen,* 25.4.1914.
55 Markievicz, Constance, Irishwomen and the Suffrage, *Sinn Fein* 27.3.1909; see also Fallon, Charlotte H., Soul of Fire: A Biography of Mary MacSwiney, Cork 1986, 17, 37.

Skeffington, the leader of the suffrage organisation, The Irish Women's Franchise League (IWFL) criticised women in the nationalist movement for trusting Irishmen so much. She claimed that women were accepted in the Gaelic League only because they raised children and used Irish products. For her this was not enough: women should organise themselves independently in order to get that key to citizenship, the vote.[56] According to Margaret Cousins, another activist in the IWFL, the suffragists were convinced that any progress relating to the position of women would help in achieving the national independence.[57]

In the prevailing situation the principal goals of suffragists and of nationalist women were different. In 1912 the suffragist paper *The Irish Citizen* defined its goal as gaining the rights of citizenship equally to men and women, and to claim from men and women equally the duties of citizenship.[58] Nationalist women on the other hand regarded their task as creating a united front forceful enough to gain independence. As regards the role of women in future, they were convinced that in a free country women would have their say when the representatives of government were chosen.[59]

After joining Inghinidhe na hEireann Markievicz defined her policy regarding nationalism and feminism. She recognised the value of the struggle of the suffragists, who were fighting "for the rights that every soul born into this world is entitled to – the right of taking up the responsibilities and duties of citizenship in the nation of which they form a part; and the right to their free share and portion of the advantages and privileges enjoyed by those who are already citizens. "[60] She did not mention any further extension of the franchise and it seems that she accepted the goal as obtaining the vote on the same terms as it was then or might later be granted to men.

In Markievicz's opinion, the "seemingly small privilege of a vote" had given men the opportunity to play a part in building up their nation whereas women were bracketed with "criminals, soldiers and paupers, and robbed of the initial right of citizenship," even though they had to obey the laws and pay their share of the expense of government. [61] The reasons Markievicz presented were the same as those the suffragists had used for decades. They were familiar to her from her activities over ten years earlier in Sligo: they were also part of the debate in which her sister Eva Gore-Booth was taking part. However, Markievicz's arguments concerning the immense moral value of a vote went even further. Granting the vote was not only means of developing a person's self-respect and self-reliance, it was also a way of developing feelings of nationality. [62]

---

56   Sheehy Skeffington, Hanna, Sinn Fein and Irishwomen, *Bean na hEireann*, April 1909; *Irish Citizen*, 23.5.1914, Editorial.
57   Cousins James & Margaret, We Two Together. Madras 1950, 185.
58   *Irish Citizen*, 25.5.1912.
59   This was the idea of Mary MacSwiney, see Fallon 1986, 15.
60   Maca, Free Women in a free Nation, *Bean na hEireann*, January 1909.
61   Ibid.
62   Maca, Free Women in a free Nation, *Bean na hEireann*, January 1909; About the rhetoric of suffragettes, see Cullen Owens, 39; Sheehy-Skeffington, Hanna, Reminiscences of an Irish Suffragette, in Sheehy-Skeffington, Andree and Cullen Owens, Rosemary (eds.), Votes for Women. Irish Women's Struggle for the Vote, Dublin 1975,12.

While Markievicz advocated women's equal rights and duties as citizens, she pointed out that the situation in Ireland differed from that in Britain. Although the freedom of a sex and the freedom of a nation were in her view both "equal and integral parts of the great ideal of liberty", and although sex should not be put before nationality – or nationality before sex –, the two matters were in fact by no means symmetrically balanced. Markievicz urged women to join nationalist-minded groups and to remain outside the "English" societies because it was a time of a nationalist struggle. According to her the "English women were with the men of England" and against the Irish, even though she admitted – possibly because of her own personal connections – that each Irishwoman could help them by every means "in her individual power".[63] Yet Irish women were in revolt against the British, not only because of the enslavement of their sex, but also because of the enslavement of their nation, argued Markievicz.[64]

Although Markievicz knew of women's battles for their rights in different countries, – she compared the situation in Ireland with the experience of other European countries and pointed out that in Russia or in Poland women had played a greater role in public life and had worked as comrades with their men far more than in Ireland[65] –, she subordinated the issue women's rights to that of nationalism.She did not address women who basically regarded their struggle for emancipation as a universal struggle, even though their practical objectives naturally aimed at bettering their position in their own country.

Markievicz, striving for "liberty", believed at the same time in evolution regarding reforms in society, except in the case of national freedom which "cannot and must not be left to evolution." [66] For her the "little Bills", though improving the conditions of the Irish, were at best a poor substitute for the nation's freedom. [67] Her positive view of evolution connected with the liberal ideas of Herbert Spencer, whose conception of society was as a part of a evolutionary process[68], even though Markievicz did not share his view that a society should not be compelled to help those of its members who were less fortunate. Liberalism saw the human race as developing and progressing by way of the removal of restrictions on individual development and achievement. Women were an obvious case where development and achievement were stunted by disabilities imposed on individuals on the basis of birth.[69] Equal rights feminism, strongly tied to and influenced by liberals, argued that once people were enfranchised, they possessed the means to work out their own liberation.[70] Eva Gore-Booth wrote that the work of evolution was founded on an everlasting

---

63   Maca,Free Women in a free Nation, *Bean na hEireann*,January 1909.
64   Irishwomen and the Suffrage, *Sinn Fein*, 27.3.1909.
65   Markievicz 1909, 1.
66   Markievicz 1909, 6-7.
67   Markievicz 1909, 6.
68   Barker, Rodney, Political Ideas in Modern Britain, London 1978, 51-52; Somervell, D.C.,
       English Thought in the Nineteenth Century, London 1929, 164.
69   Cullen 1985, 186.
70   Anderson, Bonnie S., 367.

basis of security.[71] Markievicz accepted the liberal view of evolution, but not on every respect; for her the freedom of the nation could not be left to wait.

Thus Markievicz in fact maintained that the question of women's rights should be demoted to second place when the struggle for independence was at stake. However, to bring out the question of equality between the sexes was necessary, not only because in Markievicz's understanding national liberation meant the ultimate attainment of human liberation, but because nationalist revolutions had not in fact so far embraced the emancipation of women. They had not granted equal citizenship for both sexes.[72] Therefore, while Markievicz pursued liberty, she had also to emphasize the liberty of women as a separate but related issue.

It is obvious that one cannot define Markievicz as "not a feminist ever and only a mild suffragist",[73] as a friend of hers did. However, it is true that she ignored some parts of the feminist debate. According to her message women's reproductive role was not of primary importance, and she ignored questions of sexuality and prostitution completely. Whereas British suffrage organizations apparently accepted that a woman's natural role was that of mother and child-carer,[74] Markievicz more often pointed out the possibilities and abilities of women in the public arena.

However, it is essential to realize that one cannot simply divide nationalist women and suffragists into two separate groups. In both camps there were women whose ideas were built on the goals of both movements. The observation that nationalist organisations which women founded in the closing years of Queen Victoria's reign had an important feminist motivation, although this might not form part of their raison d'etre[75] is quite legitimate. In fact, many women, gathered in nationalist-minded organisations, pointed out the need to improve the possibilities for women. Markievicz declared that the women in Ireland were doubly enslaved, with a double battle to fight.[76] Even if the interest of feminist movements seemed to be submerged in the nationalist movements[77],

---

71   Gore-Booth, Eva, Eva, Women and the Suffrage. A Reply to Lady Lovat and Mrs. Humphrey Ward, The *Nineteenth Century and After*, September 1908, 506, Eva Gore-Booth Collection, Penn State University.

72   Branca, Patricia, Women in Europe Since 1750, New York 1978,152.

73   Hanna Sheehy -Skeffington, Sheehy Skeffington Papers, MS 24 189, NLI.

74   Garner, 13; about the attitudes found in NUWSS, see Garner,21, 24 and WSPU, Garner, 50; See also Holton 1986, 12-15 on suffragists who accepted gender differentation as naturally given; suffragists stressed the states' functions of nurturance, functions which they insisted could only be adequately fulfilled with women's assistance, ibid, 14. The suffragists countered the anti-suffragist assertion that in order to keep the woman in a condition of purity they should be separated from the public duties of men, and stated that women's nurturing qualities, now muted, must come out into the public light to purify politics and to tip the balance towards peace and decency, Bethke Elshtain 1995, 5-6.

75   Sawyer, 45-46.

76   Maca, Correspondence. To Miss Nora Cassidy and the Young Girls of Ireland, *Bean na hEireann*, 9/1909. Stating that Irish women were double slaves because of their race and sex resembled the assertion of socialists that women were at a double disadvantage because of their sex and class, see Hannam in Rendall 1987, 236.

77   This is a common conclusion in the Irish discussion of women and nationalism, see for instance Condren, Mary, Sacrifice and Political Legitimation: The Production of a Gendered Social Order, *Journal of Women's History*, Vol. 6 No 4/Vol. 7 No 1(Winter/Spring); MacCurtain,

nationalist women also pursued a manysided programme, like suffragists in both Britain and in Ireland.[78] Margaret Ward has observed that throughout the history of Irishwomen's relationship with nationalism there have been countless examples of women's attempts to develop alternative discourses on empowerment within the movement and of their determined efforts to remove the constraints placed upon their participation.[79]

The Irishwoman's task and sphere

Markievicz argued that the old idea that women could serve the nation only at home[80] was not valid anymore. She remarked critically that women had long been content to dream at home, but was convinced that they were nevertheless capable of rousing themselves; because in history, when Ireland had been a great nation, her women had been great among women.[81] In her argument she might have leaned towards the views of her sister for Eva Gore-Booth had been formulating ideas rejecting "separate spheres" notions of masculinity and femininity since 1903.[82] Markievicz's words also fit well with the arguments of those suffragettes who accepted militancy and subsequently argued that their campaign was concerned with much more than votes for women and that it was about women being capable of fighting their own battle for freedom's sake and breaking down the old senseless barriers which had been the curse of their sex.[83]

However, Markievicz's view was even more centrally based on the nationalist picture of Irish women, portrayed as equal to men throughout all generations. According to the ancient tales Ireland had once had female physicians, lawyers, judges and poets.[84] Throughout history women had done their share in making Ireland what she was, "a heroic land, unconquered by long centuries of wrath

---

Margaret, Women, the Vote and Revolution, in MacCurtain, Margaret & ò Currain, Donncha (eds.), Women in Irish History: The Historical Dimension. Naas 1978, 48-51; Cullen Owens Rosemary, The Smashing Times: A History of the Irish Women's Suffrage Movement 1889-1922. Dublin 1984, 105; McKillen, Beth, Irish Feminism and National Separatism 1914-1923. *Eire/Ireland*, 3/1981, 62. See also Dana Hearne, who sees that in the context of Ireland in 1914-1916, gender-based concerns could not be fully intergrated with nationalist concerns, Hearne, Dana, The Irish Citizen 1914-1916: Nationalism, Feminism and Militarism, *Canadian Journal of Irish Studies*, Volume 18, Number 1, December 1991, 11.

78 Ryan 1995,489; Holton, Sandra Stanley, The Suffragist and the 'Average Woman', in *Women's History Review*, Volume 1, No 1, 1992, 13. About similarities and differences of the nationalist and feminist goals among women in Ireland and in Finland, see Oikarinen, Sari, Gender, Nationality and War. Irish and Finnish Women and the Struggle for Independence in the Beginning of this Century in Gullikstad, B. & Heitmann, K., Kjønn, makt, Samfunn in Norden I et historisk perspektiv. Bid I. Konferanserapport fra det 5. nordiske kvinnehistorikermøte, Klækken 08-11.08.96, Trondheim 1997, 206-221.

79 Ward, Margaret, Irish Women and Nationalism, in *Irish Studies Review*, No 17 Winter 1996/7, 9.

80 Markievicz 1909, 12.

81 Maca, Free Women in a free Nation, *Bean na hEireann*,January 1909.

82 Lewis, 72.

83 Garner, 106, quote from Richardson 1953, 103.

84 Milligan, Alice, Irish Heroines, in Dunn, Joseph and Lennox, P.J. (eds.), The Glories of Ireland, Washington 1914, 162.

and wrong, a land that had not abandoned its Faith."[85] In the words of Eva Gore-Booth, women had proved to be heroic in every great national movement.[86]

It has been observed that in Ireland women were looking for opportunities not so much to gain their freedom as to regain it by rediscovering and developing Irish culture. In Ireland written records and oral tradition reminded them that they had enjoyed privileges under Brehon law.[87] However, basing their demands on the doings of women in earlier times was not an exceptionally Irish feature. In 1780 in America, the right of women to contribute to the revolutionary cause was often defended by recalling the "heroines of antiquity, who had rendered their sex illustrious."[88] By emphasising the role of certain historical, albeit usually exceptional women figures, the national fight was in a way making its own contribution to the development of women's history.

Regarding the path Markievicz chose, it is not irrelevant that women in the past had not only done their share but had been part of a military tradition. In Irish mythology the ancient Queen Maeve was depicted as a masterful, boastful, wilful, power-loving, uninhibited woman, who regarded herself as the equal of any man, and one who must be seen as equal. She had given her name to the landscape of Sligo[89] , being thus a part of Markievicz's experience as well. There were also other dominant female fighting figures in the early sagas as well as in later retellings.[90] For Markievicz's contemporaries Maeve was seen as an expert on war, who was superior in combat.[91]

Thus, in Markievicz's opinion history promised Irishwomen a lot, were they only living in an independent nation. Moreover, her conception of Irish men supported the demand that women should join together with them rather than fight for their own goals separately.

Markievicz approached the question of men's attitude to women in politics with confidence: in her view the men, after "understanding the question", would be with the women, who were still a "new and strange element." Markievicz perceived the reason to be based on the characteristics of Irish men and suggested that:

> "The men of our race, descended like us, from a long line of martyrs in the cause of liberty, will not try to keep our rights and our duties from us, and on the day that Ireland stands free before the world shall see our emancipation too."[92]

---

85   Milligan, 166.
86   Gore-Booth, Eva, Women and the Suffrage. A Reply to Lady Lovat and Mrs. Humphrey Ward, The *Nineteenth Century and After*, September 1908, 498, Eva Gore-Booth Collection, Penn State University.
87   Sawyer, 69.
88   Rendall, 36.
89   Reynolds, Lorna, Irish Women in Legend, Literature and Life, in Gallagher, S.F. (ed.), Women in Irish Legend, Life and Literature. Irish Literary Studies 14, Buckighamshire, 1983, 12-13.
90   Ayling, Ronald, 'Two Words for Women': A Reassessment of O'Casey's Heroines, in Gallagher, S.F. 1983, 105. That Markievicz gave her daughter the name Maeve has to some observers been a sign of her rebellious aspirations, Sawyer, 43.
91   Milligan, 163.
92   Maca,Free Women in a free Nation, *Bean na hEireann*,January 1909.

Markievicz's view chimed with the prevailing nationalist-minded understanding of the remote past, where people possessed the very virtues which were supposed to make a modern nation great.[93] The idea that the inequality of women and men would be solved spontaneously in an independent Irish society and that this was possible because Irish men were by nature democratic – a view that completely contradicted that of many of the suffragists – stemmed from the idea of a unique Irish history which had been made possible by the unique Irish race. Markievicz's trust in men was most probably based on her personal friendship with men like Hobson and MacCartan. In Markievicz's vision, the common characteristics both sexes shared were courage, a striving for democracy and equality and an idealistic nature, all inherited from their ancestors. Yet she made a clear distinction: people were born either male or female, Irelander or foreigner.[94]

Therefore, Irish women had history and the character of Irishmen on their side. But they had themselves to act also in order to get their own demands met. In Markievicz's words, it was the "women's task to teach the men to look upon us as fellow-Irelanders and fellow-workers." In order to do that, they should join the movement and bring women into public life. Moreover, they should serve on all committees and boards for which they were eligible, and be taught how to work well. Also, when women gave their services to collect money, they should "insist" that they should be on the committees that had the spending of it. That she chose the word "insist" when speaking about the women's task, implicitly suggests something quite another than a complete trust in Irishmen. Markievicz crystallised her message by asserting that "no one can help you but yourselves alone; you must make the world look upon you as citizens first, as women after." The motto of women should be "All or Nothing", to be members of a free nation and with freedom to participate in the government of it.[95]

Markievicz based her argument for the need to get women involved in politics partly on the prevailing situation. Because women had, until very recently, been removed from all politics, they "should be able to formulate a much clearer and more incisive view of the political situation than men." Men, who were more or less in touch with politics, had usually in her experience the label of some party attached to them from early on. Thus, because they were so occupied in examining closely, from a narrow party point of view, all the Bills relating to Ireland, they lost sight of the fact that their separate nation also had an interest in class, sex and trade legislation. There was a chance for Irish women, to remind their menfolk that they should examine all legislation not from a party point of view, or from the point of view of one sex, trade, or class, but simply from the point of view of their nation as a whole.[96] That was possible

---

93 Matossian, 221-222.
94 Maca, Free Women in a free Nation, *Bean na hEireann*, January 1909.
95 Maca, Free Women in a free Nation, *Bean na hEireann*, January 1909.
96 Maca, Free Women in a free Nation, *Bean na hEireann*, January 1909. The understanding of women's purity in relation to male politics was also to be discerned in the speeches of the leadership of the radical British Suffragist organisation WSPU leadership, who constantly

because the women had "an inner knowledge of the right", argued Markievicz.[97] A similar view than hers had been expressed in a women's republican journal about ten years earlier when it was claimed that the task of women was to revive men's interest in national work and to "give them safe guidance out of the hurly-burly of the political faction fight into which they have wandered from the straight path."[98] This mistrust of Irish parliamentarians, who were seen possibly corrupted by living in Britain, was also expressed in other nationalist circles, for instance in the writings of D.P.Moran.[99]

In Markievicz's opinion, women should be a clear part of the nationalist movement because Irish women had also been responsible for allowing the Irish situation to deteriorate in the first place: they had

> "abandoned their Dublin mansions, to hire or buy houses in London, they followed the English court about and joined the English ranks of toadies and placehunters, bringing up their daughters in English ways and teaching them to make English ideals their ideals, and when possible marrying them to Englishmen."[100]

These words revealed the background of Markievicz: she was not addressing the majority of Irishwomen, but women of her own class, the Anglo-Irish. Obviously she was most concerned with the behaviour of the upper and middle classes, who "had been lost to their country for years, if not for all eternity."[101] She seemed to suggest that the doomed aristocracy could redeem thenselves only by following her path. At the same time, she pointed out that women should be talking about nationalist ideas to the peasants as well[102] - thus re-emphasizing the importance of awakening all Irish people. In that, her advice might well have been influenced by the programme of the Gaelic League, which urged its supporters to go among "their Irish-speaking fellow-country people."[103]

This idea of focusing on certain groups of women was to be found in the British suffrage organisations also. The question of gaining the vote was not simply a question of equality for all women. Many suffragists were satisfied with trying to secure vote only for the women of the middle and upper classes. In relation to this point Markievicz seemed to be more concerned with the attitudes and potential of only one group of Irish women: she did not draw special attention to working class women, even though she urged women to organise trade unions and publish statistics on women's wages.[104] Her wish

---

pointed out the lack of principle and the moral and political bankruptcy of their parliamentary opponents, especially those in the Liberal Party, Holton 1990, 18.
97   Irishwomen and the Suffrage, *Sinn Fein*, 27.3.1909.
98   *Shan Van Vocht*, September 1897, in Ward 1995, 10.
99   O'Brien 1995, 54.
100   Markievicz 1909, 3.
101   Markievicz 1909, 3.
102   Markievicz 1909, 11.
103   Women's role in sustaining Gaelic culture, 1901, in O'Day & Stevenson, 133.
104   Maca, Free Women in a free Nation, *Bean na hEireann*, January 1909.

seemed to be to reflect the influence of her sister, whose work at that time was focused on those problems; Eva Gore-Booth wanted to broaden the goal and include the working class women in her demands. Furthermore, Markievicz's remark that in the world of labout the vote gave men power to frame laws to protect their labour from the "rapacious capitalist, who in return has the same weapon at his service for his defence" [105] seemed merely to mirror the ideas of Eva rather than demonstrate a personal interest in working class women as such.

Markievicz and Militant Suffragettes

Despite their differences nationalists and suffragists shared one goal: women should be organised in pursuit of their rights; they should demand those rights and also safeguard them. When suffrage for women was not included in the Home Rule Bill of 1912, the IWFL organised mass meetings to back their demands and got support from nationalist women as well.[106] Hence the nationalists did not want to condemn the goal of the suffragettes, but they did not accept the methods they employed.[107] When the use of mass force did not work, the IWFL started to use the methods of its British model WSPU (The Women's Social and Political Union). It heckled at political meetings, broke the windows of public buildings,[108] and the women in prison started hunger-strikes.[109] Its conviction that "war" was the only possible method to use against the IPP[110] separated the organisation from other similar organisations in Ireland. The action these women took was shattering the view of what constituted decent suitable behaviour for women. Public opinion saw such militant tactics as either hindering Home Rule or as anti-national and anti-feminine behaviour.[111] Militantism was also a dividing issue among women as well.[112] The suffragettes defended themselves against the criticism of nationalists by reminding them that the history of the Irish was likewise a series of acts of violence, of breaking the law, and damaging property.[113]

---

105   Maca, Free Women in a free Nation, *Bean na hEireann*, January 1909.
106   *Irish Citizen* 8.6.1912; 5.7.1913. In 1913 IWFL had about 800 members, see Report of the Executive Committee of the IWFL 1913. Dublin 1914.
107   Suffragists, *Sinn Fein* 27.7.1912.
108   Cullen Owens 1984, 64.
109   *Irish Citizen,* 8.6.1912; 5.7.1913; 12.7.1913.
110   Levenson, Leah & Natterstad, Jerry H., Hannah Sheehy-Skeffington: Irish Feminist, Syracuse 1986, 24, about the objectives of it, see McKillen, Beth, Irish Feminism and Nationalist Separatism, 1914-1923, *Èire-Ireland*, 1/1982, 53. About the connections with the programme of WSPU, see Rosen, Andrew, Rise Up, Women! The Militant Campaign of the Women's Social and Political Union 1903-1914. London 1974, 72.
111   Cullen 1985, 193.
112   For instance Louie Bennett, An Appeal to Militants, *Irish Citizen* 8.11.1913; see also Bennett, Suffrage Policy, *Irish Citizen* 11.10.1913;. Ethics of Rebellion, *Irish Citizen* 27.7.1912; "A Christian Militant", A Holy War, *Irish Citizen* 29.3.1913.
113   *Irish Citizen,* 22.6.1912.

Even though it was feared that employing radical methods would alienate politicians on the women's question,[114] they were not sympathetic to women's demands in the first place. Sinn Fein, although its members included women who tried to stress the issue, rejected motions concerning women as dealing with "social questions" which were to be considered only after independence.[115] The leaders of the IPP opposed women's suffrage partly on moral grounds,[116] but also and more importantly because it did not want to irritate the British Prime Minister Herbert Asquith, who at that stage opposed it.[117] The growing militancy of some suffragettes in Britain had by the year 1913 led to arrests and consequently to hunger strikes. The law, which the British authorities employed to solve the problem, was known a "Cat and Mouse" and in the summer of 1913 the extension of the law to Ireland produced a considerable protest movement. [118]

It is interesting to note that Markievicz, who in her own words "was not a member of any suffrage group, because she was a separatist and a Republican and did not want a vote in the British Parliament", wished, however, to express her sympathy with women on hunger strike. According to her, their actions showed that the spirit of martyrdom had not died in Ireland. She declared that she was proud to be a woman and asked, how many men would face hunger-strike for anything in the world.[119] Consequently, she lent her support to suffragettes by signing a petition against the law and by naming the law as barbarous and unworthy of any civilized country.[120] In general this was not exceptional. In Victorian England women seldom chose to channel their energies into one specific area of protest, and most can be found offering at least financial support or institutional strength to a whole range of distinct but connected campaigns. Political co-operation and good friendship were often closely allied [121], as in the case of Hanna Sheehy-Skeffington and Markievicz.

The organisation arranging the meetings against "Cat and Mouse" was the IWFL, of which Sheehy-Skeffington was the leader. In September 1913 Markievicz spoke at one of its meetings emphasizing her earlier idea of the moral and educational value of the suffrage. She declared that there were three great movements going on in Ireland, the nationalist, women's and industrial movements. The reason for their greatness she saw in their having one unifying goal, because for her they were "all really the same movement in essence, for they were fighting the same fight, for the extension of human liberty."[122] Thus,

---

114 Ryan 1994, 126.
115 *Irish Citizen*, 9.5.1914; See the opinion of Griffith in Sinn Fein5.7.1913; about the Sinn Fein meeting, *Irish Citizen* 28.3.1914; about Griffith opposing women's suffrage, see *Irish Citizen*, 9.1.1915.
116 Sheehy Skeffington, Hanna, in Sheehy-Skeffington, 1975, 18.
117 Murphy 1989, 169; Ryan 1994, 125; Cullen Owens 1984, 57-61.
118 Look at Cullen Owens, 64-65.
119 Extracts of her speech, *Irish Citizen*, 5.7.1913.
120 Irish Citizen, 12.7.1913; *Irish Citizen*, 6.9.1913.
121 Levine, Philippa, Feminist Lives in Victorian England, Oxford 1990, 60,61.
122 *Irish Citizen*, 27.9.1913.

human freedom was the goal that she was striving for – and this she pursued not only within the nationalist movement. The movements which gave her hope were all shattering the status quo of society. Also, these movements employed similar, unparliamentarian methods in order to promote their cause and at least some sections of them protested visibly and radically.

Markievicz's view on whether to include a demand for the women's franchise into the Home Rule Bill had thus changed. In spring 1909 she had criticised the Sinn Feiners Jenny Wyse-Power and Arthur Griffith. They had argued that Sinn Fein women could logically join an IWFL which demanded the vote on the same terms as it was, or might be, extended to men on the grounds that the phrase did not mention "an English Parliament."[123] and other nationalist had women shared her criticism of such a view.[124]

Yet in the summer of 1912 she supported Irish suffragists who were demanding linking female suffrage with Home Rule Bill.[125] Although Markievicz did not stand for home rule as the final goal, she did not resist the demand in itself. Expressing strong demands for action by the British government was for her one form of showing rebellious spirit. While British public opinion was focused on the question of the suffrage and especially on the actions of militant suffragettes, it did not seem a good idea to oppose the Irish suffragists in such circumstances. Rather, it was essential to put further pressure on the British. In this respect – by backing up the suffragists – Markievicz went further than the official Sinn Fein policy.[126] She was also the only member of Inghinidhe who both stood for women's suffrage and was also well known to the Irish public.[127]

The hunger strikes aroused even more sympathy for suffragists than before and among radical nationalist women in particular as well as among nationalist-minded members of the labour movement. Considering the attitudes of Markievicz and other nationalists, it is obvious that this sympathy was increased by the desire of the IWFL to work independently of British organisations.[128] Thus this transfer of sympathy helped the struggle for their own political goals.

It is worth noting, however, that Markievicz, who defended the militant suffragettes, had many ideas in common with them. For Emmeline Pankhurst, a leader of the militant WSPU the "pole star" in history was revolution, allied to social disruption and the achievement of social regeneration through the exertions of noble individuals. The great qualities within individuals were forged in the fire of a great struggle. She highlighted the "joy of battle, the exultation that comes of sacrifice of self for a great object." Like Markievicz, Pankhurst valued deeds before words. Like the romantic nationalists, Pankhurst saw human progress as having advanced through the tumultuous acts of the oppressed, and

---

123   Irishwomen and the Suffrage, *Sinn Fein*, 27.3.1909. Her writing contradicts the argument that she was always sympathetic towards the IWFL, Van Voris, 64.
124   Mary A. McLarren, *Bean na hEireann*, April 1909; Levenson, 24.
125   *Irish Citizen*, 8.6.1912.
126   See for instance Griffith's writing in *Sinn Fein*, 5.7.1913; Ward 1983,84.
127   Ward 1983, 84.
128   Sheehy-Skeffington 1975, 12; Cousins 1950, 164.

identified herself and the WSPU with past revolutionaries and resistance movements. [129]

Militancy involved the idea that the progress of civilisation occures not in a steady stream but through moments of fire and tempest, not in the pursuit of reason but in the assertion of spiritual grandeur, not through the workings of established social institutions but by the actions of heroic individuals. [130] All these ideas were not only acceptable to Markievicz but also her guiding light, in her public speeches at least. It is nevertheless necessary to note that Markievicz did not comment on the goals of the militant suffragettes as such. In her view, they were unimportant, unlike their methods, which supported her opinion that important goals were not achieved by progress, but by shaking society.

The Joan of Arc of Ireland

Speaking on behalf of the hunger-strikers was also a way to defending the values of sacrifice and an overwhelming sense of responsiblity and devotion. That was a central feature of the agenda of Markievicz from the very beginning. In March 1909 she had expressed her wish to see a Joan of Arc freeing Ireland. [131] Joan of Arc was a kind of an icon for women who strove to promote their goals in the early 20th century. She can be found in the writings of suffragists and nationalist women, from Ireland to Finland. [132] She represented a woman who was as good as, if not better than men in their own field. The path she chose – that of a Catholic soldier in a struggle against the English power – combined well not only with the Irish nationalist but also with the feminist ideas held by Markievicz.

Markievicz emphasized the need to have a strong woman, who was independent of all men, to lead the Irish; she did not employ the common Irish image of a suffering mother, who was looking for her sons to fight the fight for her. Nor did she employ the rhetoric that presented Ireland as Hibernia, a matron, whose honour was guarded by her brave admirers. [133] Thus, Markievicz in a

---

129 Holton, Sandra Stanley, In Sorrowful Wrath: Suffrage Militancy and the Romantic Feminism of Emmeline Pankhurst, in Smith, Harold L. (ed.), British Feminism in the Twentieth Century, Aldershot 1990, 11-12. Pankhurst claimed to have borrowed the extreme militant tactics from the Irish nationalist movement, Käppeli, Anne-Marie, Feminist Scenes, in George Duby and Michelle Perrot, General editors, A History of Women in the West IV. Emerging Feminism from Revolution to World War, 504.
130 Holton 1990. 22.
131 Markievicz 1909, 16.
132 In Finland, see Gripenberg; Emmeline Pankhurst's favourite heroine was also Joan of Arc, a figure both she and her followers identified with closely,Holton 1990, 15; The militant suffragist Emily Davison felt the call of Joan of Arc, see Stanley, Liz with Morley, Ann, The Life and Death of Emily Wilding Davison. A Biographical Detective Story. With Gertrude Colmore's The Life of Emily Davison, London 1988, 19-20. There was also a 'Joan of Arc' at her funeral, Elsie Howey, who often appeared dressed as Joan, in full armour and on horseback, Stanley, 109.
133 Curtin 1991, 136-137.

way replaced the essentially Irish figure of Cathleen ni Houlihan with the international figure of Joan of Arc. In that, she broadened and reshaped the image of Ireland itself. At the beginning of this century Ireland was seen in England as a feminine, childlike, lazy and dreaming figure as opposed to the masculine, dynamic and rational figure of England.[134] Irish nationalists also embraced this image. In his writings D.P. Moran alleged that Ireland was sunken in "the feminine" and in need of "the masculine" principle.[135] According to Moran Ireland, personified as usual as a woman was "either in a wild carnival of screech or in a drowsy state of Oriental fatalism".[136] Sir Horace Plunkett also voiced that same concept: In 1911 he lamented that Ireland was, more than any other country, spoken of as a woman "probably due to the appearance in our national affairs of qualities which men call womanly." [137]

The criticism was not a general feature. More often, the image of Ireland as a woman, as a sorrowful Dark Rosaleen or as charismatic Cathleen ni Houlihan, was popularized. To die on behalf of this beautiful female image was an honour and a duty for men, and to raise children for such a task was the job of women, according to the common features of nationalist narrative. But even if the imagined Ireland, personified as a woman, could rouse people, it could not be perceived as the image of an actor. The 'real' people – men – were the actors. Markievicz, among other radical nationalist women who embraced feminist ideas, challenged this image. Along with her speeches, her own personal history supported the view of women as independent actors who themselves decided their destiny. While Ireland was dismissively defined as an Oriental place, the Oriental was also perceived as a metaphor for a passive women. A few years later Markievicz pointed out that Irish women should free themselves from the last vestiges of the harem.[138] Thus, she was not only striving to escape the passive role of womanhood, but was also redefining the role of the truly republican woman.

*   *   *

How do the ideas of Markievicz then relate to the ideas of feminism? It is obvious that she grasped the classic arguments within liberal feminism the attempts to reconcile of their aim that women should share the same rights as men because of their common humanity with the notion that they did after all have particular roles and characteristics.[139] In the struggle to be counted as full

---

134 For instance Eagleton, 100.
135 Moran in his Irish Ireland, 7, quoted O'Callaghan, 149.
136 Moran in Irish Ireland, 76-77, quoted in O'Callaghan, 152-153.
137 Plunkett, Horace, Pilkingon, Ellice and Russell, George ("AE"), The United Irishwomen. Their Place, Work and Ideals. With a Preface By the Rev. T.A. Finlay, Dublin 1911, 1.
138 The Future of Irishwomen. Speech at the IWFL Meeting, October 12th , Irish Citizen, 23.10.1915.
139 Both of them were evident in John Stuart Mill's famous On the Subjection of Women (1869).Garner, 3. About categories of suffragists, see Offen, Karen, Defining Feminism: A Comparative Historical Approach, Signs: Journal of Women in Culture and Society, 1988, no 1, 136.

citizens, women pursued two alternative lines: one held that women and men had the same potential and should therefore be granted the same rights, the other that female qualities were required in the public sphere.[140] Within the context of the nationalist struggle Markievicz emphasized the importance of women as the moral guardians of men. Her suggestion that women, who had been able to form a clearer vision of politics because they had been outsiders, was similar to that of many suffragists.

In Markievicz's opinion, the universal rights of all people were best served by forming a sovereign nation. One goal was thus connected with another and, in order to gain the franchise for women it was necessary to become an independent nation first. Thus she followed the ideas of Hegel, who regarded the state as the realm of universal values far beyond the petty and sectional concerns of civil society.[141] Markievicz's main concern was not to gain equal rights for women within the British Empire, but rather to strengthen Irish women's position in the ongoing battle so that their value as cultural carriers[142] and their pure vision would be acknowledged and that these, together with their active work, would then grant them equal citizenship with men in an independent state. She accepted the goals of the movements for "women's rights", in the sense of of civil and political equality[143], but these goals were for her to be realised only in an independent Ireland.

---

140 Blom 1996, 6.
141 Breuilly, John, The Sources of Nationalist Ideology, in Hutchinson 1994, 104.
142 That fight involved the important role of women as ideological reproducers; women as 'cultural carriers' of the ethnic group, see Women and the Nation-State, Floya Anthias and Nira Yuval-Davis, in Hutchinson 1994, 315.
143 Gerda Lerner has distinguished between the movements for 'women's rights' and the movements for 'woman's emancipation', in the sense of a broader striving for freedom from oppressive restrictions imposed by sex; self-determination; autonomy, Rendall, Jane, The Origins of Modern Feminism: Women in Britain, France and the United States 1780-1860, London 1985, 1.

■ Raising the Generation of the Future — Na Fianna Eireann

The founding of Na Fianna Eireann

From the very beginning Markievicz had in her speeches and writings shown a desire to raise and organise the Irish to struggle for their freedom. First she had focused especially on women, but the step which followed – founding a boys group from which a nationalist army would be formed – was even more radical. According to her own reminiscences she got the inspiration for it in 1909, when she read in the Dublin daily papers of how a number of Boy Scout organisations and Boys' Brigades had been reviewed at Clontarf by an British Viceroy and addressed by him. Reading this she realised "vividly and suddenly, that Ireland was being attacked at her most vital point, the minds of her children." These children would not learn the love of Ireland, but admiration for "a tyrannical Empire." Later they would enlist in the British army or police forces and would be used against Ireland or other countries under the rule of the British Empire.[1]

Hence in the background of Markievicz's anxiety was the principle of anti-enlisting, which she promoted in other forums as well. It was part of the programme of Sinn Fein and Inghinidhe na hEireann.[2] To make Ireland impossible to govern it was of vital importance not to provide England with soldiers and police. However, for Markievicz the promise that one would not enlist in the British army was not enough. According to her own words, she wanted to start a Boy Scout Organisation as quickly as possible, "with the object of training the boys mentally and physically to achieve the Independence of Ireland."[3] In May 1909 she boldly suggested that an Irish army should be formed through training boys.[4]

Markievicz did not get much encouragement for her idea, which she mooted at several meetings. Even though many nationalists were concerned with the Baden-Powell organisation, none of them thought of the possibility of forming an Irish nationalist boys organisation as a counter-blow to the English one. To

---

1   C.De M, A Few Memories. II. The Fianna, *Eire*, 9.6.1923.
2   Maca, The British Soldier as a Paying Guest, *Bean na hEireann*, 7/1909; also extracts of her lecture on the Women of '98, *Bean na hEireann*, 14/1909; Some years earlier the women of Inghinidhe had organised a mass meeting of Irish children in Dublin, where they swore to cherish an undying enmity towards England until the freedom of Ireland had been won, Yeats 1953, 221.
3   C.De M, A Few Memories. II. The Fianna, *Eire*, 9.6.1923.
4   Van Voris, 67.

this she is said to have replied, "In 10 years these boys will be men."[5] When Markievicz brought her idea to the Executive of Sinn Fein, it was not met with the enthusiasm that she had expected. Sinn Fein, whose programme contained no provision for organising an army, would not undertake the work. However, its members could help her individually if she decided to start it herself.[6] Despite the negative response Markievicz decided to go on. She got help from Helena Molony, and two young IRB men, Patrick McCartan and Sean McGarry. Also the Fenian veteran Tom Clarke gave her words of help and encouragement. However, in the beginning they got all in all "amazingly little support from the young men, and the public for the most part laughed at us."[7]

In the summer of 1909 Markievicz started two projects connected with her new idea. In late summer she rented a cottage in Raheny, near Dublin, in order to start a co-operative market garden together with Bulmer Hobson, Helena Moloney and a group of boys, who were members of the Fianna.[8] She herself has neither explained the reason for the experiment nor the reasons for its failure after a few months.[9] The idea of setting up co-operative businesses was not in itself unusual. The co-operative movement was widely supported in Ireland, including by members of her own family.[10] The Raheny experiment, even though it was a poorly designed and an incomplete idea as such, drew on the ideas of self-reliance and co-operation. For Markievicz they were the central features of the ideal Irish society she wanted to create. The co-operative idea of self-help, of active work in order to win through hardships[11], could also be linked with her experiment as well. The Raheny experiment indicates that she perceived co-operative ideas as important in teaching the boys to become citizens.

The more succesful of her two projects in the summer of 1909, which led to the formation of Fianna, was the formation of a boys group "The Red Branch

---

5   Gifford, 348-349.
6   C.De M, A Few Memories. II. The Fianna, *Eire*, 9.6.1923.
7   C.De M, A Few Memories. II. The Fianna, *Eire*, 9.6.1923. About the negative attitude see also Fianna Handbook. Introduction by Countess Markievicz, 7: Markievicz, Constance de, Tom Clarke and the First Day of the Republic. A Memory, *Eire*, 26.5.1923.
8   O'Faolain, 91; Norman, 67 It has been suggested that she read about the co-operative experiment in Ralahine, see Marreco, 130-131; Van Voris, 72-73. The Irish landowner Vandeleur had in 1831 employed an Englishman E.T. Craig to solve the problems on his land by Owenite methods. Craig established the Ralahine Agricultural and Manufacturing cooperative Association, which after a good start ended in 1831 after Vandeleur lost his property by gambling, Harrison, J.F.C., Robert Owen and the Owenites in Britain and America: The Quest for the New Moral World, Oxford 1969, 170-171. E.T. Craig remarked that the experiment had shown the possibility of settling Ireland without force when people were given the oppostunity to raise themselves from poverty, Craig, E.T., An Irish Commune: The History of Ralahine, with an Introduction by George Russell (AE) and Notes by Diarmuid Ó Cobhthaigh, Dublin 192,167.
9   The house had been uninhabited for a long time, etc, see O'Faolain, 91.
10 Sir Horace Plunkett had in 1894 established The Irish Agricultural Organisation Society, which in 1903 had 800 branches and 80 000 members, Plunkett, Sir Horace, Ireland in the New Century, Dublin 1982 (Dublin 1905), 192.
11 See Rauter, Anton, Co-operative Principles and Their Importance for Co-operative Progress, in Co-operatives to-day: Selected Essays from Various Fields of Co-operative Activities, Geneva 1986, 377.

Knights." The first camp with the eight boys convinced Markievicz that a boys' organisation could be made a success.[12] Her humorous, detailed account of the difficulties during the camp weekend does not provide any particular reasons for her optimism. When Markievicz wrote about it, years after the Fianna had become a permanent element in Irish political life, she obviously wanted to stress her own belief in the movement from the very beginning.

However, her two projects were too small and unorganised to result in something lasting. To get the boys' organisation started properly Markievicz asked Bulmer Hobson to help. She had heard that he had run some boys' football clubs on Gaelic lines in Belfast, and that he "understood boys." In fact Hobson had for a short time organised hurling clubs and lessons in the Irish language and history for boys. Now Markievicz suggested that the expriment should be carried on in Dublin and offered to pay for the rent of a hall. She also asked him to be president of the boys' organisation.[13] At the first meeting, in which about a hundred boys participated, Hobson was chosen as President and Markievicz as secretary. The objective of Na Fianna Eireann – the Soldiers of Ireland – was to re-establish the independence of Ireland, and in order to do that, to train the youth of Ireland by teaching scouting and military exercises, Irish history and the Irish language. The members promised to work for the independece, never to join England's armed forces, and to obey their superior officers.[14] The new organisation got no words of encouragement from Sinn Fein and the Gaelic League, who dissociated themselves from it in their public announcements.[15] Despite their reluctance Na Fianna Eireann now concentrated on its work.

Training Irish nationalists

The value of educating youth was recognised in different civic movements throughout Europe at the beginning of the century.[16] For instance the temperance movement, different Christian societies and emerging political parties highlighted the need to raise a new generation which was to be the champion

---

12 The National Boys Brigade, which was called the Red Branch Knights, was formed in June 1909, Fianna, Christmas 1914.

13 C de M, A Few Memories. Larkin, The Fianna and the King's visit, *Eire*, 16.6.1923; Hobson 1968, 16.

14 Hobson 1968, 17. These were the first three clauses of its Constitution as amended by the Ard Fheis 1913.

15 *Sinn Fein*, 21.8.1909. According to one observer this was due to the growing hostility of Griffith towards Hobson, Greaves, C.Desmond, Liam Mellows and the Irish Revolution, Southampton 1988 (1971), 43. He forgets that it was Markievicz who first presented the idea. On the other hand there was some co-operation from the start: Sinn Fein lent its rooms for the Fianna, see *Sinn Fein* (daily paper), 1.10.1909, and the advertisements of Fianna were publicised in *Sinn Fein*.

16 Concerning the first steps of the Boy Scout Movement in Finland and the ideas behind it, see for instance Halmesvirta, Anssi, Riiviöistä ritareiksi. Verneri Louhivuori, suomalaisen partio-aatteen synty ja nuorkirkollinen luonteenmuokkausideologia 1910-1924, in Historiallinen Arkisto 19, Suomen Historiallinen Seura, Tampere 1997, 7-59.

of moral values, temperance and purity. Their aims and ideas were often coloured by patriotism. In the Fianna's case, that was the driving force. According to a contemporary, the organisers focused on building the Fianna on nationalist lines by going for the earliest system of organisation and education known in Ireland. They studied the methods by which the Irish champions were disciplined in the pre-Christian era and applied them, with modifications, to the modern organisations.[17]

The "especial Irish method" which was to be the guiding line of the Fianna was not explicitly defined by Markievicz or anyone else. In the background of it can be found the basic nationalist idea of following and reconstructing the old Irish heritage. According to Markievicz, the Fianna boys should be "Irish in their knowledge of Ireland's history; Irish in their use of her language, Irish in their adoption of the fine code of honour of the old Fianna, and Irish in their prowess in arms and in their attitude as honourable soldiers waiting faithfully for the hour to come when they too should serve Ireland with all the passion of their glorious youth."[18]

The educational ideas of the Fianna reflected the idea of a special Irish education promoted by Irish Ireland thinking. According to Douglas Hyde, the founder of the Gaelic League, the same education that suited the English did not suit the Irish; on the contrary, there should be an Irish education, which taught the student everything relating to Ireland and the Irish; her language and her history.[19] For Fianna boys, the Irish legends of the warriors were of special importance. At the first annual meeting of the Fianna Markievicz held up as a moral for the boys the reply of Ossian of the old Fianna to St.Patrick. "We, the Fenians, never used to tell an untruth; a lie was never attributed to us; by truth and the strength of our hands we used to come safe out of every danger". She wished the boys to be self-reliant, honest, and to have a great sense of honour and self-sacrifice.[20]

Markievicz was not the only one who took the ancient tales of warriors as an example for contemporaries. The traditions of the ancient Fianna and especially of the mythological warrior Cuchulainn played an important part in the teachings of the prominent Gaelic Leaguer, writer and teacher Patrick Pearse whom Markievicz got to know better in 1911.[21] Pearse, who had founded a school for Catholic boys, St. Enda's, also found the source of Irish ills in English influence. He believed that the English educational system made Irish children into "willing slaves."[22] These ideas were also shared by Markievicz, who maintained that only the ignorance resulting from an English education separated the boys from the work Ireland demanded of them.[23]

---

17   Gifford, 349.
18   C.De M, A Few Memories. II. The Fianna, *Eire*, 9.6.1923.
19   Hyde, Douglas, What Ireland is Asking For, in Lady Gregory (ed.), Ideals in Ireland, 58-60.
20   *Bean na hEireann,* 19/1910.
21   Markievicz, Constance de, Memories. The King's Visit, *Eire*, 14.7.1923.
22   Moran, Sean Farrell, Patrick Pearse and the Politics of Redemption: The Mind of Easter Rising 1916, Washington d.c. 1994, 192.
23   Armid, A Woman With a Garden, *Bean na hEireann,* 14/ December 1909.

In Na Fianna Eireann politics in itself was considered a forbidden area, because the boys came from different backgrounds. But as they were "trained to be Irish nationalists"[24], they were in fact educated to adopt a certain political view. The exclusion of party politics reflected the idea of Wolfe Tone that the Irish should be united into one people despite their differences. Both Markievicz and Hobson shared this idea.

The activities of the Fianna branches or sluaghs varied in practice from boxing to scoutcraft, from the Irish language and irish history to first aid and Flag-signalling.[25] To a large extent the programme followed the lines of Baden-Powell; in both groups the boys were taught signalling, first aid, tracing, and the ideals of both were chivalry, obedience and honesty. But there was, of course, an important difference. The Fianna-boys were taught to be Irish nationalists and to use the guns. Markievicz, who was an excellent shot, taught them herself.[26] Markievicz seemed to think that the boys should already prepare for the future struggle; she did not try to discourage or punish boys who attacked the Baden-Powell boy groups.[27]

The First Years of Na Fianna Eireann and its impact

Markievicz was chosen as President of the Fianna in 1910. At that time there were seven branches; five in Dublin, one in Waterford and one in Glasgow. Each branch consisted of twenty to sixty members.[28] By July 1912 there were 22 branches.[29] To spread the organisation all over Ireland the Fianna named a special organiser, Liam Mellows.[30] Although the number of the branches of the Fianna grew, Markievicz was sometimes concerned about its progress. Even though a branch could be born spontaneously, the boys disappeared after they "found they were not to go out fighting the English the next week."[31] Another problem was money.[32] In addition to the lack of material resources and the number of members Markievicz was concerned with the question of inner improvement. In speaking at the Annual Conference in 1913 she emphasized the need for " improving and perfecting the material." She considered every boy to be worth all the trouble taken to improve his education and character and pointed out that the very act of a boy enlisting was a proof in itself of character and a willingness to play his part in the great national work. Therefore the officers should study the theory and modern methods of education in order to better train the boys under their command. Furthermore, they should

---

24 Gifford, 350.
25 An example of the activities of An Cheud Sluagh from Dublin in *Sinn Fein*, 18.12.1909.
26 Czira, 55; Jones 1919, 171.
27 Gifford, 356.
28 Van Voris, 72-73.
29 *Irish Freedom*, August 1912.
30 *Irish Freedom*,May 1913. By June Fianna was established in most of the south-west counties, *Irish Freedom*, June 1913.
31 O'Faolain, 96.
32 Gifford, 349-350.

remember that more could be achieved by kindly sympathy and mutual help than by punishment or reprimands.[33] Her words reflected a wider concern among the Fianna in general; for in December 1913 it was being argued that the culture of the body had monopolised attention while the culture of the mind had been overlooked.[34]

Markievicz was apparently impressed by the ideas of Pearse, who had studied continental educational thinking and applied it to the Irish situation. According to him, real education consisted of forming the child's character, drawing out his faculties, and disciplining his intellect. He also strongly condemned corporal punishment. In his school he wanted the boys to be taught an active love and reverence for the Christian virtues, such as purity, temperance, fortitude, truth, and loving-kindness. They should have a spirit of chilvalry and self-sacrifice, charity and a love of nature. Patriotism was to be systematically taught and the formation of a sense of civic social duty promoted. [35]

Both Markievicz and Patrick Pearse paid attention to the civic education of the boys, whom they perceived as the future Irish citizens who should transform society according to special Irish values. The handbook of the Fianna, published in 1914, stressed the educational role of the movement. The first work of the members should be to train themselves to be fit citizens of a free nation. The most important thing was that the Fianna was governed by the boys themselves, something which prepared them to serve Ireland in other organisations when they were older. A sluagh of the Fianna should be a little self governing community - a boy's Republic. Fianna aimed at making Irish boys strong and self-reliant and self-respecting:

> "By working for Irish Freedom they are taught the lesson of self-sacrifice and service. By obedience to their officers and the discipline of their sluagh they learn to obey and to be self-controlled. By becoming officers they learn to command. By governing their organisation they gain experience and confidence, and learn to think for themselves."[36]

For Markievicz it was logical that the boys who had been trained to be Irish nationalists would strive to be future martyrs. In 1914 she wrote with feeling:

> "This year has felt the spirit of Cathleen ni Houlihan moving once more through the land. This year we have heard again her imperious demands, her call to those who would serve her, to give her all, to give her themselves...It will take the best and noblest of Ireland's children to win Freedom, for the price of Freedom is suffering and pain. It is only when the suffering is deep enough and the pain almost beyond bearing that Freedom is won...The spirit of Ireland is free because Ireland's children have never shirked to pay the price. The path of freedom may lead us the same road that Robert Emmet and Wolfe Tone trod. Treading in their footsteps, we

---

33   The Fourth Ard Fheis, *Irish Freedom*, August 1913.
34   *Irish Freedom*, December 1913.
35   Dudley Edwards, 105-106, 116.
36   Fianna Handbook, Dublin 1914, 12—23.

will not fear, working as they worked we will not tire, and if we must die as they died we will not flinch."[37]

The boys had in themselves the love of country, which for Markievicz was a feeling that few people were born without. She asserted that the list of Irish martyr patriots was exceptional; and because the blood of these men ran in the veins of the Irish and because they lived in the same air and on the same earth, it was natural that the Irish had inherited a tiny part of the great love that was in patriots' hearts. She appealed to the boys by comparing the road of nationalists to the road of Christ and promised that their reward would be greater than "money or advancement, success or luxury, for they would be patriots and heroes."[38]

The need for sacrifice that Markievicz emphasized was shared in Fianna circles as well.[39] It was also becoming more important for Pearse. In his play An Ri (The King) written in 1912 he expressed the necessity of sacrificing the young and the sinless to save a decadent nation.[40] Pearse's idea of the Irish Hero, a man who exemplified the virtues of Cuchulainn and the mythological heroes of ancient Gaelic Ireland, who was modelled on Christ in self-abnegation, suffering, death and ultimate victory, and who was identified with the previous leaders of the rising[41], was an ideal of which Markievicz apparently approved and wanted the boys to approve. The Fianna boys and the boys at St.Enda's were also directly connected. For instance, in 1913 the Fianna put on displays at a fete at St.Enda's.[42]

The founding of the Fianna created a new interest in the educating of children and youth in Sinn Fein. Early in 1910 Sinn Fein announced that an "Irish Brigade" for children had been established and a column for children was also started in the paper.[43] There were in addition others who were even more interested in the rebel boys' organisation. For Hobson, who had by now left Sinn Fein, the Fianna offered a way to recruit members for the IRB. In 1912 he created a special Fianna circle for the older boys into the Central branch of the Dublin IRB.[44] The Circle discussed matters of Fianna Policy on the eve of every Ard Fheis (Convention) and the voice of the convention was that of the IRB.[45] Thus the Fianna was becoming a part of the organisation designed to start a rebellion.

---

37   Markievicz, Introduction in Fianna Handbook, 6-8.
38   Love of Country. Extracts from a lecture by Constance de Markievicz, *Bean na hEireann* 20, July 1910.
39   E.g. in the articles written for Fianna in *The Irish Freedom*, a paper of the IRB. See e.g. "Art" in *Irish Freedom*, November 1910, who writes that the only road to freedom is the red road of war.
40   Dudley Edwards, 142. See also Gilley, Sheridan, Pearse's Sacrifice and Cuchulain Crucified and Risen in the Easter Rising 1916, in Jonah Alexander and Alan O'Day (eds.), Ireland's Terrorist Dilemma, 32.
41   Martin, F.X., 1916 - Revolution or Evolution?, in Martin 1967, 247.
42   Dudley Edwards, 172.
43   *Sinn Fein*, 26.3.1910, 15.1.1911.
44   Hobson 1968, 13, 17.
45   Van Voris, 89.

For boys only? – the role of female in Na Fianna Eireann

The idea of the Fianna came from a woman, but that did not mean that the organisation was intended for both sexes equally. At the first meeting of the Fianna the only two women attending were Markievicz and Moloney, and they were not accepted unanimously by the boys.[46] Girls were not admitted as members in the beginning. The situation changed at the annual meeting of 1912, when the motion to open the doors to girls was accepted by one vote before motion was reached suggesting that girls should start their own independent organisation. The journal voicing the views of the IRB described this as the most revolutionary decision made at the meeting.[47]

Behind this revolutionary decision lay the activities of Markievicz and the two daughters of the socialist James Connolly, Ina and Nora, who had started their own branch in Belfast earlier.[48] The Connolly girls had, according to Markievicz, faced endless opposition in organising young girls on the same lines as the boys.[49] It is likely that the influence of the IRB was reflected in this opposition. There were still strong prejudices against women who were not content to be merely passive supporters of the nationalist cause.[50] It has also been asserted that the IRB hindered the development of the girls' branches overall, except in Glasgow and Belfast.[51]

Organising girls was thus not immediately successful, and it was certainly not the first thing on the agenda of Markievicz. Nonetheless, it would be incorrect to say that her attitude was shaped by the traditional view that men did the fighting and women bound the wounds.[52] When one looks at her speeches and actions, it is clear that she was breaking these traditional roles in many areas of activity. The answer to the question why there were so few girls' branches can best be found by looking at the situation in general. The organising of a radical nationalist movement was still facing difficulties: the movement for promoting passive resistance was many times stronger. In addition, the organising of the Fianna in Ireland was not in the hands of Markievicz alone but was being mainly done at a grassroot level by men and boys who, it seems, were rarely as interested in organising girls as they were in organising boys. Possibly Markievicz thought that organising the girls inside an already established movement would be easier than starting something entirely new. It is logical that she did not want to divide girls and boys between separate organisations when one remembers that her object was to provide both sexes with common goals in pursuing the nationalist task. Moreover, it should be noted that the Fianna was established – at least in part – to confront recruitment into the police force and the British Army, something which did not endanger girls and women.

---

46   Hobson 1968, 16; Van Voris, 70. Markievicz does not write about this personally.
47   Irish Freedom, August 1912.
48   Connolly-Heron, Ina, James Connolly: A Biography, *Liberty*, June 1966, 15.
49   Constance de Markievicz , James Connolly; as I knew him, *The Nation*, 26.3.1927.
50   See Ward 1986, 86.
51   Norman, 73.
52   Haverty, 87.

Markievicz had criticised men who had adopted conventional party politics and thus did not see the "right" nationalist path as clearly as women did. Instead of trying to change their attitudes, she focused on raising the younger generation of males. She did not address young girls as often as young boys, but found it important to remind the former that they should above all cultivate ideals. Her vision of women as moral guardians is revealed in her comments on the fact that character and deeds influenced people more than empty words. [53] She also regarded the action of women during the previous rebellions as an example worthy of being followed by the boys of the Fianna. [54]

In speaking to the young women of Ireland in March 1909 Markievicz had asserted that "if in your day the call should come for your body to arm, do not shirk that either" and had concluded by hoping for a Joan of Arc that would free Ireland.[55] In Markievicz's view women were therefore entitled to fight alongside the men. Moreover, they could even lead them. Yet as regard the founding of a nationalist army the role of women was not of primary importance. That was not in a contradiction of her overall ideas of radical women. The only organisation that welcomed Fianna with open arms at the very beginning was Inghinidhe na hEireann, which had been concerned with what it described as the consistent neglect of the children in nationalist organisations.[56] It saw the boys of Fianna as future soldiers of a nationalist army which was important not only for gaining independence but for sustaining it.[57]

Nevertheless the fact that the radical women's organisation supported the Fianna nor the speeches of Markievicz and other nationalist women on the ancient warqueens had an impact on the division of labour between sexes in the new organisation. The later decision to accept girl members did not essentially change the situation, even though it in principle gave both sexes the same opportunities. Apparently women, including Markievicz, found it more important to promote the development of the nationalist army than to fight for the right to be in the army themselves, at least in a situation where the building of the the army was still not finished. For them the equality of the sexes in that matter was of secondary importance.

---

53   Correspondence: To Miss Nora Cassidy and the Young Girls of Ireland, Maca, *Bean na hEireann* 9/1909.
54   Extracts from her lecture on the Women of' 98 in the Na Fianna Eireann, *Bean na hEireann* 14, December 1909. That men and women were equally important in the struggle was declared also in the nationalist play *The Memory of the Dead* written by Casimir Markievicz. In the play the leading lady, Norah —who was played by Constance Markievicz — uttered the words:"If there are men in Ireland ready to die for their country, there are just as many women", Markievicz, Casimir Dunin, The Memory of the Dead: A Romantic drama of '98 in Three Acts, Dublin 1910.
55   Markievicz 1909, 16.
56   Editorial Notes, *Bean na hEireann*, 9, July 1909.
57   Na Fianna Eireann, *Bean na hEireann* 11, September 1909; Editorial Notes, *Bean na hEireann* 15, January 1910.

Markievicz as a Rebel Actor

The Fianna played an important part in the life of Markievicz. Her home became a meeting place for Fianna boys and "rebels of all sorts."[58] She gave lectures[59], camped out with the boys in Dublin mountains and accompanied them on their marches, when the boys dressed in kilts, played Irish pipes and carried banners. At the same time she sticked anti-recruiting bills to lamp-posts.[60] For adults the activities of the Fianna may have seemed ridiculous, but for their children Markievicz was an ideal figure. The respect and enthusiasm the boys felt for her impressed her contemporaries.[61]

The work with the Fianna meant that Markievicz had taken a step further towards being an active actor in nationalist politics. In less than a year after joining the Inghinidhe na hEireann Markievicz had forsaken laces and ball-gowns and had started a para-military organisation for boys. She had achieved fame as a rebel speaker and had placed herself in the radical nationalist camp, despite the suspicion.[62] It has been asserted that the Fianna was Hobson's idea[63] or that the Fianna only continued the activities he had started in Belfast. However, there is a clear difference between the programme of the boys group in Belfast and the programme of the Fianna. The latter declared openly that they wanted to re-establish Irish independence and trained militarily in order to achieve it. The militaristic nature of the organisation was emphasized in the uniforms Markievicz designed for the boys. Her idea of the Fianna was the first sign of an emerging militarism in Ireland before the First World War. She strove to recruit a new group, young Irish boys, to her army to free Ireland. Her "army" already included young idealistic women.

Although Markievicz shared most of her ideas with Hobson, she did not follow him when he, along some other radical nationalists, left Sinn Fein when the small organisation seemed to be near its end.[64] Her decision to stay has been described as illogical, and it has been maintained that she stayed because at that time only Sinn Fein admitted women.[65] However, Markievicz strongly

---

58   Sheehy-Skeffington, Hanna, Countess Markievicz, Sheehy Skeffington Papers, MS 24 189, NLI.
59   For instance she spoke about revolutionary movements in Belfast 23.11.1911, *Bean na hEireann* 23, 1911.
60   Jones 1919, 172.
61   Lyons Thornton, Brighid, in Griffith, Kenneth & O'Grady, Timothy E. (eds.), Curious Journey: An Oral History of Ireland's Unfinished Revolution, London 1982,39; Skinnider, Margaret, Doing my Bit for Ireland, New York 1917,18; Jones 1919, 171; O'Faolain, 95. On the other hand Hobson tells that he had on many occasions to point out privately that the boys could not accept the financial help of Markievicz and must refuse her membership or office. According to him, the feeling against the presence of a woman in a boys' organisation continued in varying degrees of intensify for several years, Hobson 1968, 16.
62   See Cronin, Sean, McGarrity Papers, Tralee 1972, 25-26; Later Markievicz was suspected of having given information concerning a secret meeting of Sinn Fein, Markievicz, Constance de, Mr. Griffith and Mr. Tim Healy, *Eire*, 1.9.1923.
63   E.g. "In August 1909 Hobson, with the aid of Countess Markievicz, founded Fianna Eireann..." McCullough, Martin, Hobson, and Republican Ulster, in Martin 1967,101; Kee, 206.
64   In September 1910 it was claimed that Sinn Fein was in the last stages of its existence, Davis, 65. Also Markievicz, Constance de, Memories. The King's Visit, *Eire*, 14.7.1923.
65   According to Davis she said that herself, Davis, 68.

objected to the quarrels: even though she criticised the road Griffith seemed to have taken[66] she simultaneously lamented the lack of unity in Ireland during previous rebellions[67] and criticised the extremists, especially Hobson, maintaining that the only result of their dropping out of the movement was the further dwindling and melting away of the organisation without anything more extreme being started in its place.[68]

To Markievicz demonstrating of the rebel spirit was one of the most important – if not the most important – things in Irish nationalism. When the King of England came to Dublin, she was among the small group of nationalists consisting mainly of women of Inghinidhe na hEireann and Fianna boys, who wanted to exploit the visit for propaganda. The majority of Sinn Feiners – including Hobson and other members of the IRB – decided not to provoke an uproar by staging demonstrations in Dublin. Markievicz and others who stayed in Dublin distributed handbills all along the route and waved a black flag but created little disturbance.[69] By now it was clear that Markievicz wanted to show rebellious spirit on every possible occasion. Under her guidance Fianna was one of the most visible organisations in that respect.

The idea of training young people to confront the ideas and educational system of the coloniser and to promote patriotism was not a unique one in Ireland or elsewhere in Europe. In addition, the similarities between the educational objects of Pearse and Markievicz are evident – even though the connections have often remained unnoticed. What is special regarding Markievicz is that she was a woman who taught the boys to take up arms against her own class. It is obvious that training the boys for future fighting was more important to her than training them to speak the native language fluently or teaching them to promote Irish culture. This does not mean that she did not appreciate the national culture in itself . Rather, her character and personal capabilites led her to try a different way. Interestingly, the road she chose was a road which the men of her class had rejected. Markievicz, who strove to undo the conquest her soldier ancestors had done, wanted to achieve her aim in a similar way – by the use of arms. She believed firmly in the need for sacrifice, for "giving it all." Only that would make independence acceptable. The Irish boys, whom she wanted to raise as Irish nationalists, should be prepared to give their life for Ireland.

---

66   Before Christmas 1909 it was suspected that Griffith was going to join up with Tim Healy and bring Sinn Fein and the "All for Ireland League" together with a new policy. The first activity of the joint party would be to fight Mr. Redmonds's candidate in the South Dublin election. The rumours caused an uproar in Sinn Fein, Markievicz, Constance de, Mr. Griffith and Mr. Tim Healy, *Eire*, 1.9.1923.
67   She compares the rising in Poland in 1830 with the Irish ones. Armid, A Woman with a Garden, *Bean na hEireann* 13, November 1909.
68   Markievicz, Constance de, Mr. Griffith and Mr. Tim Healy, *Eire*, 1.9.1923.
69   Markievicz, Constance de, Memories. The King's Visit, *Eire*, 14.7.1923 and 21.7.1923 ; see also C de M , A Few Memories. Larkin, The Fianna and the King's visit, *Eire*, 16.6.1923. For text of the handbill, see Ward 1983, 78.

■ The Red Countess[1]

Socialism – a way to promote nationalism?

In the autumn of 1910 Markievicz was drawn into another movement that was gathering strength in Ireland. In the labour movement she saw a potential force and support for the nationalist struggle. Among the first things that impressed her was the speech of Jim Larkin. One morning at that time she read a piece of news which filled her "with hope, admiration, sympathy & delight." The news was that "a man had arisen in Ireland with an illuminating new idea. The man was Jim Larkin, and the idea was that Irish Labour must not be controlled from England." She decided to go and listen to him. Markievicz, among other contemporaries, was greatly impressed by the oratorial skills of Larkin. From that day she looked upon Larkin as a friend and wanted to help him.[2]

The few words Markievicz spoke at the same meeting as Larkin reveal her vision of the Larkinite movement as a force opposed to British influence: she urged all nationalists to help him, whether they were workers or not.[3] The black- and -white nationalism Markievicz had adopted was guiding her vision of the labour movement as well. Thus, the notion of international solidarity between workers was ignored in her claim that the message of Larkin was that "international socialism stood for free nations or national units who, on a basis of absolute equality, associated together to preserve peace, and to further ensure the just distribution of the fruits of man's labour."[4]

In addition, Markievicz pointed out that before the activities of Larkin, when the unions were mainly organised and controlled from England, "the Irish interests were neglected and Irish Nationalism obscured." She connected Larkin even more strongly with the nationalist tradition by asserting that Larkin knew this instinctively because of the rebel blood in his veins; "his stock had contributed a martyr in '98."[5] Thus, she understood the activities of Larkin as a separate programme arising from the national situation, which was unique to

---

1   This name was given Markievicz later, in 1923. She preferred herself the appellation given her on the Continent, where she was the Green Countess. Fox, R.M., Rebel Irishwomen. Dublin 1935, 19.
2   Markievicz, Constance de, A Few Memories. Larkin, The Fianna and the King's visit, *Eire*, 16.6.1923. About Larkin's oratorial skills e.g. Lyons 1973, 276. Larkin was released from prison in September 1910, Berresford Ellis, Peter, A History of the Irish Working Class, London 1985 (1st edition 1972),185.
3   Larkin, Emmet, James Larkin: Irish Labour Leader 1876-1947, London 1965, 74.
4   Markievicz, Constance de, A Few Memories. Larkin, The Fianna and the King's Visit, *Eire*, 16.6.1923.
5   Markievicz, Constance de, A Few Memories. Larkin, The Fianna and the King's Visit, *Eire*, 16.6.1923.

Ireland. It has been claimed that because Markievicz only had to read about Larkin to attend a meeting, she was already thinking as a socialist.[6] However, if her reason for going there came from the idea that the workers of Ireland should not be guided from England, she was not thinking as a socialist, but more or less as a nationalist.

At the time Markievicz first saw Jim Larkin[7], then a 34-year-old trade union activist, he had already gained a reputation as an organiser of the workers. Ireland was at that time a dominantly agricultural country. Of the skilled working force, the organised workers were members of English-based trade unions.The constituency of old unionism amounted to only about 10 per cent of the waged workforce. As a rule the Irish employers totally ignored trade unions and condemned them. The right of combination for workers was fought town by town: Belfast in 1907; Dublin,1908 and Cork in 1909.[8]

In the year 1909 Larkin established the Irish Transport and General Workers' Union (ITGWU) which laid the cornerstone of an Irish labour movement. It argued that Irish workers could rely on their own resources and build a movement geared to tackling native conditions.[9] Larkin summed up his philosophy regarding the ITGWU in one phrase "The land of Ireland for the people of Ireland." The people of Ireland included equally Protestants and Catholics; in Belfast Larkin strove to unite the workers despite religious differences.[10] His aim to unite different sections of the population in Ireland reflected the notion of Tone and was certainly approved by Markievicz . In addition to that, the fact that Larkin was sympathetic to republicanism and the ideology of Irish Ireland[11], certainly brought her closer to him. In turn, Larkin was friendly to the Fianna and lent them a bigger room at the Union headquarters. [12]

The other prominent labour leader, James Connolly (1868–1916), influenced the ideas and policy of Markievicz even more. She met him in 1910 in Belfast through his daughters who had started working along the lines of the Fianna there, and spent "pleasant and interesting evenings...listening to James Connolly and his friends talking and I, trying to learn all I could." The conversation covered a very wide ground, but everything discussed led back to the same question - "how can we work out Ireland's freedom?" Aware of her own ignorance, Markievicz started "to read the books recommended to me and tried to fit myself for the work I had started on" [13], a project she had gone

6   Marreco, 136.
7   James Larkin was born in Liverpool of Irish parentage in 1876. As a child he became a labourer and worked as a seaman and as a dock foreman in Liverpool. Working for the National Union of Dock Laboureres, he was sent to Belfast in 1907 and organised there a wave of strikes.
8   Berresford Ellis, 178; O'Connor, Emmet, A Labour History of Ireland 1824-1960, Dublin 1992,69. The new line of Larkin was not accepted unanimously in the labour movement; the Belfast socialists wanted to preserve connection with the English movement whereas the Dublin socialists wanted to sever it, Mitchell, Arthur, Labour in Irish Politics, Dublin 1974, 31.
9   O'Connor, 68-69.
10   Berresford Ellis, 180, 183.
11   See Berresford Ellis, 178, 192-193.
12   Markievicz, Constance de, A Few Memories. Larkin, The Fianna and the King's visit, Eire, 16.6.1923.
13   Markievicz, Constance de, James Connolly; as I knew him., Nation, 26.3.1927.

through earlier regarding the ideas of Irish nationalism. Connolly and Markievicz became friends and when Connolly was later in Dublin, he stayed with her for months at a time.[14]

The man whose ideas Markievicz wanted to learn and promote was, like Larkin, a son of Irish emigrants born in Scotland and originally a worker. James Connolly had in 1896 founded the Irish Socialist Republican Party (ISRP), a small and largely Dublin-based group, which broke up in 1903. The principal objective of ISRP was the "establishment of an Irish Socialist Republic based upon the public ownership by the Irish people of the land and instruments of production, distribution and exchange."[15] In 1903 Connolly migrated to America and absorbed the current syndicalist ideas there. He joined Daniel De Leon's Socialist Labor Party and worked for the Industrial Workers of the World.

Connolly's syndicalism was based on the straightforward premise that workers should take hold of the daily fight in the workshop and organise it in a revolutionary manner, giving it a revolutionary purpose and direction.[16] In *Labour in Irish History*, published in 1910, Connolly wrote that

> "...the Irish toilers would henceforward base their right for freedom not upon the winning or losing the right to talk in an Irish parliament, but upon their progress towards the mastery of those factories, workshops and farms upon which a people's bread and liberties depend.
> As we have again and again pointed out, the Irish question is a social question...Who would own and control the land? The people, or the invaders..."[17]

Ultimately, the workers would take over the state and their industrial unions, the trade unions, would then form the basis for governing the new commonwealth.[18]

Connolly returned in Ireland in 1910 at the invitation of the Socialist Party of Ireland (SPI), the successor of ISRP, and strengthened his position as the most influential socialist theoretician in the Irish labour movement. Unlike most syndicalists, Connolly did not completely forsake political action.[19] In the spring of 1912, he was engaged in founding a new party, the Independent Labour Party of Ireland. It supported a socialist programme and labour political action, and advocated home rule for Ireland as a step towards ending the division of Irish workers on religious - political issues.[20] However, Connolly was first of all committed to the militant ITGWU, which he greatly admired, and later to the Irish Citizen Army (ICA), which he saw as the primary revolutionary vehicles.[21]

---

14   Markievicz, Constance de, James Connolly; as I knew him., *Nation*, 26.3.1927.
15   Anderson, 41-42.
16   Anderson, 40. Quotation from *Harp*, 8/1908, 8.
17   Connolly 1910, 166.
18   Cahill, 24.
19   Cronin 1980, 110.
20   Mitchell 1974, 32.
21   Anderson, 38, 57. About syndicalism in Larkinism, see MacCarthy, Charles, The Impact of Larkinism on the Irish Working Class, *Saothar*, 4/1978, 55-56.

It is rather difficult, given the ideas Markievicz had so far presented, to imagine her to accepting a committed syndicalist and a Union leader in the way that she did. But she was not choosing Connolly's ideas because of their syndicalism. She agreed with Connolly's final goal: the revolution which would crush British government and sever all the links with it[22] with the help of the Irish poor – the small tenant farmers, the agricultural labourers, the workers in towns and cities – who, in his view, had been the only group to resist foreign rule and who formed the rank and file of every rebel movement.[23]

Another central feature that enabled Markievicz to embrace Connolly's ideas was his notion of the struggle for national independence as an inseparable part of the struggle for socialism. In 1896 he wrote: "The struggle for Irish freedom has two aspects: it is national and it is social. The national ideal can never be realised until Ireland stands..as a nation, free and independent."[24] On the other hand, national liberation would have been in vain without a Socialist Republic . Otherwise England would still rule through her array of commercial and individualist institutions.[25] Thus, socialism and nationalism were two sides of one great democratic principle.[26] According to Connolly, "the cause of labour is the cause of Ireland, the cause of Ireland is the cause of labour. They cannot be dissevered."[27] His declaration was not acceptable to most of the supporters of labour movement, who advocated Home Rule and were not interested in radical nationalism.[28]

Thus, in a situation where the politics of Sinn Fein did not seem to gain the support of the Irish to the extent Markievicz had hoped, the labour movement, now gaining strength through the militant ITGWU, offered a new way to demonstrate the rebel spirit. In addition, both Larkin and Connolly had adopted the Irish Ireland ideas that Markievicz was devoted to. Like Larkin, Connolly had a patriotic passion; he studied Irish history, admired Irish music and song and supported the Gaelic revival movement and Sinn Fein.[29] He approved the Irish Renaissance as a way to strengthen democratic consciousness.[30]

Markievicz had now redefined her policy. Even though she supported, albeit not without reservations, the policy of Sinn Fein, she also accepted the goals of the labour movement, especially those promoted by Larkin and Connolly. In

---

22   Connolly 1910, 23-24; Connolly, James, Socialism and Irish Nationalism (1897), in Berresford Ellis, P. (ed.), James Connolly: Selected Writings, London 1988, 128.
23   Cronin 1980, 110-111.
24   Anderson, 41-42. In his own day Connolly's ideas were novel and radical and he was ridiculed and misunderstood by many of his contemporaries, ibid.
25   Connolly, James, Socialism and Nationalism, *Shan Van Vocht*, 1897, in James Connolly: Selected Writings, 124.
26   Berresford Ellis, 173.
27   Connolly, James, The Irish Flag, *Workers' Republic*, 8.4.1916, in James Connolly: Selected Writings, 145.
28   Greaves 1961, 224; See e.g. Gallagher, Michael ,Socialism and Nationalist Tradition in Ireland 1798–1918, *Éire-Ireland* 2/1977, 85.
29   Anderson, 48; Metscher, Priscilla, Republicanism and Socialism in Ireland: A Study in the Relationship of Politics and Ideology from the United Irishmen to James Connolly, Frankfurt 1986, 315-316.
30   Greaves, 195.

Sinn Fein that was a divisive factor. When it came to social and economic questions, both Sinn Fein and the IRB were conservative.[31] Griffith attacked the Irish working class movement and blamed Larkinism for unemployed fathers, grieving mothers, hungry children, broken homes and rising food prices.[32] The tradition of the nationalist movement had constantly demanded that social questions should be left until after successfully solving the national question. Socialism and nationalism were seen as opposing forces.[33] Socialism was even seen as a foreign influence which would divide the nation. This conception was supported by references to the old co-operative community by cultural nationalism and also by the negative stand against socialism taken by the Catholic church.[34]

In years 1910–12 there is no indication that Markievicz was giving priority to the goals of the working class movement over nationalist goals. Her involvement with and acceptance of labour issues did not push aside the ultimate goal, a rising, which would establish an independent Irish nation. She focused her energy at that time for the most part on organising the Fianna. Her connections with women workers give evidence of this.

Markievicz and women workers

Larkin and Connolly were not the only ones who were actively involved with the labour movement among Markievicz's circle. Her closest relative and younger sister Eva Gore-Booth had for several years been organising working class women with her life-long friend Esther Roper in Manchester both as a speaker and secretary of different groups. [35] In Lancashire, where she worked, the suffragist activists had strong links with the Independent Labour party (ILP) and trade union circles.[36] Eva Gore-Booth also wanted to widen the franchise to include not only a particular group of women but all women. She stressed the need of political power for the defence of the workers, especially women, who were paid at lower rates than men and whose work was restricted to the poorer and less remunerative sections of those trades.[37]

31 Rumpf, E., & Hepburn, A.L., Nationalism and Socialism in twentieth-century Ireland, Liverpool 1977, 10; Garvin 1987, 35, 132.
32 *Sinn Fein*, 30.9.1911.
33 Gallagher, 65.
34 Patterson, Henry, The Politics of Illusion: Republicanism and Socialism in Modern Ireland, London 1989, 17-18.
35 See reports of Manchester & Salford Women's Trades and Labour Council in 1900-1908, Box 3, File 8,Eva Gore-Booth Collection, Penn State University, Pennsylvania, USA; She was also leading the Lancashire and Cheshire Textile and other Workers Representation Committee, Liddington, 197; in 1908 she attended the Labour Party Conference as a delegate from the Association of Machine, Electrical and Other Women Workers, Liddington 237.
36 Garner, 16.
37 Lewis, 64-65; See e.g. Gore-Booth, Eva, The Women's Suffrage Movement Among Trade unionists, in Villiers, B.(ed.), The Case for Women's Suffrage, London 1907, 50-65.

The activities of Eva Gore-Booth were not unusual themselves. By the twentieth century, women participated in and occasionally influenced socialist movements throughout Europe. Socialists and feminists shared same goals. Both wanted to change contemporary society. Markievicz also referred to the importance of getting women workers into the Parliament in 1909 when she asserted that a man, who had the privilege of a vote in the labour world, had power to frame laws "to protect his labour from the rapacious capitalist, who in return has the same weapon at his service for his defence."[38] Again, in 1911 when she was speaking at the foundation meeting of the Irish Women Workers' Union (CIWWU), she highlighted the importance of a vote:

> "Without organisation you can do nothing and the purpose of this meeting is to form you into an army of fighters...As you are all aware women have at present no vote, but a union such as has now been formed will not alone help you to obtain better wages, but will also be a great means of helping you to get votes...and thus make men of you all."[39]

This extract from her speech contains two ideas which usually formed part of her appeal to an Irish audience: that they should organise themselves and become fighters. It is interesting to note that Markievicz, who earlier was careful to put the nationalist struggle before the struggle for "votes for women" now underlined the importance of the vote. Of course, she was speaking alongside with the suffragist Hanna Sheehy-Skeffington, but it seems that she assumed her audience would be more interested in organising themselves into a union if they saw it as a way of getting the vote. In fact, it is unlikely that latter was the greatest concern of women workers in Dublin, who lived and worked under difficult conditions. Apparently Markievicz in her own mind connected these two things because of the activities of her sister.

In any case neither her appearance at the meeting nor her address do not in themselves prove that her socialist ideas were fully formed, as has been pointed out.[40] It would be interesting to know, however, what kind of a speech she gave to the factory girls of Belfast. The topic of her lecture was "Strikes as a Revolutionary Weapon".[41] She had also spoken at the gates of factories,[42] in the same way as her sister. However, she was not actively involved with the IWWU despite being elected a Vice President of the organisation in 1915.[43] Her friend, the nationalist Helena Moloney became more active in the women workers' cause.[44] Markievicz, despite her involvement with and acceptance of the women workers' movement, did not see the issue being as important as the nationalist struggle or the organising of Irish workers as a whole.

---

38   Maca, Free Woman in Free Ireland, *Bean na hEireann*, January 1909.
39   Women Worker's Union. Great Meeting in Antient Concert Rooms, *The Irish Worker*, 9.9.1911.
40   Haverty, 95.
41   According to William McMullen, Introduction in Ryan, Desmond (ed.), Connolly: Workers' Republic, Dublin 1951, 22.
42   Connolly-Heron, Ina, *Liberty*, July 1966, 51.
43   *Workers' Republic*, 13.11.1915. Molony was chosen as the General Secretary and James Connolly as the other Vice President.
44   E.g. Connolly-Heron, 17.

The importance of action – the Lock-Out

The Dublin Lock-Out in 1913 was important to Markievicz in two respects. On the one hand it placed her firmly on the side of the workers; on the other hand it represented a policy that she wanted the Irish to adopt. According to her own words she was by then sure of her stand and thus joined with the workers in the fight. [45]

From 1910 onwards there was a series of strikes in vital sections of the economy, including the docks, the mines, the railways and shipping in Britain.[46] By the summer of 1913 the ITGWU stood at the summit of its pre-war strength, embracing about 30,000 men, in the main unskilled Dubliners.[47] In Dublin the workers' unrest was especially forceful. In the summer of 1913 the employers wanted to crush the ITGWU for good and demanded that the workers either left the unions or left their jobs. The Lock-Out, which started in August, had by September left about 25 000 workers without work. Larkin and Connolly were arrested and the police attacked a crowd. The British TUC supported the Dublin workers.[48]

In this situation the sympathy of Markievicz was without hesitation on the side of the workers. In a poem written during the unrest she declared her support for Jim Larkin and his followers in their opposition to William Murphy, the leader of the employers:

> "Who fears to wear the blood red badge
>   upon his manly breast?
> What scab obeys the vile command
>   of Murphy and the rest;
> He's all a knave, and half a slave
>   Who slights his Union thus,
> But true men, like you men,
>   Will show the badge with us.
>   ...
> We rise in sad and weary days
>   To fight the worker's cause,
> We found in Jim, a heart ablaze,
>   To break down unjust laws,
>   ...
> Good luck be with him. He is here
>   to win for us the fight;
> To suffer for us without fear,
>   To champion to the right.
>   ...   " [49]

---

45   Markievicz, Constance de, James Connolly; as I knew him., *Nation*, 26.3.1927.
46   Garner,8.
47   O'Connor, 83
48   Berresford Ellis, 194-196.
49   "Maca", Who Fears To Wear the Blood Red Badge, *Irish Worker*, 11.10.1913. The name was an adoptation of the old republican rebel song "Who Fears To Speak of '98" and was sung by its tune, Van Voris, 362.

Markievicz commented on Larkin's arrest in a similar vein, portraying him as a hero for all the Irish, not only for the workers:

> "Jim Larkin is in jail. In jail for fighting the workers' cause. In jail for championing the poor against the rich, the oppressed against the oppressor...He dared attack "capitalism." Under the flag of "capitalism" you find the British Crown with its all minions, its judges, magistrates, inspectors, spies, police, the Ancient Order of Hibernians – even some of the clergy – all the worshippers of Mammon...In the little Court House in Green Street Jim stood...many a fight in the cause of Freedom has been fought in the Green St. Dock; it was one of the last stations on Robert Emmet's road to gallows. It bears a great tradition of noble souls who gave their all in the cause of freedom...All honest men and women must love, respect and honour him...to carry on the fight as he would have it carried on; to give their all in the cause of freedom – the workers' cause...Jim is in jail for us; what sacrifice can we make for Jim? What offering of work and self sacrifice can we lay at his feet? Let none of us think that we are of no importance and that we don't count; every little one of us is something to Jim..."[50]

Instead of attacking the employers, Markievicz juxtaposed Larkin with the representatives of British government and the others who had condemned his activities. By putting the word capitalism in quotation marks, Markievicz seems to be uncertain of its suitablility to describe the group Larkin fought against. She saw Larkin first and foremost as a martyr following in the steps of Emmet and fighting the British, rather than as a Socialist championing for workers. In her opinion it was British rule that had caused the crisis, and not merely the contradictory interests of employers and workers. In the same way as she had earlier categorized all English people as worshippers of Mammon, she now labelled all representatives of British government as "capitalists". In her writings, Larkin's sentence was defined in a way which resembled the fate of Christ who also sacrificed everything. The words "every little one of us is something to Jim" brought the image of Christ even nearer, but recalling also the nationalist idea that every Irishman or woman should fulfil his or her duty as well.

The activities of Markievicz supported her words. She organised a soup kitchen to better the worsening situation of Dublin workers. It took her time right round the clock for about half a year. Furthermore, she collected funds for the kitchens – for example by selling her jewels – and she visited sick people.[51] Her charitable work has even been regarded as her greatest achievement. On the other hand, she faced a lot of opposition because of supporting such an unpopular cause.[52] During the Lock-Out two influential

---

50   In Jail by Madame Markievicz, *Irish Worker*, 1.11.1913.
51   Connolly O'Brien, Nora, Portrait of a Rebel Father, Dublin 1935, 152; Coxhead, 89; Skinnider, 13.
52   Sheehy-Skeffington, Hanna, Constance Markievicz, *An Phoblacht*, 5.5.1928. She got bad reputation especially in Catholic church circles when there emerged a scheme to board the children of distressed parents with families in England for the duration of the Lock-Out, O'Connor, 86; Van Voris, 114 There was also a pamphlet of her, which advised that "Belfast

nationalists, Griffith and Moran denounced "the sway of socialist doctrines" as one more manifestation of the tide of anglicization now engulfing Irish society[53]. However, some of the leading intellectuals were on the side of the workers.[54]

The Lock-Out continued until the British relief fund organised by the British TUC closed on 10 February 1914. The defeat was a severe set-back for trade unionism in Dublin and for general unionism throughout Ireland. Bitterly Larkin and Connolly blamed the British TUC for the failure.[55] Markievicz did not personally comment on the result of the Lock-Out, during which she had served the workers and their families full-time. Bearing in mind her policy in the coming years, perhaps a more important factor in the Lock-Out so far as she was concerned was the creation of workers' military guard, the Irish Citizen Army.

The Irish Citizen Army – representing equality and sacrifice

The unrest during the Lock-Out gave Markievicz the opportunity to attack the representatives of British rule. She organised a Fianna "stretcher squad" for duty on the streets, and they were amongst the first to get into trouble with the police.[56] By joining the Irish Citizen Army Markievicz was directly connected to the the objectives of the emerging militant labour movement in Ireland .

The Irish Citizen Army (ICA) was initially a defence force designed simply to protect the workers during the Lock-out. However, after ITGWU's defeat and the great bitterness which it engendered, Connolly saw the ICA as a revolutionary vehicle. From the Dublin Lock-Out onwards his commitment to a democratic transition to socialism was increasingly superseded by a revolutionary strategy employing physical force.[57]

In its constitution the ICA declared that its first and last principle was that the ownership of Ireland, moral and material, was vested by right in the people of Ireland. Its principal objects were to arm and train all Irishmen capable of bearing arms to enforce and defend its first principle and to sink all differences of birth, privilege and creed under the common name of the Irish people. The members should be, if possible, members of unions recognised by the Irish Trades Union Congress.[58] The idea that the Irish people were entitled in the ownership of Ireland, had been promoted by James Fintan Lalor in the 19th

---

Catholics should ask Madame Markievicz what part she played in Dublin at the time of the deportation of the poor Catholic children, when Larkinism and Liberty Hall tactics brought the Working people to the verge of starvation!" Madame Markievicz and Liberty Hall, Pamphlet, 1913, NLI.

53   Hutchinson, 187.
54   Men like Patrick Pearse, W.B.Yeats, Padraic Colum and AE, Berresford Ellis, 195.
55   O'Connor, 88; Berresford Ellis, 202.
56   Murphy, 286.
57   Anderson, 61-62.
58   Berresford Ellis, 207-208.

Century. It was also accepted generally in the nationalist movement as a goal intended to unite all the Irish. Even though the ICA was a guard formed for the defence of the working class, the struggle against capitalists was not highlighted in the constitution. Therefore, to join forces with the workers of the ICA was not a big leap for Markievicz given her policy during the Lock-Out.

Connolly was the President of the new organisation, Markievicz became treasurer and and the young dramatist and socialist activist Sean O'Casey the Secretary. Markievicz, ranking as an officer of the Citizen Army, wore uniform and carried arms; she was also head of Fianna and a trusted friend of the leaders of the Volunteers, a militant group of the nationalists formed in autumn 1913. Thus she formed a link uniting the three organisations and was, according a sympathetic evaluation, influential in preventing the discords that tended to arise.[59] However, Markievicz, who strove to reconcile the goals of the nationalist and socialist military organisations in the name of co-operation and who promoted unity in the pursuit of independence, did provoke suspicions about herself. Sean O'Casey's antipathy towards Markievicz broke out openly when he criticised her for general bourgeois tendencies and demanded that she either to sever her connections with the Volunteers or leave the ICA. Markievicz refused to forsake either of the organisations. In a vote on the subject she won. O' Casey left the ICA and Markievicz continued her work in both the nationalist and labour arenas.[60]

Markievicz worked actively in the ICA and tried to recruit new members for it in the countryside.[61] However, the number of ICA activists remained small and outside Dublin it not only did not have much support but actually raised hostile feelings.[62] In addition of promoting the ICA, Markievicz apparently contributed to the establishing of a boys' group in the ICA (Citizen Army Scout Corps), for whom she designed the uniforms. The ICA also had female members. The women were given training in first-aid and ambulance work and the girls were taught handling of a rifle and drill.[63] That the ICA gave equal tasks to both sexes was yet one more thing that probably inspired Markievicz in the new movement. Another was the symbolism of sacrifice.

When Connolly was arrested during the Lock-Out he decided to start a hunger-strike. According to an admiring Markievicz, he continued writing when most people would have been occupied in getting well: "to work for the cause, sweeping aside all personal suffering, as well as all pleasure, comfort, ambition

---

59   Macardle, Dorothy, The Irish Republic: A Documented Chronicle of the Anglo-Irish Conflict and the Partitioning of Ireland, with a detailed account of the period 1916-1923, Dublin 1951, 108.

60   O Cathasaigh, [O'Casey, Sean], The History o f the Irish Citizen Army, Dublin 1919, 45-46; Robbins, 19. Markievicz was the only member of Sinn Fein who took part in the demonstration that ICA arranged when Asquith was visiting Dublin, Sinn Fein and Socialism: The Cork Workers' Club. Historical reprints no 19, Cork 1977,2.

61   O Cathasaigh, 21-22. She also tired to get more support for ICA in her writings urging for support and cooperation, ibid., 9-23.

62   Cronin,117.

63   Fox, R.M., The History of the Irish Citizen Army. Dublin 1943,108.

was the rule of his life."[64] Connolly, who used the strategy of the suffragettes and who spoke about them approvingly,[65] was for her someone capable of the ultimate sacrifice in the way that the hunger-striking Irish suffragettes had been. Like Jim Larkin, whom she portrayed as a Christ-like martyr prepared to suffer for the Irish people, Connolly now showed himself even willing to offer his life. For Markievicz, who had been searching for and offering encouragement to people willing to do this, and who undoubtedly believed in the idea that one of the community could represent the whole race and show the right way to others,[66] this was an important factor. Moreover, she – like nationalists in general – had found in the early Christians an example of an unyielding spiritual fight against materially stronger oppressors,[67] an idea which Connolly also shared.[68]

Against the British in the ranks of the workers

Writing later about the differences between the leader of Sinn Fein, Arthur Griffith and James Connolly Markievicz distinguished them clearly. The most important factor , in her view, was that Griffith failed to understand that Ireland could "never rest content with a British constitution, a British social and economic system...". Griffith, who saw Ireland merely free politically, possibly as Gaelic speaking, had no sympathy with the cause of the tenants or with the Co-operative society, but his paper advocated the attraction of foreign capitalism to start factories in Ireland because labour was so cheap there. This idea, argued Markievicz, was instinctively disliked by all who had a Gaelic outlook, and, of course, by Labour: "We did not want a black country with all its slums, misery and crime to be built among the "fair hills of Holy Ireland." "[69]

On the other hand there was James Connolly, who "came from a stock that was both Fenian and socialistic, and approached the question of Ireland's misery and subjection from a broader standpoint than any man previously in his generation." Markievicz praised Connolly for clearly demonstrating that it was faith in a Gaelic ideal that was the real massive power throughout the whole struggle against the English invader. This meant that political "freedom" would be futile if it were bound by British ideals.[70] Her words stem from Connolly's *Re-Conquest of Ireland* where he in autumn1915 promoted a two-fold thesis: that the conquest was capitalist and the re-conquest must be socialist. In Markievicz's view, the socialist re-conquest meant going back to Irish ancient society, in which the Gaelic ideals had been at their purest.

---

64   Markievicz, Constance de, James Connolly; as I knew him., *Nation*, 26.3.1927.
65   *Irish Citizen*, 15.11.1913.He also urged everyone to act and vote against the Liberal government as long as Larkin was in jail, which was a tactic the English militant suffragette organisation WSPU used, Berresford Ellis, 200; Cullen Owens, 40.
66   See O'Neill, Daniel J., The Cult of Self-Sacrifice, 1/1989, *Éire/Ireland*, 95.
67   See for instance Markievicz 1909.
68   Berresford Ellis, Introduction, 38-39; Connolly, James, Labour, Nationality and Religion, written in 1910, in Berresford Ellis, Peter (ed.).Selected Writings of James Connolly, 105.
69   Markievicz, Constance de, Memories, Mr. Griffith, *Eire*, 25.8.1923.
70   Markievicz, Constance de, Memories, Mr. Griffith, *Eire*, 25.8.1923.

Unlike what has been claimed, Markievicz did not combine the goals of the nationalist and socialist movements because she saw the same problems in England and thus concluded that nationalism could not be the sole answer in Ireland.[71] It is quite clear that she did not view Ireland and England in the same way; Ireland was a unique nation which was drawing from its own history the answers for the future. For her the labour movement offered at that stage a way to create unrest, to show revolutionary force which would eventually lead to a Rising against the conquerer. It also promoted equality between the sexes and accepted the goals of the Irish Ireland movement. The Lock-Out and the activities of Markievicz during it have usually been seen as forming a watershed, after which Markievicz clearly belonged to the ranks of the socialists. It is equally important to ask, however, what did the Lock-Out as an action and a symbol mean for her and her nationalist ideas? It represented a struggle against the British, it represented giving all to the cause. It divided the ranks of the nationalists, those who wanted to take the side of – in Markievicz's opinion – the materialist English or the English garrison in Ireland and those who wanted to help and join in the rebel movement, which Markievicz understood as a primarily nationalist movement striving for the ancient Irish equality. Her speeches or actions do not indicate that she pondered very much on socialism as a political or economic doctrine. The policy of the labour movement was for her the policy of one section of the Irish people desiring independence.

---

71   Haverty, 94.

■ "A Terrible Beauty is Born" — the Easter Rising and Markievicz

Home rule is not enough

The prospects for Irish nationalist radicals – like Markievicz – did not appear bright between 1910 and 1912. While the IPP was holding the balance in the House of Commons, it seemed that the English Liberals would, at last, have to put a Home Rule Bill through parliament. Enthusiasm for John Redmond and Home Rule was high and Sinn Fein and the radicals generally suffered as a consequence. At that time the revolution seemed far off.[1]

Home rule dominated Irish discussion in 1912-1914. It was not a discussion Markievicz wanted to concentrate on. On the contrary, she had constantly expressed her desire for complete Irish freedom, and consequently did not accept the Home Rule Bill which Prime Minister Asquith proposed in April 1913. In it the responsibility for relations with the crown, defence and foreign policy, customs and excise, and land purchase, was reserved for Westminster. A Home Rule parliament clearly could not exert much immediate authority on Irish affairs.[2]

Markievicz, who had been chosen for the executive of Sinn Fein in 1911[3], attended the Sinn Fein meeting in which the party refused to accept as a final solution the proposed settlement, or any settlement that would leave any trace of British government in Ireland.[4] Sinn Fein described the year 1912 as a year of disillusionment and disaster, because the high hopes of the majority of the Irish people for a satisfactory Home Rule Bill were disappointed.[5] During the course of negotiations in 1913 Sinn Fein announced that the sooner the question of Home Rule was out of the way, the sooner it would be realized that it did not mean national freedom or material paradise.[6]

The discontent with Home Rule was shared in Ulster, but for other reasons. Ulster Unionists wanted the province of Ulster to be excluded from the operation of the Home Rule Act. According to Edward Carson, the leader of the Unionists,

---

1   Nowlan, Kevin B., Tom Clarke, MacDermott, and the I.R.B., in Martin 1967,113; Thompson, 77.
2   Lee, J.J., Ireland 1912-1985. Politics and Society, Cambridge 1989,7.
3   *Sinn Fein*, 7.10.1911.
4   *Sinn Fein*, 20.4.1912.
5   *Sinn Fein*, 4.1.1913.
6   *Sinn Fein*, 3.5.1913.

they were convinced that Home Rule would be "disastrous to the material well-being of Ulster as well as the whole of Ireland, subversive of our civil and religious freedom, destructive of our citizenship, and perilous to the unity of the Empire."[7] In January 1913 the Ulster Volunteer Force was established. Soon it enrolled about 100 000 men, who were prepared to resist the implementation of Home Rule by arms.

As militant unionism gathered strength, some Irish nationalists decided that the time had come to follow the example of the north, and in November 1913, under the inspiration of the Gaelic scholar, Eoin Mac Neill, and strongly backed by the men of the I.R.B., the Irish Volunteers were inaugurated. By July 1914 they stood at 160 000.[8] In its manifesto the organisation declared that its object would be "to secure and maintain the rights and liberties common to the whole people of Ireland." Their duties were to be defensive and protective, and they would not contemplate either aggression or domination.[9]

The formation of the Irish Volunteers gave hope to those who were determined to rouse Irish against British rule. The old Fenian veteran Tom Clarke wrote that "...it is worth living in Ireland these times - there is an awakening ...things are in full swing on the up side..."[10] These developments satisfied Markievicz as well. She had recently joined the ICA and had through her work with the Fianna manifested her idea that Irish independence had to be fought for in the future. The discussion of Home Rule and the exclusion of Ulster were for her of minor importance. Actually, she did not directly comment on developments in Ulster at all. However, she no doubt agreed with Connolly[11], Redmond and the nationalist groups who opposed the partition of Ulster. Markievicz had embraced the aim of Tone "to unite the whole people of Ireland" and seemed to assume that the problems in Ulster would be solved simply by severing all links with England. After all, at that time, the republican tradition was dominated by Tone's doctrine of the Common Name of Irishman obliterating, in theory, all political differences between Catholics, Protestants and Dissenters. [12] Also, many of the nationalists held that Ulster Protestant attitudes were basically the consequence of British duplicity.[13]

"Buy a revolver" – women's opportunities

The developments that resulted in the formation of the Irish Volunteers as well as the ICA offered also , in Markievicz's view, a chance for women. Given that the awakening of Irish women was one of her goals, it is not surprising to find

7   Coogan 1987, 23.
8   Boyce 1995, 282-283.
9   The Manifesto of the Irish Volunteers. Read at the Inaugural Meeting in Dublin, November 25th,1913, in Macardle, 910.
10   Clarke in a letter to McGarrity on 8. 12.1913, quoted in Cronin, 105.
11   In Connolly's view, Labour would not have a chance in the Home Rule parliament without Ulster, Thompson, 86.
12   O'Brien 1995, 35-36.
13   Lee 1989, 19.

her supporting the female counterpart of the Irish Volunteers in the spring of 1914. The part intended for women was, however, carefully defined. It was to be

> "different from that of the men, and rightly so. It is not ours to undertake physically and directly the defence of the nation except in a last extremity and in the direct stress of war...Our first duty is to give our allegiance and support to the men who are fighting the cause of Ireland...We women are not politicians, but we know what we want...we pledge ourselves...to give...support morally,financially, and in every way we can....of helping to arm and to equip...We shall start first-aid classes,and later on, if necessary, an ambulance corps....we shall take no part in sectional politics, nor shall we take up the time of what is meant to be a purely practical organisation in discussing them."[14]

Although both the supportive role designed for women and the idea that women could not be politicians seem to contradict the goals of Markievicz, her interest in the new women's organisation was evident from the very beginning. At this point, Cumann na mBan was needed to bring together all the potential forces for the military-minded nationalist movement. Hence Markievicz gave "many practical suggestions", as the central branch of Cumann na mBan, which the new organisation was called, was being organised in Dublin[15] and collected money for it.[16] Apparently she estimated the chances of the new group as quite bright since she led the negotiations that resulted in integrating Inghindhe na hEireann as a branch of Cumann na mBan. Probably Markievicz believed that merging into a bigger organisation that was gaining strength – in October 1914 Cumann na mBan had altogether 63 branches [17] – could also further the goals of more radical women. The executive of Cumann na mBan was, after all, composed of different opinions[18], which meant that a more radical policy could be pursued within it. Markievicz did not belong to the executive of Cumann na mBan in the first years of the organisation, but she seems to have been a member, because she once called Cumann her organisation.[19]

The policy of Cumann na mBan was not generally approved among women activists. For some suffragists its establishment was a backward step for women's emancipation. The Irish Citizen called its members "slave women" who were placing party nationalism above the cause of their sex. [20] Markievicz did not

14   Inaugural address by Agnes O'Farrelly, *Irish Volunteer*, 18.4.1914.
15   *Irish Volunteer*,25.4.1914.
16   Van Voris,147.
17   Ward 1983, 93-95.
18   About the executive, MacCurtain, Margaret, Women, the Vote and the Revolution, in MacCurtain, Margaret & Ò Currain, Donncha, Women in Irish History: The Historical Dimension, Naas 1978,52: Bean de Barra, Leslie, in Voices of Ireland, Conversation with Donncha Ò Dulaing, Dublin 1984,93.
19   Conlon, Lil, Cumann na mBan and the Women of Ireland 1913-1925, Kilkenny 1969,12. From that period there are no membership books left, if there ever were any.
20   For the debate on this, see *Irish Citizen* especially for April and May of 1914. According to Beth McKillen the debate had a negative influence both on membership and public opinion, McKillen 1981, 59-61.

take part in the heated debate that followed immediately after the forming of Cumann na mBan. However, she strongly criticised the role of the Cumann women – but not their nationalism as such – while speaking in a meeting of the IWFL in late autumn 1915.[21]

In her speech, after touching on the history of ancient Ireland, that" bred warrior women", Markievicz declared that women were now "in danger of being civilised by men out of existence." In her opinion, Ireland was distinguished by the number of fighting women who had held their own against the world, who had owned no allegiance to any man, who were super-women - the Maeves, the Machas, the Warrior-queens. Nevertheless, in later times the Irishwomen had as a rule taken no prominent part. Judging from the glimpses from the male chroniclers, their role seemed to have been passive, lamented Markievicz. The Ladies Land League had to her mind promised better things. However, when it had started to do the militant things that the men only threatened to do and merely talked of doing, the men, "as usual", had discarded the women and disbanded their organisation.

After discussing the role of Irish women in history, Markievicz argued that women were now attached to national movements chiefly to collect funds for the men to spend. In her mind, these Ladies' Auxiliaries demoralised women, set them up in separate camps, and deprived them of all initiative and independence. Women were left to rely on sexual charm, or intrigue and backstairs influence, which was not right. Rather than trust their "feminine charm", women should take up their responsibilities and be prepared to trust their own courage, their own truth, and their own common sense, and not the problematic chivalry of the men they might meet on the way, urged Markievicz.

Markievicz's conception of the methods women should and should not employ was characteristic of many women in the suffragette movement. Her sister Eva Gore-Booth denounced the idea that women did not need the vote because they could always influence their husbands. [22] In addition, the notion that in order to be taken seriously women should dress sensibly[23], was demonstrated in the disgust with which Markievicz described a type of a young lady who "started to walk round Ireland with all her jewels on, a golden wand in her hand, and a sly appeal to "man" from out the corner of her down-cast eyes. According to her, a woman like that was "like the lap dog which, when it meets a larger animal, rolls over on its back, turns up its toes, and looks pathetic." Instead women should dress suitably in a short skirt and strong boots, leave

---

21   The Future of Irishwomen. Speech at the IWFL Meeting, October 12th , *Irish Citizen*, 23.10.1915; Markievicz had continued participating in the activities of the IWFL; she had dressed up as Joan of Arc in full armour in a feminist tableau at a Suffragist Fête in Dublin, had given "dramatic selections"on another occasion and had written in their paper about the heroic women of '98. Writings in *Irish Citizen*, Women of '98, 6.11.1915; 13.11.1915; 27.11.1915.

22   Gore-Booth, Eva, Women and the Suffrage. A Reply to Lady Lovat and Mrs. Humphrey Ward, *The Nineteenth Century and After*, September 1908, 500.

23   Romero, Patricia W., E. Sylvia Pankhurst. Portrait of a Radical, New Haven 1987, 73; Dudley Edwards, 55.

jewels and gold wands in the bank, and buy a revolver[24], advised Markievicz, who often dressed in a uniform herself.

Markievicz contrasted the 'lap-dog like' women with suffragettes and trades union women, who gave her hope, since they were following "higher ideals" and were not in a position of inferiority as elsewhere. She argued that the reason for this was to be found in Catholic and Protestant churches, who fostered the tradition of segregation of the sexes. A consciousness of dignity and worth should now be encouraged in women. They should be urged to get away from wrong ideals and false standards of womanhood, to escape from their domestic ruts, their feminine pens: "It would be well to aim at bringing out, as it were, the masculine side of women's souls, as well as the feminine side of men's souls..We have got to get rid of the last vestige of the Harem before woman is as free as our dream of the future would have her."[25]

In emphasizing the need for liberation not only for the female sex, but also for the male as well, Markievicz was introducing to her Irish audience notions similar to those that her sister Eva and Esther Roper were presenting in Britain about the same time. Eva Gore-Booth was acknowledged as leader by a group of women and men who were interested in the reform of relations between the sexes and who founded a journal *Urania*, which demanded the abandonment of traditional sex-roles, believing them to be completely artificial and dishonest.[26] Yet there was a difference: Markievicz did not ponder the issue of sexuality whereas her sister believed that the inequalities in male/female relationships arose from the nature of the sexual union and its consequences for women. Eva Gore-Booth coined a phrase which later became the motto of *Urania*:'Sex is an Accident'-with no bearing on the essential nature of a human being.[27]

Thus, both sisters shared the opinion that being a woman in contemporary society was a hindrance from doing things. But whereas Eva Gore-Booth contemplated the issue on a more general philosophical level, Markievicz was concerned with the outcome of the rigid division of labour between masculine and feminine spheres in Irish society. Actually, what mattered most, was that by designing and fostering separate spheres the nationalist fight would be less powerful than it otherwise would be. As long as women chose not to enter the masculine, political and public arena – because Markievicz strongly believed that women should take and were capable of taking initiatives themselves – they were not playing the part that belonged to them. On the other hand, she was well aware of the hostility women were bound to meet.

---

24   The Future of Irishwomen. Speech at the IWFL Meeting, October 12th , *Irish Citizen*, 23.10.1915.

25   The Future of Irishwomen. Speech at the IWFL Meeting, October 12th , *Irish Citizen*, 23.10.1915. About women and their back-door influence, see also Eva in 1908; Ward 1995,6.

26   Lewis, 160. "Uranism" was one of the new words to describe sexual love between women, Anderson, Bonnie S., 221.

27   Lewis, 103.

Markievicz gave her support to Cumann na mBan, but trained and marched with the ICA. Even though the activities of both organisations – training in first aid, drilling, signalling, rifle practice and the organising of boy scouts[28] – were virtually similar, there were two main differences. First, unlike the women in Cumann na mBan, the women of ICA were "absolutely on the same footing as the men"; they took part in all marches and manoeuvres and did have information from them.[29] Secondly, women were actually only taught to shoot in a few branches of Cumann na mBan [30], which certainly was a distressing weakness in Markievicz's view; she made it clear that women should learn to shoot.[31]

The greater degree of equality in the ICA most probably measured up to the way in which Markievicz saw the role of women in military organisations. Its leader, James Connolly treated women members as the equals of men.[32] His attitude was later fondly remembered by Markievicz:

> "When he began to organise the I.C.A. he brought me along, treating me, as he got to know me, as a comrade, giving me any work that I could do, and quite ignoring the conventional attitude towards the work of women. This was his attitude towards women in general: we were never, in his mind, classed for work as a sex, but taken individually and considered, just as every man considers men and then allotted any work we could do." [33]

Connolly was not only treating women as equals, he also wanted to encourage them to be independent. A belligerent article in the *Workers' Republic* in December 1915 resembles Markievicz's speech to the IWFL a couple of months before:

> "Women...If you want a thing done do it yourself. Buy a revolver and shoot any man... who attempts to injure you...If men wanted to protect you there would be no war and no prostitution...Sex distinctions must go. Women must protect themselves. Sex distinctions are harmful alike to men and women."[34]

The author of the article is not certain [35] – be it Connolly or Markievicz, it is clear that they both wanted to raise their military spirit amongst women. Along with the Irish developments, Markievicz welcomed the ongoing war, because it was "shaking them [women] out of old grooves and forcing responsibilities on them."[36] Her words reflected the discourse on role of women during the

28 Ward 1983, 93,95.
29 Markievicz, Constance de, Some Women in Easter Week, in Prison Letters of Countess Markievicz, 37; see also Connolly O'Brien, Nora, in Voices of Ireland, 80; Anderson 1994, 24.
30 Ward 1983, 104.
31 Conlon, 12
32 Anderson 1994, 24.
33 Markievicz, Constance de, James Connolly as I knew him,*Nation*,26.3.1927.
34 *Workers' Republic*, 18.12.1915, quoted in Anderson 1994, 24.
35 Anderson suggests it as Connolly's, 24.
36 The Future of Irishwomen. Speech at the IWFL Meeting, October 12th , *Irish Citizen*, 23.10.1915.

First World War. Throughout, British newspapers were full of articles about "women in men's jobs" and women's changing role in industry and the repercussions this might have for "society". Women's "new-found self-confidence" was also widely discussed.[37] But Markievicz was not satisfied with this changing role as long as Irishwomen belonged to the British Empire. She welcomed the war as an opportunity to start a rebellion.

England's Difficulty is Ireland's opportunity – Markievicz the Activist

In the summer of 1914 the situation in Ireland was tense. In addition to the British army, there were military organizations which were prepared to fight either for or against Home Rule. According to a contemporary evaluation, there was a possibility of civil strife.[38]

When war broke out in Europe, the situation changed. Almost a quarter of a million soldiers enlisted in Ireland. The immediate effect of the war upon Irish society was to raise living standards, especially for farmers; but in the longer term it destabilised Irish politics and helped to create the conditions for the revolution which followed.[39]

After the war the Home Rule would be awaiting Ireland. Ulster would get a special legislation and the question of partition was left open.[40] Most Irish nationalists must have been reasonably satisfied with Home Rule even with partition.[41] It was a victory to Redmond, who encouraged the Irish to join the British army. The Irish Volunteer organization split on the question of whether to co-operate in Britain's war with the German Empire or stand neutral in defence of Ireland. The majority – the constitutional nationalists – chose to serve under the British flag.[42] The minority, including Cumann na mBan, took their lead from MacNeill and kept the old name of the Irish Volunteers.[43]

It was not surprising that many radical nationalists opposed participating in the war on the British side and that Sinn Fein speakers argued the case for Irish neutrality in the war.[44] Markievicz had joined the short-lived Irish Neutrality League, which declared that true patriotism required Irishmen to remain at home.[45] Propaganda against conscription had for a long been on the

37   Braybon, Gail, Women and the War, in Constantine, Stephen, Kirby, Maurice W., Rose, Mary B., (eds), The First World War in British History, London 1995, 141; Anderson, Bonnie S, 197.
38   Dickinson, 115.
39   Preface in Fitzpatrick, David (ed.), Ireland and the First World War, Dublin 1988, viii.
40   Laffan 1983,47
41   Cruise O'Brien 1995, 95.
42   O'Donoghue 1967,190; Lee 1989, 22.
43   In the minority belonged only 13 000 out of a total 188,000, Lee 1989, 22.
44   Figgis, Darrell, Recollections of the Irish War, London 1927, 99.
45   O'Brien, Introduction, in Ryan, Desmond (ed.),Labour and Easter Week: A selection from the writings of James Connolly. With introduction by William O'Brien, Dublin 1966 (1949), 3-4. The president of the League was James Connolly and Markievicz belonged to its committee with Arthur Griffith and Francis Sheehy-Skeffington.

agenda of Sinn Fein and other nationalist-minded organisations such as the Inghinidhe and the Fianna and the Irish Volunteers as a whole declared that it would resist any attempt to impose conscription on Ireland.[46] In the course of war Markievicz wrote against conscription remarking that talking about defending "small nationalities" was hypocritical. She suggested jail as an alternative to enlisting and promised that not going to war would give peace to one's soul.[47]

The war offered Markievicz a chance to condemn British policy not only in Ireland but on a larger scale. Using every opportunity to blacken Britain's name Markievicz championed the goal of peace and even employed the pacifist vocabulary of the women in the British peace movement – to which her sister Eva Gore-Booth belonged [48] – to stress the difference between the "wrong" ideals of the British who were at war, and the "right" ideals that motivated the Irish struggle. She portrayed the Irish as a small, righteous vanguard of Christians were fighting a battle against a materialistic and "evil" empire. [49] It was a comparison she had used before and in time of war it recalled the way in which the "enemy" was portrayed, at least initially, in all the combatant nations.[50] But a time of upheaval when imperiums were trembling, was also an opportunity to rise. Markievicz said openly that she did not want the war stopped until the British Empire was smashed.[51]

Markievicz was not the only one who took the war and Britain's participation in it as an opportunity for rebellion and a chance to obtain independence at last. In the autumn of 1914 the IRB committed itself to organising a rising before the war ended and a very secret special IRB Military Council whose members alone shared the details of the intended Rising was established in 1915.[52] The old principle of the IRB was that whenever England was in trouble,

---

46 Macardle, 123.
47 Markievicz , Constance de, Love your Enemies, *Fianna*, January 1916.
48 Both Eva Gore-Booth and Esther Roper had joined Sylvia Pankhurst on platforms in the East End, condemning the war and calling for an early peace,Romero, 114; Eva was also a member of the British organising committee of the International Women's Peace Conference, held in April 1915 at the Hague, Lewis, 164.
49 " In every church where John Bull can get a grip on the soul of the clergy in charge, the red God of war is throned on the Altar of the Prince of peace, while the message of love is suppressed and Christian men are urged from the pulpits to line up and kill English enemies..."Markievicz, Constance de, Love Your Enemies, *Fianna*, January 1916. The women of British peace movement had in 1915 composed a letter to their German sisters, in which they expressed their concern by writing e.g. in similar way like Markievicz : "...The Christmas message sounds like mockery to a world at war...Do you not feel with us that the vast slaughter in our opposing armies is a stain on civilisation and Christianity..." Lewis, 164-165.
50 Also many feminists joined in the war enthusiasm, Bethke Elshtain, 111-112.
51 *Irish Citizen*, 8.1.1916. She spoke at a meeting which was held to give Francis Sheehy Skeffington a welcome on his return to Dublin from America. She expressed similar ideas also in February 1916, O'Brien, Conor Cruise, Ireland's Fissures, and My Family's, *The Atlantic Monthly*, January 1994. According to a contemporary feminist and union activist Louie Bennett Markievicz only quoted some wild, flowery phrases and talked a lot about dying for Ireland, Fox, R.M., Louie Bennett: Her Life and Times, Dublin 1958, 47.
52 E.g. Dangerfield,136; Lynch, Diarmuid , in F. O'Donoghue (ed.), The IRB and the 1916 Rising, Cork 1957, 25. The members of the Military Council were Tom Clarke, Sean MacDermott, Patrick Pearse, Eamonn Ceannt, Joseph Plunkett and from 1916 James Connolly and Thomas MacDonagh.

action should be taken. But the opinions differed within the secret society. Hobson was against a rising as he saw it as violating the constitution of the IRB which demanded that any such rising must have the support of the people.[53]

Thus, the question from now on was not basically about being a member of the IRB or not; rather, the division between nationalists was between activists and those who wanted to pursue a more passive, waiting and defensive policy.[54] The activists had the support of James Connolly, for whom the outbreak of the the World War was a bitter blow.[55] However, he made it clear that he preferred fighting "for our own country than for the robber empire."[56] In July 1915 he declared that the members of the ICA were prepared to

> "...lay down their lives for Ireland...the laying down of their lives shall constitute the starting point of another glorious tradition - a tradition that will keep alive the soul of the nation."[57]

Connolly had always judged every political crisis with an eye to its revolutionary possibilities.[58] He joined the IRB Military Council in January 1916. Soon after that he wrote that the working class had also betrayed the national liberation movement and could be purified only through an armed rebellion; socialism in Ireland was unthinkable before national independence. [59] However, within the labour movement Connolly was quite unique in his belligerent attitude. The majority was afraid that trade unionism would be suppressed if the movement showed a willingness to take part in a rebellion.[60]

Like Connolly, Markievicz belonged to the activists. She wanted to train the Irish in different arenas to be able to use the changed situation to their advantage. She remarked later, that the section opposed to a rising were the "not yets".[61] She claimed that the strained relations between the ICA and the Volunteers had

---

53   On Hobson, Townshend, 287. According to Hobson, " We must not fight to make a display of heroism, but fight to win.", Hobson 1909,55.
54   Wall, Maureen, The Background of the Rising: From 1914 until the issue of the countermanding order on Easter Saturday 1916, in The Making of 1916. Studies in the History of the Rising, ed. by Nowlan, Kevin B., Dublin 1969,165.
55   He believed that the war could have been prevented if only the socialist proletariat had refused to march against their brothers. Connolly, Revolutionary Unionism and War, International Socialist Review, March,1915, quoted in Ryan 1966, 55.
56   Connolly's Speech on War's Outbreak, *Irish Worker,* September 5,1914, quoted in Ryan 1966,49.
57   Connolly, Why the Citizen Army Honours Rossa, Rossa Souvenir, July 1915, quoted in Ryan 1966, 70; see also Connolly, The Man and the Cause, *Workers' Republic,*July 31, 1915, quoted in Ryan 1966, 72; Connolly, Ireland's Travail and Ireland's Resurrection, *Workers' Republic,* August 7,1915, quoted in Ryan 1966, 76-77.
58   Anderson 1994, 67.
59   Newsinger, John, Easter Rebellion - Defeat or Victory, *Monthly Review* 7/1982, 34; Greaves 1961,288: Fox 158,49.
60   Jones, 13.
61   Markievicz, Constance de, James Connolly as I knew him, *Nation,* 26.3.1927.

not been rooted in class differences only, but also to difference about the timing of a rising.[62]

The division between those who wanted the rising as soon as possible and those who opposed it, and between Markievicz and her former mentor, Hobson, was evident in discussion of how to place the Fianna on a more military footing in 1915. The emerging militarisation had meant a growing interest in training along Fianna lines.[63] The handbook of Fianna was used among the Irish Volunteers[64] – which had tried to incorporate the Fianna itself [65] – and it is likely that it was also being used by Cumann na mBan. Thus the methods of the Fianna, which Markievicz had to a great extent copied from the guides designed for British boy scouts, and to which she had added military training, influenced other movements as well.

The discussion of a direction for the Fianna took place at the Annual Meeting in 1915. According to some representatives, the movement was essentially a military one and could be changed organisationally to serve that purpose even more effectively. Hobson, with some support, opposed the scheme, because he belived that the civil side of their activities and character-building were more important than the military side. Nevertheless, the majority was for reorganising. At the same meeting Markievicz became a member of a committee to arrange the new executive, but was not herself elected to that executive[66], something that might well have been the goal of the IRB. Yet she continued her work with the boys, gave lectures to them and stressed the need for spiritual education[67]

---

62 "Some Labour men branded the Volunteers as a middle class, capitalist army, all for show, which never would fight; while some of the Volunteers looked down on the I.C.A. as a mob of undesirable and wild scalliwags, who wanted to fight in season and out of season more especially at the wrong moment, before everybody else was ready", Markievicz, Constance de , James Connolly; as I knew him, Nation, 26.3.1927; About the relations between the ICA and the Volunteers see Fox 1943,71; Nevin, Donal, The Irish Citizen Army, in Nowlan, Kevin B. (ed), 123.

63 In September it was announced that an Irish Boy Volunteer movement had been started by a subcommittee of Cumann na mBan and officers of the Irish Volunteers, Irish Volunteer,12.9.1914. Liam Mellows and other officers of the Fianna were helping to train the Volunteers, Macardle, 100.

64 Van Voris,145. The Fianna Handbook, which was printed in Dublin in 1914, had some army drill, signalling and First Aid instructions while its drawings resembled those in Baden-Powell's handbook for scouts.

65 See articles on this in Irish Freedom,To the Boys of Ireland, February; Fianna column in May 1914; A Word With the Boys and Girls, June 1914. Also Irish Volunteer had a column for Fianna.

66 Fianna Congress, Fianna, August 1915.

67 Ever since the war began the Fianna had gone about to recruiting meetings, putting speakers to rout and sometimes upsetting the platforms. Markievicz took the boys to an anti-German play, where the boys sang a German song and made fresh words for an anti-recruing song titled 'The Germans are Winning the War, Me Boys, Skinnider,23, 25, 222. She reminded Fianna boys of the importance of duty and loyalty, Fianna, November 1915. In a same number she wrote in her poem "The Dreams" that freedom would come through blood and suffering, pain and tears. The aim of spiritual education is implied in a letter from AE 25.10.1915 to his publishers in which he asked for a permission on behalf of Markievicz to use his poems with the Fianna. AE described Markievicz as "an enthustiastic lady who believes in boy scouts and has organised companies of them and wishes to combine poetry and scouting and makes her boys into poets as well as heroes. She is certainly not looking for profits...I don't think her experiment will be a success but I wish it well and I like the idea of boy scouts with a pocket book of poetry...", in Denson, 109.

although she later agreed that the time when she worked hardest for the Fianna was before that, in the years 1909–13.[68]

In spite of having constantly emphasized the importance of spiritual growth, Markievicz did not like Hobson raise her voice against the reorganising of the Fianna on a more military lines. Hobson did not want to guide the Fianna towards rebellion, which in his opinion would not succeed. Markievicz, on the contrary, demonstrated her willingness to support a rising by marching openly with the ICA and the Fianna boys.[69] In the summer of 1915 she had, in that respect, more companions than before. After the public funeral of the old Fenian chief, O'Donovan Rossa in August, twelve hundred Volunteers marched openly with their arms through Dublin and the members of Cumann na mBan began to parade in uniform.[70]

Officer Markievicz

Along with others who were pledged to a rising, Markievicz strove to rouse a rebellious spirit among the Irish: she stressed that the rebels of past risings had been "simple, common men".[71] In a battle hymn written for the ICA she prayed for God's blessing in the fight. The tone of the hymn was nationalist - it declared that fighting for Irland was under God's protection and that those who fell for freedom would never die.[72] Her words, which in no way suggested a connection with the ICA as the labour movement's army, were nevertheless valued by the Workers' Republic editor - Connolly - who described the poem as "brilliant".[73]

On the eve of the rising Markievicz encouraged people to sacrifice in her poems:

"We are ready to fight for the land we love,
  Be the chances great or small;
We are willing to die for the flag above
  Be the chances nothing at all.

   ...

So we're waiting till "somebody" gives us the word
  That sends us to Freedom or death;
As freemen defiant we'd sooner fall
  Than be slaves to our dying breath."[74]

---

68 Markievicz to Eva Gore-Booth, 1.1.1921, PL,266.
69 Fox 1943,92 She led with Connolly a sham attack on Dublin Castle on October 6th. Boys of the Fianna took part in the manouvres, Macardle,137.
70 Macardle, 137.
71 Markievicz, Constance de, The Manchester Martyrs, *Workers' Republic*,27.11.1915.
72 Markievicz, Constance de, "Hymn on the Battlefield. Dedicated to the Citizen Army.",*Workers' Republic*, 13.11.1915. She had also written a play which was presented by the Irish Workers' Dramatic Company, see *Workers' Republic*, 1.4.1916.
73 *Workers' Republic,* 13.11. 1915.
74 Markievicz, Constance de, Our Faith, *Workers' Republic*, 22.4.1916. In another poem she claimed that the Irish race was being called for self-sacrifice, courage and faith, "To Arms! for the day has come.", The Call, *Workers' Republic*, 15.4.1916.

Markievicz's belligerent lyrics were by no means unique as such. The Great European War promised cleansing and redemption to intellectuals of both left and right on the eve of the War.[75] According to Freud the use of massive warfare meant that "Life has indeed become interesting again; it has recovered its full content."[76] Considering this, it has been correctly observed that the words of Patrick Pearse about cleansing and sanctifying bloodshed – which often have been used to underline the absurdness of the ideas the planners of rising had – must be seen in the context of their time. The rhetoric of blood was in keeping with much contemporary political writing in Irish republican and socialist papers; it reflected the romantic convention of bloody revolution.[77] It was a rhetoric Markievicz often used. In March 1916 she asserted that the only way to speak to England was with guns in hand.[78] In time of War millions of soldiers were fighting for their countries - that was what Markievicz wanted the Irish do as well.

The Rising was timed to begin on Easter Sunday 1916. According to the plans strategically important points in Dublin would first be taken so that the city could held its own until the rest of the country had risen, but the plans were incomplete and there was no certainty at any stage that the whole of a widely dispersed and only partly trained force of about 18 000 could be brought into action.[79] Two major factors obstructed the plans - the confusion caused by conflicting orders and the failure of the arms landing coming from Germany.[80] After discovering the secret plans, MacNeill and Hobson were shocked and opposed them firmly. MacNeill gave a countermanding order after Pearse had sent the groups a message to prepare. Thus only a tiny part of the expected force turned up and there was no support from the countryside.[81] That did not stop the principal architects of the Rising. They were idealists for whom it was both an imperative national necessity and a means to an end.[82]

Markievicz, who had written about the willingness to die "be the chances nothing at all", shared the idealist and romantic vision of the inevitability of the Rising in order to gain freedom. She was "horrified" to read MacNeill's

---

75   Bethke Elshtain 1995, 85; Anderson, Bonnie S., 198.
76   Kiberd,17.
77   Dudley Edwards, Ruth, 179.
78   Conlin, 18. Markievicz was lecturing at Cork on March 7, on anniversary of Emmet's death.
79   Coffey, Thomas, Agony at Easter. New York 1969,99; Townshend, 298. About the plans, see e.g. Introduction in Edwards, O.Dudley and Pyle, Fergus, 1916: The Easter Rising, London 1968,22; O'Donoghue 1967,190, 200. The rank and file of the organisations were not so strongly committed to a rebellion as their leaders were. Fitzgerald, Desmond, Memories 1913-1916, London 1968, 28. The majority of Volunteers were prepared to act only if the Ulster Volunteers tried to block the Home Rule, Coogan 1987,34.
80   The British captured a German arms ship which was bringing arms to Ireland , an attempt which was a result of negotiations between Roger Casement and the Irish American organisation Clan na Gael on the one hand and the Germans on the other. The idea of a rebellion came as a surprise to Dublin Castle. Early in 1916 Under Secretary Nathan had reported to Chief Secretary Birrell that things were for the time being fairly quiet. Ò Broin, Leon, Birrell, Nathan, and the men of Dublin Castle, in Martin, F.X., (ed.) Leaders and Men of the Easter Rising: Dublin 1916;1967,3.
81   Ryan 1966, 110-118; 1/5 of the force came into the fight, MacDonagh, Oliver, The Union and its Aftermath, London 1967, 82.
82   O'Donoghue, Florence, Ceannt, Devoy, O'Rahilly, and the military plan, in Martin 1967, 189.

countermanding order[83] and claimed years later that the failure of the Rising was largely his fault; that the prospects had been bright and the possibility of winning, even though "remote and small", had still been there.[84] Apparently, she shocked not so much when the arms were lost and the plans revealed but when the unity of the nationalists was shattered.

The Easter Rising began on Easter Monday, 24 April 1916 at noon, when the tricolour was hoisted at the General Post Office in Dublin. Patrick Pearse declared Ireland a Republic and read the Proclamation of the Provisional Government that had been designed by himself and Connolly.[85] It declared that the action was taking place in "the name of God and of the dead generations from which she (Ireland) receives her old tradition of nationhood." It declared the right of the people of Ireland to the ownership of Ireland. The republic guaranteed religious and civil liberty, equal rights and equal opportunities to all its citizens and promised suffrage for all men and women.[86]

Thus the republic aimed at the unity of the whole of Ireland and equal citizenship for the sexes as well. Markievicz also believed in a republic.[87] She had already declared herself a republican at a meeting of the IWFL in 1913. But what did the republic mean? It has been claimed that in 1916 establishing a "republic" only meant overthrowing the British government in Ireland.[88] The structure of any such republic had not been clearly determined. Wolfe Tone had been convinced that separation under a republican government was the only way to achieve democratic principles in Ireland[89], but the details were still vague.

The Rising was over in less than a week. Outside Dublin very little happened.[90] On the Saturday Pearse gave the order to surrender to about 1 600 members of the Volunteers and the 200-strong ICA who had held sections of the city centre of Dublin. The Republic had endured only for six days and had left behind 400 dead and 3000 wounded. The Rising surprised the Irish and their reactions towards it appear to have been initially hostile. Prisoners herded through the streets of Dublin to the docks, for internment in Britain, were booed. The people did not rebel and did not agree with the rebels or their goals in a situation when the Irish farmers were more prosperous than at any time in their history and Home Rule was on the statute book. [91] The reaction of the

---

83   Markievicz, Constance de, James Connolly as I knew him, *Nation*, 26.3.1927.
84   Markievicz, Constance de, "1916", *Nation*,23.4.1927.
85   Dangerfield, 179.
86   See O'Day, Alan & Stevenson, John (eds.), Irish Historical Documents Since 1800, Dublin 1992, 160-161.
87   She for example remarked that there was a parallel between Emmet and the nationalists of her day in their belief in an Irish republic, Conlon,18.
88   Martin, F.X., 1916 - Myth, Fact, Mystery, *Studia Hibernica*, 7/1967, 69. It is important to note, however, that one of the main architects of the proclamation, Pearse had plans for an independent Ireland ruled by a German prince, who could help in diminishing English influence. See for example Fitzgerald, Garrett, Our Republicanism is more recent than we realise, *Irish Times*, 29.5.1993: O'Brien, Conor Cruise, 56: Lee 1919, 26.
89   Metscher, 54.
90   Lyons 1973, 365-366: Kee,274.
91   Cronin,117;O'Donoghue 1967,190.

crowd was quite understandable, because a great number of the victims and wounded were unarmed civilians and everyday life had been disturbed by shootings, bombings and looting. Many people treated the rebels as traitors, because their relatives were away fighting in the World War. [92]

For Markievicz the inevitable step toward freedom was an armed rebellion. A romantic nationalist, she stood for a rising where flags were raised, songs of dead patriots were sung and where uniformed, pure-hearted people marched against the materialist, corrupt and oppressive coloniser. After fighting in St. Stephen's Green and at the College of Surgeons, Markievicz was among the two thousand prisoners walking through an abusing crowd. Her role in the Rising was an exceptional one for a woman, not just because of her sex - there had been approximately 90 women taking part in the Rising[93] – but because she was one of the leaders of the ICA and had been appointed an officer, a Staff Lieutenant under Connolly. She also knew enough about the plans to carry on should anything happen to Connolly.[94] During the week she had been a sniper, second in command in St.Stephen's Green. She found her work "very exciting when the fighting began. I continued round and round the Green, reporting back if anything was wanted, or tackling any sniper who was particularly objectionable."[95]

Markievicz, who acted like a soldier and was dressed like one, has been described as bloodthirsty and fearless to the last.[96] That there was a strain of ruthlessness in her talk is certain. Nevertheless, there is no evidence that she committed unusually cruel acts during the week.[97] She regarded the Rising as a confrontation of two armies, representing two nations. Her ancestors had belonged to the conquering army she fought against. Her involvement with nationalist politics had led her to the opposite group, with whom she was prepared to die.

Prisoner for Life – a personal sacrifice

For Markievicz the Easter Rising represented a link in an inevitable chain of risings and it should not be left in their shadow when it came to sacrifice. All the preceding nationalist rebellions in Ireland had ended in executions. Nationalist 'faith' maintained that ultimate sacrifice had to be made in order to

---

92 Fitzpatrick, David, Ireland Since 1870, in Foster, R.F. (ed.), The Oxford History of Ireland,Oxford 1992, 198-199.; Van Voris, 196.

93 Anderson, 76. Ward has obseved that what happened in practice, when the time for armed rebellion finally arrived, was a traditional division of labour between the sexes within the ICA, and a discernible reluctance by many Volunteers about having women involved at all, Ward 1983, 107.

94 Markievicz, Some Women in Easter Week, in Prison Letters of Countess Markievicz, 38- 39.

95 Ibid.

96 Caulfield, Max, The Easter Rebellion, Dublin 1995 (1963 & 1995), 128,252,282.

97 Caulfied on about Markievicz shooting a police constable to her great delight, 66, but Diana Norman has found no evidence to back that story, Norman, 138-140.

awaken coming generations; Pearse said that the rebels had kept faith with the past and handed a tradition to the future.[98]

It is obvious that Markievicz stood for the conception that a nation could not be born without blood and suffering. In fact, belief in the necessity of the blood-sacrifice to redeem Ireland had became increasingly widespread in the nineteenth century. In Cathleen ni Houlihan Yeats could advocate it as the duty of each Irish generation and Pearse could preach that the blood of the sons of Ireland was needed to redeem Ireland, which was "a sacrifice Christ-like in its perfection."[99] According to a writer witnessing the Rising, Ireland could not accept freedom as a gift.[100]

In Markievicz's thought, idealism and a spirit of self-sacrifice were the keynote of the true Irish character.[101] Later, she claimed that it was through unfolding these features the Rising was turned into a victory.[102] However, the stress on martyrdom and sacrifice was not a uniquely Irish feature, even though many Irish national histories tend to overemphasize it. Not only in the context of the First World War, but also earlier 'martyrdom' – the assumption of responsibilty and duty, the willingness to devote oneself to the cause and to sacrifice other things for it – had been a very strong current running through all the suffrage organisations, and also through other reforming social movements dating from the last quarter of the nineteenth century.[103]

Markievicz had not wanted to surrender[104] but was prepared to die in Kilmainham jail. On 4th May she was court-martialled and condemned to death. In her defence she said: " I went out to fight for Ireland's freedom and it doesn't matter what happens to me. I did what I thought was right and I stand by it."[105] On 6th May her sentence was commuted to penal servitude for life and she was removed to Mountjoy prison with some other women. The reason her life was saved was that Prime Minister Asquith considered it best that no capital sentence should be carried out in the case of a woman.[106]

During the Rising Markievicz had shown bravery. However, in his memoirs the head prosecutor W.E.Wylie contradicts the common view that Markievicz was prepared to die.[107] It seems plausible that Markievicz preferred a sudden

---

98   Thompson, 104. The philosophy of sacrifice was an essential part of separatist philosophy. O'Hegarty,P.S., The Victory of Sinn Fein. How it won it and how it used it. Dublin 1924, 165.
99   Hawkins 1983, 127; Thompson, 89.
100   Stephens, James, Introduction in The Insurrection in Dublin, New York 1916.
101   Markievicz in a letter for playwriter Frank J. Hugh O'Donnell 5.12.1918, in preface of The Dawn-Mist: A Play of the Rebellion, Dublin 1922.
102   "We conquered by telling them that each one of them must learn to carry the cross for Ireland, and that without pain and self-sacrifice our country would be lost."Markievicz to Eva Gore-Booth, 6.1.1919, PL, 189.
103   Stanley, 178.
104   Roper, 48.
105   Court Marital Proceedings, Dublin May 4 1916. Trial of Constance Georgina Markievicz, Colonel Maurice Moore Papers, MS 10 580, NLI. About Markievicz eagerly waiting for execution, Roper,97: O'Faolain, 158; Sheehy Skeffington Papers, Countess Markievicz, MS 24 189, NLI.
106   Ó Broin 1989, 14.
107   He claims that in the court Markievicz " curled up completely. " I am only a woman', she cried, "and you cannot shoot a woman. You must not shoot a woman." Her behaviour had "slightly disgusted" Wylie, Ó Broin, Leon, W.E.Wylie and the Irish Revolution 1916-1921, Dublin 1989, 27.

death on the battleground. The shots of executions she heard in her cell had a strong impact of her.[108] Connolly's death devastated her.[109]

Nevertheless, the deaths and the personal losses she felt were not allowed to blur the vision. In her symbolic poem on the tragic death of a thrush Markievicz left no room for regrets:

> " No effort is lost though all may go wrong
> And death come to shadow and change.
> He gave his best, and simple and strong
> Broke the darkness which lasted the winter long
> With Spring-time's triumphant melodious song,..."[110]

The leaders of the Rising believed that they had fought the first successful battle for freedom, so they could "die happy."[111] Markievicz, who was saved from execution, pledged to give her life to Ireland.[112] There were no "dead dreams",[113] she wrote in prison a year after the Rising.

If dying for Ireland was an essential element in winning the struggle, it seems logical that Markievicz did not want to complain about life in prison: " ...it's only a mean spirit that grudges paying the price."[114] She claimed that "little comforts and luxuries" meant little to her. This ascetic attitude reflected the ideas of republicans overall: the weak would be triumphant against the physical power of the strong.[115]

In prison Markievicz portrayed herself as a follower of the call of Cathleen ni Houlihan who had gained immortality:

> " You remember 'They shall be remembered for ever.' What we stood for, and even poor me will not be forgotten, and 'the people shall hear them for ever?' That play of W.B.'s was a sort of gospel to me. 'If any man would help me, he must give me himself, give me all.' "[116]

---

108   She described her feelings later in a poem, Countess de Markievicz, In Kilmainham, *New Ireland,* February 1918; see also her letter to Gertrude Bannister, n.d., Roger Casement Papers, MS 13 074, NLI.
109   Roper, 54.
110   Markievicz to Eva Gore-Booth, 27.2.1917, PL, 165.
111   For instance Clarke, Thomas J., in MacLachlainn, Piaras F. (ed.), Last Words: Letters and Statements of the Leaders Executed After the Rising at Easter 1916, Dublin 1971, 45; Dudley Edwards, Ruth, 314
112   See Marreco, 217. According to Haverty the poem suggests that the Markievicz's most vital emotional bond was to dead comrades, especially Connolly, Haverty, 167. However, this idea dismisses the importance of her sister Eva.
113   Easter 1916, in the prison notebook of Markievicz, National Museum of Ireland.
114   Markievicz to Eva Gore-Booth, 16.5. 1916, PL, 140.
115   Garvin 1987, 156-157.
116   Markievicz to Eva Gore-Booth, 21.9.1916,PL, 155. Markievicz mentions the play also later, see letter to Eva Gore-Booth, 6.1.1919, PL, 189. The prison letters are interesting in the sense that they show another side of Markievicz, whose writings are mostly inteded for publication. On the other hand she also knew that the Censor would be reading them. Writing letters was quite unusual for her, see letter to Eva Gore-Booth, 9.6.1917, PL, 175. Her letters reflect a similar optimistic tone to the prison letters of women during the Civil War, see Walsh, Oonagh, Testimony from Imprisoned Women, in Fitzpatrick, David (ed), Revolution? Ireland 1917-23, Dublin 1990, 70.

Furthermore, Markievicz regarded her own part in the Rising to be her destiny:

"All my life, in a funny way, seems to have led up to the last year, and it's been such a hurry-scurry of a life. Now I feel that I have done what I was born to do. The great wave has crashed up against the rock, and now all the bubbles and ripples and little me slip back into a quiet pool of the sea....that's how I feel, quite peaceful and calm."[117]

Markievicz, who presumably was prepared to spend a long time in prison, found comfort in the thought that she had done her share. It gave her a sense of being important.[118] It gave her peace.[119] She was committed to the establishing of an Irish republic, which entailed the duty of sacrifice. By picking on the wave as a symbol Markievicz viewed the rising as an unavoidable force of nature. Every generation encountered their own high tide - after the crushing came a new wave.

Logically therefore Markievicz regarded the situation in Ireland as a great chance for the generation of the youngest rebels and had great faith in them.[120] She stressed that "there is nothing I can do in my own country that others can't do as well."[121] Markievicz was ready to remain in jail; she declared that her only desire was to be of use in struggle with England[122]. Yet life in prison was not easy. In Mountjoy Markievicz suffered from hunger, which forced her to steal food from the rubbish heap.[123]

In June 1916 Markievicz was removed to Aylesbury prison in England, where she served the rest of her sentence. Her removal caused concern to her friends and various organisations, because she was under the same discipline and treatment as the "lowest criminals."[124] Nevertheless, she was known as a good prisoner, who did prison work and kept to the rules.[125] Despite her co-operation she was determined to do something in order to change thingsand smuggled letters to Eva urging her to get questions asked in parliament on the condition of her and other political prisoners. She also suggested that trade unions should examine the situation of the poor people in jail and start a reform there.[126] Later she sharply criticized the English jails and held prison, as a punishment, to be a remnant of barbarity.[127] It was characteristic of Markievicz to tackle the

117   Markievicz to Eva Gore-Booth, 29.12.1916, PL, 158.
118   "...I would have felt very small and useless if I had been ignored.', Markievicz to Eva Gore-Booth, 8.8.1916, PL, 150.
119   Markievicz to Eva Gore-Booth, 29.12.1916, PL, 159.
120   Markievicz to Eva Gore-Booth, 14.5.1917, PL, 169.
121   Markievicz to Eva Gore-Booth, 9.6.1917, PL, 172.
122   Markievicz to Eva Gore-Booth, Unofficial paper, no date, PL, 143.
123   Ni Chumhaill, Eithne, The History of Cumann na mBan, An Phoblacht,15.4.1933.
124   Irish Citizen, March 1917; Nationality, The Prisoners, 17.2.1917.
125   Roper, 98; Countess Markievicz, Hanna Sheehy-Skeffington Papers, MS 24 189, NLI.
126   Unofficial paper, no date, PL, 145: four unofficial papers to Eva, no date, PL, 143-145; Later she showed her frustration in a comment about the policemen's strike: "Why don't the jailers do ditto! and by way of sabotage, destroy the jails?" Markievicz to Eva Gore-Booth, 11.9.1918, PL,185.
127   Countess Markievicz on English Jails, New Ireland, 8.4.1922; also Countess Markievicz, Conditions of Women in English Jails, New Ireland, 15.4.1922.

problems she confronted in her environment. However, elsewhere in Europe other women, who had been imprisoned because of their political activities, also showed similar concern throughout.[128]

A Catholic nationalist

It has been asserted that the Easter Rising was essentially a rebellion by members of the Catholic nation, for the Catholic nation.[129] The leaders of the Rising regarded themselves as fighters for a cause that God had sanctified and were prepared to die for faith and fatherland thus linking together Catholicism and Irish nationalism.[130] The belief in a sacred cause as a motive in a fight is not unusual. In terms of this study it is more relevant that in the aftermath of the Easter Rising, some protestants were converted to catholicism.

One of the converts was Markievicz, who asked a Catholic priest to be with her as she was awaiting her expected execution. In Mountjoy she registered as a Catholic. The last night before surrender, when she had wanted to join in the prayers of her comrades, had led her to the decision of conversion.[131] She had been impressed by the great devotion of the boys of the Fianna and the men of the ICA.[132] Markievicz explained her decision in a similar way to her earlier decision to join the nationalists; through one eye-opening experience. Even though she presented her conversion in such a dramatic way, the act as such was in fact of a minor importance in her life compared to her involvement with nationalist politics. Even so, choosing the religion of the colonised set her ultimately apart from her Anglo-Irish and protestant family and background. It was the final touch, in a way, the creation of an "ideal " Irish rebel. By her conversion, Markievicz defined Catholic faith as a characteristic of the Irish nationalists. In her prison notebooks Markievicz drew pictures on angels saluting a woman with a sword and a rosary[133] – a woman who with these symbols combined the religion and struggle like herself. In a way, religion and nationalism merged into one faith.[134]

---

128 English suffragette Emily Davison linked prison conditions and the social charasteristics of prisoners ina wide-ranging programme of social reform, Stanley, 167.
129 Boyce 1995, 309-310.
130 Newsinger, John, " I Bring Not Peace But A Sword": The Religious Motif in the Irish War of Independence, *Journal of Contemporary History* 1978, 625.
131 Events of Easter Week, *Catholic Bulletin*, February 1917, 130; see also Markievicz's poem "The Rosary" , *Capuchin Annual* 1968, 240. Later she remembered how William Partridge recited the Rosary each night in the College of Surgeons, Markievicz, Constance de, " 1916", *Nation*, 23.4.1927.
132 Hanna Sheehy-Skeffington, in Roper,73.
133 Prison Notebooks of Constance Markievicz, National Museum of Ireland. After being released from prison she gave a crucifix of hers to Gertrude Bannister, who was a cousin of Roger Casement and a friend of Eva's. Constance de Markievicz to Gertrude Bannister, n.d., Roger Casement Papers, MS 13 075, NLI.
134 Her conversion has certain similarities with that of Maud Gonne's, who felt it important "*not* to belong to the Church of England", O'Brien 1995, 72.

In Ireland the Catholic faith remained a true sign of nationality.[135] It was also something that many Anglo-Irish longed to embrace in order to be nearer the people.[136] As a whole, the conversion has been interpreted as a removal of the last barrier between Markievicz and those with whom she worked[137] even though it is arguable whether her conversion was the "most radical action of her life."[138] According to Esther Roper, Markievicz had not been a religious person.[139] By all accounts, it seems that in this respect, she did not change very much. She had wanted "to be with the boys in death by baptism of desire, if need be" and was not particularly interested in learning the instructions of the Catholic Church.[140]

Markievicz did not refer to her conversion or contemplate religious issues in her letters. Only in one letter do her words suggest that in a prison, excluded from the hectic politics of the day, one had the ascetic environment needed for developing one's spiritual side. [141] Her ponderings about the "subconscious self...in tune with the subconscious soul of the world"[142] reflect most likely the interest in mysticism that she and her sister Eva Gore-Booth possessed. Rather than being engaged with Catholicism, Markievicz was fascinated with the occult and astrology, like her sister and their family friend W.B. Yeats.[143]

When Markievicz chose the Catholic faith, she already had many Catholic friends. She had also direct connections with the Church; before the Rising she had often helped "the poor and the destitute" with the Capuchin brothers in Dublin.[144] Markievicz's conversion brought her closer to certain sections of the Catholic Church. Before the Rising the Church had been generally hostile to secret societies and favoured the IPP.[145] Accordingly, the Rising was

---

135   Rumpf & Hepburn,15; Phillips, 52; O'Brien 1995, 9-10. Garvin has criticised the view that joining together revolutionary ideology and Catholic faith was unique in Ireland, Garvin 1987, 169.
136   This was the opinion of Lady Gregory, who eventually did not convert to Catholic faith, Yeats 1953, 242.
137   O'Faolain, 153; Marreco,234; Van Voris,202-203; Haverty,171; Norman,173. On the other hand Roper remarked that the ritual and the ceremonies, the music, art and cultural background of the Catholic Church attracted the mystic in Markievicz, Roper,75. Haverty sees her conversion as being in harmony with the side of her which had "naively" fallen for idealistic nationalism before the Rising, Haverty, 178-179.
138   Norman makes the assertion because she sees that most of Markievicz's life had been spent in a society where Catholics were seen in the same way as anti-semitics saw Jews. She forgets that Markievicz had for a long time been working in larger arenas outside that society. Also the claim that joining the Catholic Church would have been a reactionary move to her socialist friends does not seem relevant in Ireland, where many socialists – for instance Connolly and Larkin – were openly Catholic. Furthermore, the argument that Markievicz converted to Catholicism because she wanted the Church to be going in the direction she considered it should seems to be far-fetched. Norman, 173.
139   Roper, 21.
140   Sheehy-Skeffington in Roper 1934, 73-74.
141   Markievicz to Eva Gore-Booth, 9.6.1917, PL,173. She mentioned also having thought about S. Francis, 9.6.1917, PL, 172.
142   Markievicz to Eva Gore-Booth, 9.6.1917, PL,173.
143   Markievicz to Eva Gore-Booth, 29.12.1917, PL, 160-161; Eva Gore-Booth to Ella Young, n.d., Ella Young Papers, Library of Congress; W.B.Yeats to Ella Young, n.d., ibid.; Markievicz speaking about ghosts and supernatural powers, Young 1945, 190-194.
144   Father Albert to Eva Gore-Booth, 30.3.1917, Constance Markievicz Papers, MS 5770, NLI; also 23.7.1917, ibid.
145   Whyte, John H., 1916 - Revolution and Religion, in Martin 1967,216-7; O'Brien 1995, 26-27..

condemned by individual bishops. However, some members of the lower clergy were in outright sympathy with the rebels, who were often portrayed as martyrs with exceptional piousness because of their religion.[146] The desire to represent the rebels as Catholic martyrs was mirrored in an article on Markievicz, where she was described as a born and religious rebel.[147] Furthermore, there was a tendency to emphasize her good work among the Dublin poor, for whose sake "she has given up everything that makes life dear to the worshippers of Mammon..."[148] A sympathetic priest, who sometimes met her in prison, wrote admiring letters about Markievicz and wished that after getting out of the jail she would visit "her best friends", the Capuchin brothers in Dublin.[149]

A Famous or a Notorious Heroine

Markievicz's participation in the Easter Rising was a big story outside Ireland. She, the"rebel Larkinite Countess Markievicz", dominated the reports of the Rising. [150] She was described as "one of the strangest figures in the whole Rebellion" and her ambition in life was, "according to one account", to shoot a British soldier.[151] In one of the stories she was pictured in "male attire, smiling and garrulous".[152]

In Ireland Markievicz got some sympathy from Sir Horace Plunkett, who remarked that "[s]he is deeply dyed in blood, but her motives were as noble as her methods were foul".[153] Her old friend AE expressed his admiration for her courage in a totally different tone from W.B. Yeats, who in his famous poem wrote:

---

146 Boyce, 310-311; Miller, David W., Church, State and Nation in Ireland 1898-1921, Dublin 1973, 341: Newsinger, 616-618; also F.X.Martin, The Evolution of a Myth - The Easter Rising, Dublin 1916, in Kamenka, Eugene, (ed.) Nationalism: The Nature and Evolution of an Idea, London 1973, 67.

147 Events of Easter Week, *Catholic Bulletin*, February 1917, 125-130. A few years later she was described as "an ardent zealous child of the Church" while travelling in the United States, Martin, John H., Countess Markievicz: Brilliant Irishwoman and Convent to the Catholic Church, Joseph McGarrity Papers, MS 17 463, NLI.

148 Father Lynch in *Irish Citizen*, March 1919.

149 Father Albert to Eva Gore-Booth, 30.3.1917, Constance Markievicz Papers, MS 5770, NLI; also 23.7.1917, ibid.

150 Appendix II, in 1916:The Easter Rising, 251-252; see also Ireland's Joan of Arc, *The Literary Digest*,July 15, 1916; The Dublin Massacre, *The Gaelic American*,13.5.1916; Lady Gregory, who was in Dublin a little later, wrote:" Dublin cynicism has passed away and was inventing beautiful, instead of derisive, fables. They told me that Madame Markiewicz had kissed her revolver..", in Smythe, Colin (ed.), Seventy Years. Being the Autobiography of Lady Gregory, London 1974, 549.

151 The Sinn Fein leaders of 1916 with fourteen illustrations and complete lists of deportees, casualties, etc., Dublin 1917,11.

152 Gore-Booth, Eva, The Irish Rebellion, in PL, 58.

153 West, Trevor, Horace Plunkett: Co-operation and Politics. An Irish Biography, Buckinghamshire 1986, 151.

"That woman's days were spent
  In ignorant good will,
  Her nights in argument
  Until her voice grew shrill..."[154]

In her home country – especially in Dublin – Markievicz was a more familiar figure than abroad. Her status as an officer was nevertheless such an exceptional thing that it caused some confusion. According to one of the participants in the Rising Markievicz, who carried arms, could not be counted among the women.[155]

Her imprisonment and active life in politics were an embarrassing thing for Markievicz's family. She did not speak much about the revolutionary side of her life even with her closest relative Eva , knowing her pacifist views.[156] However, Eva did not forsake her sister although their views regarding violence differed completely and represented two different poles in their approach to the question of women and militarism.[157] Taking the side of the rebels, Eva Gore-Booth sharply criticised British policy in Ireland both before and after the Rising.[158] Actually, she felt that the two sisters, two "wild rebels", were comrades in their work.[159]

Markievicz was pardoned on 16th July 1917 and was among the last rebels to get free. When she arrived in Dublin, she was received like a hero.[160] The first prisoners who came home in December 1916 had, to their great amazement, become heroes, their release being marked by the burning of bonfires on the hillsides and general celebration.[161] Attitudes towards the rebels were changed soon after the executions of the leaders of the Rising.[162] The financial situation of the returned heroine was nevertheless not a very good one: she had no home and no money.[163]

---

154   O'Faolain, 166-167.
155   O Briain, Liam, Saint Stephen's Green Area, *Capuchin Annual* 1966,220: "I do not count among "the women" Countess Markievicz, pictoresque in her own special uniform, second in command to Michael Mallin, or Miss Skinnider with her Scottish accent, as they were armed combatants."
156   In a letter soon after the Rising Markievicz wrote:" ....I knew all the time that you'd try and see me, even though I'd been fighting and you hate it all so and think killing so wrong.", letter to Eva Gore-Booth, 16.5.1916, PL, 137. Much of her poetry written at this period is full of horror at militarism, the triumph of mindless violent aggression and the loss of Christ, Lewis,143.
157   The last two years of the war Eva and Esther spent attending trials of conscientious objectors for the No-Conscription Fellowhip. Lewis, 149; In her pacifist plays Eva often returned to 'manliness' and its associations with might and the exercise of power. Lewis, 166.
158   Gore-Booth, Eva, The Irish Rebellion, in PL, 62.
159   Eva Gore-Booth's poem "Comrades", in PL, 128:
160   Young, 133: O'Faolain, 189-190.Her home town Sligo and Kilkenny added her name to their rolls of honorary citizens, Van Voris, 235-236.
161   Ward 1983, 121; Macardle, 204.
162   Though J.J. Lee has criticised this prevailing opinion by remarking that the basics of it lay on the consensus of historians rather than in scholarly review of the evidence., Lee 1989, 28-29.
163   Countess Markievicz, Hanna Sheehy-Skeffington Papers, MS 24 189, NLI; Markievicz gave thanks for money aid, letter in Irish National Aid Association and Volunteer Dependants' Correspondence, no date, MS 24 357, NLI.

Markievicz had sought to broaden the rebellious potential in a nationalist rising. Not only men, but the joint power of Irish women, youngsters and workers should accomplish the task. The sacrifices were not too much. Rather, they were necessary in order to keep alive the Irish nationalist spirit. That the spirit was essentially Catholic as well, was not of primary importance to Markievicz personally. The fight was about politics, not religion. However, she understood her ideals in the political struggle to be similar to those of early Christian martyrs as well as the martyrs for the nationalist cause. The celebration she faced after getting out of prison, most certainly strenghened her opinion of the rightness of the Rising which had fulfilled its purpose and changed public opinion to sympathize with and thus to promote the nationalist cause. It also most probably gave her personal confidence.

■ Pursuing the Policy of Sinn Fein and Connolly

Markievicz and the new goals of Sinn Fein

The aftermath of the Rising changed the political situation in Ireland. Traditionally, the Easter Rising has been seen as a watershed in Irish history.[1] During the last two decades it has been argued that the violent birth of a modern independent Ireland was foolish and unnecessary, because the democratic politics of consensus, reasoning and bargaining would have achieved independence more easily and without bloodshed. Tom Garvin has criticized this point of view by maintaining that pre-independent Ireland had no democratic politics.[2]

It is not surprising that the nationalist emotion which has encompassed – and still does, in some people's minds – the Easter Rising, has led to re-evaluations concerning the whole process and the ideas behind it. However, in terms of this study it is more relevant to look at the way in which it possibly affected the policy and ideas of Markievicz. The situation for the Sinn Feiners released from prison was a new and fascinating one: now they not only had the voice, but were also listened to. Since the rebellion had been blamed on Sinn Fein, it inherited the glory when it came to be seen as a noble deed.[3]

The most important result of the Rising was the birth of a united separatist party. The IPP had been in crisis even before the Rising and lost its seat in the Roscommon by-election to a Sinn Fein candidate.[4] The attempt of Lloyd George to achieve a Home Rule settlement in a Convention of all Irish groups was doomed because of the variety of goals. Sinn Fein, organised Labour and the "All for Ireland League" ignored it.[5] In November 1918 Lloyd George made it clear that Home Rule with the exclusion of six counties of Ulster must be postponed until the condition of Ireland made it possible.[6]

---

1   As Sean O'Casey wrote, Easter Week "became the Year One in Irish history and Irish life", Marreco, 232. The view of its importance and inevitablility was re-evaluated only five decades after, see Martin, F.X., in his "1916 - Revolution or Evolution? "It is a prevalent belief in Ireland that the Easter Rising was...'necessary and inevitable'", 241.
2   See Garvin, Tom, The Rising and Irish Democracy, in Màirìn Nì Dhonnchadha and Theo Dorgan (eds), Revising the Rising, Dublin 1991, 21-28.
3   Cronin, 121.
4   Ibid. However, it has been noted that the support for the republican side grew from the failure of the Irish Parliamentaty Party not to secure the Home Rule rather than from a shift in domestic politics, Patterson, 12.
5   For instance Cahill, 30; Johansson, Rolf, Irish Labour and the Downfall of Home Rule 1916-1918, in Tammisto, Antero, Mustakallio, Katariina, Saarinen, Hannes (eds.), Miscellanea, Vammala 1989, 263-268; Macardle, 219.
6   Macardle, 261.

During the first part of the year 1917 Sinn Fein had built a strong grassroots level organisation and in the same summer it had merged the competitive organisations into itself.[7] The nationalists of Sinn Fein were out to get international recognition for a sovereign Ireland and support from the people. According to Eamon de Valera, the only commandant left alive after the Easter Rising and a rising politician, Ireland should first claim absolute independence in order that her case might be heard at the coming Peace Conference. To maintain that in making that claim they were "only voicing the feelings of every Irish heart"[8], he implicitly declared Sinn Fein to be the representative of the Irish people in the new situation.

Markievicz had been concerned about the Irish wasting of "precious time"[9]; for her own part she was eager to seize the moment. In the summer of 1917 she toured Ireland making speeches about the policy of Sinn Fein.[10] In a changed situation there was no need to emphasize the need of a rebellion, and although she remarked that "no one speaks more strongly than I", she simultaneously pointed out that all in Sinn Fein were talking of "organising the country into a strong constitutional movement, with the Volunteer Force behind, whose immediate duty is to keep order..."[11]

The message Markievicz gave was a mixture of old and new. She followed the new policy of Sinn Fein by describing her party as a constitutional movement, and by referring to Parnell, the charismatic leader of Irish Parlimentary Party between 1880 and 1890, she presented Sinn Fein as the inheritor of the position of predominance that the IPP had lost. According to Markievicz "the first battle would be the election", and their men had to win every seat for Parliament. [12] In addition to that, she emphasized the importance of being recognised at the Peace Conference.[13]

However, the old message of serving Cathleen ni Houlihan even if it required one's life, was there as well. She told her audience that the Irish had to be prepared to die, as she had been, for Ireland.[14] She argued that "they would gain nothing unless they were armed and trained"[15], because they might be

---

7   Laffan, Michael, The Unification of Sinn Fein in 1917, *Irish Historical Studies*, vol XVII, 1970-71, 368-369, 374.
8   Macardle, 225.
9   "Now they'll be able, on all the committees in Ireland, to waste all their precious time tying up their minds and other people's in red tape. Notices of motion about rubbish taking the place of the divine inspiration of the moment..." Markievicz to Eva Gore-Booth, 9.6.1917, PL, 174 - 175.
10 For instance *Cork Examiner,*17, 20 and 27 of July; *Nationality*, July, September, October and December 1917.
11 Markievicz to Eva Gore-Booth, 26.9.1917, PL, 296.
12 Countess Markievicz, Cork Examiner, 13.8.1917;Kilkenny Election, *Cork Examiner*, 20.7.1917. Eamon de Valera proclaimed that Sinn Fein were the logical followers of Parnell, Boyce, 316
13 Countess Markievicz, *Cork Examiner*, 13.8.1917; Markievicz to Eva Gore-Booth, undated letter (1918-19), PL, 201. She believed that by International Law Ireland should earn the right to be at the Peace Conference by Easter 1919, Markievicz to Eva Gore-Booth in 1918, no date, PL, 296.
14 Countess Markievicz, *Cork Examiner*, 13.8.1917
15 Kilkenny Election, *Cork Examiner*, 20.7.1917.

attacked. The Easter Rising had welded "the policy of Wolfe Tone and Parnell" together, which meant that physical and moral force would together achieve freedom.[16]

In the new situation Markievicz endorsed a policy that focused on gaining and using political power, which would then be backed by a strong volunteer force. Her view reflected the ideas of de Valera, who declared that Sinn Fein stood for the principles of Easter week, but not for the methods of the men of 1916.[17] If those methods meant ending up again in a military fiasco, then Markievicz agreed. Yet the heroic spirit that she had, in her view, witnessed in the Rising should be kept alive. She found it hard to forgive or forget any statement hinted at the failure of the Rising. [18]

Markievicz was one of the participants at the Sinn Fein Annual Convention held in October 1917. There it was decided to continue under the old name, which had now become a synonym for the entire nationalist movement, but with a new President, Eamon de Valera. The objectives of Sinn Fein were deliberately defined in vague so that everyone could accept them:[19]

> "Sinn Fein aims at securing the international recognition of Ireland as an independent Irish Republic. Having achieved that status the Irish people may by Referendum freely choose their own form of government." [20]

Participation in the Peace Conference was set as the immediate objective of the nationalists.[21] According to de Valera the time for discussion on the best forms of government was not yet - its turn was to be after freedom was obtained. [22] It has been observed that in this context the term 'republic' probably became, for the public, simply another word for independence.[23] However, it is important to note that Markievicz wanted it to be made clear nevertheless that Ireland was to be a nation where everyone had equal opportunities.[24] The Easter Rising Declaration with its promises of equal citizenship was for her a guide line which had to be followed. In public she was always hopeful therefore: they were aiming at an Irish Republic.[25]

---

16   Countess Markievicz, *Cork Examiner*, 13.8.1917
17   Boyce 1995, 316-317.
18   When Eoin MacNeill was elected to the executive of Sinn Fein in 1917, Markievicz protested it because of the countermanding order that MacNeill had given prior to the Rising, but with only little support, Typescript report of Sinn Fein Annual Convention 1917, MS 21 523, NLI, 21-23.
19   After the Rising Sinn Fein consisted not only of republicans and members of old Sinn Fein, but also of those who were not satisfied with the Home Rule policy and the party which had been backing it, Johansson, 260 The young priests were also joining the strengthening party, Newsinger 1978, 618.
20   Sinn Fein Annual Convention 1917, 51.
21   Sinn Fein Annual Convention 1917, Griffith's speech, 7.
22   Sinn Fein Annual Convention 1917, 49-50.
23   Laffan 1970-71, 377; Townshend, 319.
24   Sinn Fein Annual Convention 1917, 18-19.
25   Kilkenny Election, *Cork Examiner*, 20.7.1917; See Proclamation of the Irish Republic: "...The Republic guarantees religious and civil liberty, equal rights and equal opportunities to all its citizens...".

Although the main struggle was to achieve the recognition of Ireland as a sovereign state, the Sinn Feiners also discussed the everyday arrangements of Irish life. Markievicz followed the old economic nationalist line of Sinn Fein by stressing the need for the protection of the Irish cattle and horsetrade and also by supporting the suggestion of establishing an afforestation and agricultural department in Sinn Fein.[26] Earlier in the summer she had already reminded the Irish of the importance of buying Irish goods in order to increase employment.[27] She was invited to make decisions regarding everyday life by being made a member of a Sinn Fein committee which was to concentrate on matters concerning the home food supply in war-time Ireland.[28]

Sinn Fein did not concentrate only on general political objectives. It aimed to improve the morals of its members as well. It stressed that each individual was the Irish nation in miniature. Therefore he or she ought to make themselves as near as possible to what they thought the Irish nation ought to be; they ought to have courage, temperance and manliness.[29] Although Markievicz valued the moral ideals connected with the national movement and approved every attempt to improve the national character, she was not an obedient member of Sinn Fein in this respect – she smoked and did not refuse to have a drink.[30] This, together with her failure – so far – to learn the Irish language and, it seems, her quite superficial conversion to the Catholic faith reveals something about her personality. Markievicz was willing to fight, even die for Ireland and she gave all her time for the nationalist cause, but the characteristics usually connected the nationalist cause – learning the native language, or the religion, or living an ascetic life – all these did not appreciably impinge on her personal life. She would always enjoy her art, her friends, good food, drink and tobacco. This desire to embrace life was as central to her character as was the desire to work in all possible arenas to further her cause.

Leading Cumann na mBan and Na Fianna Eireann

The other nationalist organisations were committed to work for the same objectives as was Sinn Fein. Two of them, Cumann na mBan and Fianna na hEireann, were under the guidance of Markievicz. She had been elected President of Cumann na mBan in August 1916 while she was in prison[31], a gesture that in itself indicated now that the policy of the organisation was changing. After

---

26   Sinn Fein Annual Convention 1917, 55-56.
27   Countess Markievicz, *Cork Examiner*, 13.8.1917.
28   *Nationality*, 1.12.1917. At that time there was concern about food supplies and even famine in Ireland, because food was being exported from Ireland, see e.g. *Irish Citizen*, March-April 1917; Notes and Comments, *Irish Opinion: Voice of Labour*,15.12.1917; Hunger in Ireland? How Shall We Avoid It?, Johnson, Thomas, *Irish Opinion: Voice of Labour*, 5.1.1918; Macardle, 240. Sinn Fein Food Control Committee organised a census of supplies and improved distribution, Macardle, 242.
29   R.U. Floinn, The Ethics of Sinn Fein, [pamphlet] n.d.
30   See e.g. Litton, Helen (ed.), Revolutionary Woman. Kathleen Clarke 1878-1972. An Autobiography, Dublin 1991, 162, 164.
31   Norman, 162.

the Rising and while the rebels were in prison women had been in the forefront of resistance. Their priority was to gain the support of the people. Some of them were also determined to show that women would not be passive victims but would continue the struggle so that they too would gain their independence.[32]

The Proclamation of Easter Rising 1916 had opened up a new way for the women's organisation, which now strove to see that women took up "their proper position in the life of the nation." Women should participate in public affairs, take part in the nomination of candidates, and be educated in order to be fit to occupy public positions. More importantly, the organisation was now committed to the arming and equipping of both sexes.[33] Markievicz, who was confirmed as president of Cumann na mBan in the autumn of 1917 and who continued to speak to women under the auspices of Cumann na mBan, [34] was almost certainly satisfied with this new, more active policy. She had hoped that war would shake women "out of old grooves"[35] and it seemed that the Rising had assisted in the same process.

Nonetheless, the position of women in the new situation was not her main concern. In the autumn of 1917 she did not participate in the discussion of women's rights in relation to the new constitution of Sinn Fein. At the annual convention of the party it was her friend, Kathleen Lynn, who spoke strongly on behalf of women emphasizing that the brains of both men and women were now needed: they were complementary to each other. She supported her claims by referring to the peculiarly feminine features of her sex; women, as a whole, were, she claimed, more honest than men, and worked directly for their ends. Furthermore, the influence of the women had been vital in the Easter Rising when " they urged the men to take action boldly." Lynn got support from Sean T.O'Kelly, who reminded the audience of the ancient traditions of Gaelic Ireland. The result was that the equality of men and women in Sinn Fein was to be emphasised in all speeches and pamphlets[36], Consequently, four women were elected to the new 24-member executive, among them Constance Markievicz.

The reasons Lynn gave in support of her demands were ones often heard in contemporary discussions relating to women and their participation in public life. Her logic resembled that of Markievicz, who from 1909 onwards had portrayed women as an honest and virtuous moral force much needed in the nationalist struggle. After the Easter Rising, Markievicz wanted women to take the initiative. In January 1918 she , together with some other Sinn Fein women, appealed to Woodrow Wilson to include Ireland in the list of the small nations for whose freedom America was fighting.[37] Also, when growing resistance towards British government was manifested in the wide scale of conscription, Markievicz joined in the process by calling the IWFL, Cumann

---

32   Ward 1983, 117- 123; See Farrell, 235.
33   Cumann na mBan. Policy for 1917-1918, leaflet, no date, NLI.
34   Conlon, 50, 54.
35   The Future of Irishwomen. Speech at the IWFL Meeting, October 12th , *Irish Citizen*, 23.10.1915.
36   Sinn Fein Annual Convention 1917, 16-17; *Irish Citizen*, November 1917.
37   Ward 1983, 121.

na mBan and other women's organisations together to express their own opposition.[38] The nationalist women were also getting further support from suffragettes and the IWFL was gradually becoming more and more sympathetic to the separatist movement.[39]

The other organisation Markievicz led was the Fianna. In a similar vein to before the Rising, she pointed out the need to train the youth of Ireland.[40] However, she was suspicious of the idea that all Irish people of military age should be trained in the use of arms and preferred leaving the choice to the individual.[41] Nevertheless, both the Fianna and the Cumann were training militarily with the consent of Markievicz. It is obvious that she believed in the need of voluntary military organisations, which she wanted to connect with the nationalist movement led by de Valera. In August he was elected Chief of the Fianna at her suggestion, while Markievicz herself was chosen as Chief Scout[42] thus placing her once more in the forefront of Fianna. It is most likely that this appointment was the result of two factors: her personal participation in the Easter Rising and also the deaths of a number of prominent members of the Fianna, who otherwise would possibly have taken her place.

Markievicz's policy represented the general attitude among nationalists that despite their chosen peaceful political path they were eager to enlist more and more of their countrymen into organised military groups. The Volunteer Convention had been held under cover of the Sinn Fein Ard-Fheis. De Valera, who was elected as the President of the Volunteers' Executive, thus became President of both the political party Sinn Fein and of the military organisation, the Irish Volunteers.[43] However, Markievicz's aims were not focused in the nationalist sphere only. She attempted also to link the cause of Labour to that of Ireland.

"To Ireland and you I have pledged my life"

Soon after the Easter Rising Markievicz wrote a poem in memory of James Connolly. In this she, in a typically fiery way, committed herself to continue the work he had started:

---

38   Van Voris, 242-243. When the ITUC organised a one-day general strike, Cumann na mBan organised a flag day, the flags bearing the inscription 'Women won't blackleg' and the IWWU demonstrated in support, Ward 1983, 128.

39   Hanna Sheehy-Skeffington, one of the leading suffragettes, valued the Easter Proclamation that gave equal citizenship to women, McKillen 1982, 72.

40   Speaking for Fianna, see e.g. Kilkenny Election, *Cork Examiner*, 20.7.1917. Her poem, dedicated to the Fianna, was full of the usual belligerent spirit, see Markievicz, Constance de, Heroes and Martyrs, Dedicated to Na Fianna Eireann, *An Phoblacht*, 19.4.1930.

41   Sinn Fein Annual Convention 1917, 11.

42   Van Voris, 241. The fact that de Valera was the leader of the nationalist movement is a more plausible reason for Markievicz's proposing him than the alternative suggestion: that de Valera had managed to satisfy her that his heart was on the left politically, Norman, 182.

43   Coogan, Tim Pat, De Valera. Long Fellow, Long Shadow, London 1993, 97 ; de Valera declared that IRB was no longer needed; he was against secret societies, Fitzpatrick, David, De Valera in 1917: the Undoing of the Easter Rising, in O'Carroll, John P. and Murphy, John A. (eds.), De Valera and His Times, Cork 1983, 105. Markievicz shared his dislike of secret societies, see Markievica, Constance de, Memories. The King's Visit, *Eire*, 21.7.1923.

"...

On your murdered body I'll pledge my life
With its passionate love and hate
To secret plotting and open strife
For vengeance early and late
To Ireland and you I have pledged my life
Revenge for your memory's sake!"[44]

In her election address two years later, in 1918, she was less poetic but as fervent as before when she declared that she stood for a

"...Republic [such] as James Connolly wrote about, worked for and died for. Real <u>democratic</u> control with <u>economic and industrial</u> as well as political Freedom. To organise our new nation on just and equitable lines, avoiding the mistakes other Nations have made in allowing the powers of Government, law, force, education, foreign policy etc., to be the birthright of the moneyed classes to be used by them for the further accumulation of wealth and the building up of a class tyranny daily more subtle and more difficult to seize and overthrow..."[45]

Socialism was thus the right way to build a new Ireland. Like Connolly, Markievicz believed that the national revolution would be in vain if the social structures were left intact. But the national revolution would not be possible without Sinn Fein. In her own words, Markievicz explained that she belonged to both organisations – Sinn Fein and Labour – because her conception of a free Ireland was "economic as well as political." She was convinced that the bulk of workers were with Sinn Fein, which was composed of "both Labour and Capital."[46]

However, there were also different viewpoints in Sinn Fein. Taking a completely opposite stand, P.S.O'Hegarty wrote that Sinn Fein was neither socialist nor capitalist.[47] The majority in Sinn Fein was not interested in the labour question, following their old policy. Even though it was emphasized that Sinn Fein strove for social justice more than the Labour movement[48] and Sinn Fein defined itself as a heir of Connolly's policy[49], it was not committed to the establishment of a socialist republic. De Valera wanted Labour to join Sinn Fein in freeing the country; in a free Ireland workers would have a better chance than within capitalist England. However, he advised Labour not to act too radically. In Sinn Fein there were suspicions about socialist infiltration

---

44   The poem is cited in Marreco, 217.
45   Holloway Prison, Countess Markievicz, To The Director of Elections (Sinn Fein), 6 Harcourt St., Dublin, Ireland, 6.12.18, CO 904/164, page 33, Public Record Office (PRO), London.
46   Markievicz to Eva Gore-Booth, 17.8.1919, PL, 238.
47   Mitchell, Arthur, Revolutionary Government in Ireland: Dàil Eireann 1919-22, Dublin 1995, 45: He writes thus in summer 1919.
48   For instance Ó Geallchobair, Proinnsias, Labour, Sinn Fein and the Future, Old Ireland, 7.2.1920.
49   For instance Anderson 1994, 116-117; After the Rising, Connolly was widely praised in Ireland, and many individuals and organisations proclaimed adherance to his beliefs and objectives, Anderson, 13; Lee 1919, 38.

into the movement, even though similar hostilities such as the earlier ones between Griffith and Larkin had not increased.[50] Equally, leaders of the Labour movement were not convinced by the social and economic views of many members of Sinn Fein.[51]

Markievicz maintained her connections with the Labour movement after the Rising.[52] In 1917, together with her nationalist friends Helena Moloney and Kathleen Lynn she joined forces with trade union activists Louie Bennett and Helen Chenevix to push forward the organisation of women workers. Two important strikes were settled by the IWWU in the following months.[53] However, even though Markievicz held the position of honorary chairman of the IWWU[54], the cause of women workers did not play a major part in her activities. Her complex relationship with Delia Larkin who was leading the movement, might in part explain this. A more important reason was, however, that Markievicz focused first and foremost on organising all the Irish to complete the nationalist struggle. She urged all ranks and sections to work together for the complete separation from England and the establishment of an Irish Republic.[55] She wanted Sinn Fein to embrace the cause of the workers: she supported the proposition that Sinn Fein should ensure that workers were paid a living wage.[56] On the other hand, she sought to assure Labour about the democracy of Sinn Fein.[57]

It is probable, that Markievicz's activities in the Labour movement were more acceptable in the nationalist sphere because – similarly with Larkin[58] – she wanted Irish unions to severe all their connections with the English ones.[59] Evidently, Markievicz did not trust any English organisation, even if it fought for the same goals as its Irish counterpart. Speaking of a strike in England she

50   Laffan 1985, 211; Fitzpatrick, 110; Berresford Ellis, 245-246. According to Dunphy, many of the post-1916 Sinn Fein leaders, de Valera included, shared fully Griffith's hostility to working-class politics, Dunphy, Richard, The Making of Fianna Fáil Power in Ireland 1923-1948, Oxford 1995, 31.
51   Anderson 1994, 117; about Larkin's warnings of attitudes in Sinn Fein, Introduction, in Sinn Fein and Socialism.., 6-7.; Macardle, 265. Sinn Fein was believed to be just a new name for capitalism, "Charles Russell", Should the Workers of Ireland Support Sinn Fein? in Sinn Fein and Socialism..., [1918]; Mitchell 1974, 85. For example Sinn Fein's resolution on a living wage was considered too modest. Notes and Comments, *Irish Opinion: Voice of Labour*, 1.12.1917; About distance – or even tension – in the labour-republican relation-ship in the years 1917-21, English, Richard, Radicals and the Republic. Socialist Republicanism in the Irish Free State 1925–1937, Oxford 1994, 36.
52   Markievicz sat on the Executive of the ICA, Murphy, H.L., 290; Robbins, 218; raised money for the James Connolly Labour College; *Irish Opinion: Voice of Labour*, 14.6.1919; *Watchword of labour*, 17.1.1920. She sat also on the executive of the college, *Irish Citizen*, May 1920; about her addressing speeches to workers, see e.g. Greaves, Charles D., The Irish Transport and General Workers' Union: The Formative Years, Dublin 1982, 185, 193.
53   Two important strikes were settled by the IWWU in the following months, MacCurtain 1978, 56. IWWU, led by Bennett and Chenevix, was in 1920 at its strongest with 5000 members, Anderson, 83.
54   Jones, Mary, 24.
55   Sinn Fein Annual Convention 1917, 17.
56   Proposition made by Sean T.O'Kelly, Sinn Fein Annual Convention 1917, 16. It was accepted unanimously.
57   Labour in Ireland, *Irish Opinion: Voice of Labour*, 9.2.1918.
58   Introduction, in Sinn Fein and Socialism..., 6-7.
59   Sinn Fein Annual Convention 1917, 17.

argued that wages were the only thing that would motivate an Englishman. Consequently she suspected that the British Government was counting on establishing an 'aristocracy' of Labour, "well-paid and satisfied, who will go to Parliament, compromise, sell every cause, act with the police, and trample on the underdog."[60] The features of the English national nature were thus twisting the workers' cause in England; according to Markievicz greed there was more powerful than principle. Irish Labour should be independent and separated from the British Government that was ruling Ireland.

After the Easter Rising Markievicz accepted the programme of Connolly but also supported the current policy of Sinn Fein. In a recent study of socialist republicanism Markievicz's thinking is described as blurred, because she was committed to a "Workers' republic" and yet simultaneously she wholeheartedly supported Sinn Fein, which endorsed conservative politics.[61]

In order to understand Markievicz's attempt to promote Irish independence in company with both nationalists and Labour, it is important to recognise the significance of Connolly's view that "the cause of labour is the cause of Ireland, the cause of Ireland is the cause of labour. They cannot be dissevered."[62] That is the key to understanding why it seemed essential for Markievicz to work on both arenas. It was impossible to leave the cause of Labour aside, because the nationalist struggle was fundamentally tied to it. As will be seen later in the work, her support for Connolly's policy went beyond the rhetorics of those Sinn Feiners who especially highlighted the nationalist ideas of Connolly.

Another key to any understanding of Markievicz's commitment to Connolly's cause is found in what she saw as the necessity of having the support of the workers in the Irish independence struggle. In her appeal to all ranks and sections of the nation to work for the establishment of an Irish Republic she depended on the celebrated utterance of Wolfe Tone, which, as she remarked, was also found in Connolly's first pamphlet:

-"If the people of property will not support us they must fall. We can support ourselves by the aid of that numerous and important portion of the community, the people of no property." [63]

Working simultaneously in the nationalist and the Labour movement did not necessarily meet with the approval of either of the camps. Although Markievicz was welcomed with Red Flags and the people were singing the Internationale when she got back from prison[64], doubts regarding her within the ICA were

---

60 Markievicz to Eva Gore-Booth, 8.10.1919, PL, 246. On the other hand, she told Eva that she would always back Labour, even English Labour, Markievicz to Eva Gore-Booth, 1.10.1919, PL, 244.
61 English, 37-38.
62 Connolly, James, The Irish Flag, *Workers' Republic*, 8.4.1916, in James Connolly: Selected Writings, 145.
63 Sinn Fein Annual Convention 1917, 17-18. In fact, Tone's reference to "the men of no property" was largely misunderstood; the men of no property were for Tone the middle classes who owned no land, Elliott, Marianne, Wolfe Tone. Prophet of Irish Independence, New Haven and London 1989, 418.
64 Young, 133.

not completely forgotten.[65] Nor was she unanimously accepted in nationalist circles. The Sinn Fein Club at Tulla threatened to burn a look-a-like model of the "dreaded" Countess[66] and in 1918 Griffith is said to have been displeased by her flamboyant rhetoric and would have liked to silence her, "but such a thing would be taken as a division in the camp, so she is allowed to go on making idiotic revolutionary speeches."[67] Some of those Irish who were not directly involved in nationalist or Labour politics, also opposed her activities[68]

Pursuing the policy of Connolly in the Labour movement also caused problems. After the Easter Rising Markievicz faced a situation where the leadership of the Labour movement was not as nationalist-minded as Connolly had been. The new Labour leader, Thomas Johnson, was a moderate home ruler, not a revolutionary committed to linking together nationalism and socialism in the way that Connolly had done. However, party politics were not of importance before the year 1922; the Labour movement on the whole concentrated on the economic rather than political goals in the ranks of the ITGWU led by William O'Brien.[69] The mainstream of workers did not connect nationalism with their work in the unions[70] and thus did not share the ideas of Connolly and Markievicz. Moreover, the ITGWU was hostile towards co-operation with the ICA, of which Markievicz was a member.[71] Her personal relationships with Johnson or O'Brien could not be compared with the friendship she had with Connolly and Larkin, who had moved to the United States. That is apparent when one looks at the speeches she made to workers; she did not urge them to back new leaders, but rather the ideas of James Connolly, the martyr of a nationalist Rising.

In spite of the complexity of the relationship on a personal as well as an organisational level, Markievicz found it necessary to believe in co-operation between the nationalist and workers' movements. According to her, both Labour and Sinn Fein had been able to act loyally towards each other and their disagreements had been open and without any spleen. As long as they continued to do so, "they will both be for the good of Ireland." She admitted that some did not agree with her in this respect, but did not consider that to be " a sore

---

65   See her letter to William O'Brien July 14, 1917, MS 15 673, William O'Brien Papers, NLI.
66   Fitzpatrick, 110.
67   Mitchell 1995, 161.
68   Her visit in a Catholic boy school was considered suspicious because of her political activities, Couldrey, B.M., Faith and Fatherland: The Christian Brothers and the Development of Irish Nationalism 1838-1921, Dublin 1988, 237; and although she had been received as a hero in Dublin, the audience threw mud and made impudent remarks when she spoke in other parts of Ireland, see, for example, Tomorrow is Another Day by Seamus O'Connor, Dublin 1987, in Haverty, 181.
69   Laffan, Michael, "Labour Must Wait": Ireland's Conservative Revolution, in Corish, Patrick J., Radicals, Rebels & Establishments: *Historical Studies XV*, Belfast 1985, 207;The change was dramatic: when ITGWU had by April 1916 only 5000 members, its membership had grown to almost 68 000 by 1918, Cahill, 16. In Britain also the union membership rose dramatically after the war, see Kirby, Maurice W., Industry, Agriculture and Trade Unions, in Constantine etc., 1995, 60. SPI, the party that Connolly had established and reorganised, was alive, but it was weak and controlled by the ILPTUC. Later it became the Communist party, Anderson 1994, 125-127; Fitzpatrick, 101-102.
70   Robbins, 223.
71   Fox, R.M., 1943, 193-195; Robbins, 201-203.

point" because she believed that the comrades of Easter Week had not fallen out despite their differences.[72]

Reference to Easter Week reveals what was at the core of her ideas on the Labour movement: she always saw it in terms of her experience of the Rising. The problem was that only the members of the ICA had participated in that. The Rising had thus linked only a tiny part of the Labour movement with a group of extreme nationalists. Even so, Markievicz still understood the Rising to have been a kind of fulfilment of Tone's goal of uniting all Irishmen.

At that stage the most important movement for Markievicz was Sinn Fein, which in her words was not a "solid, cast-iron thing like English parties...[but] just a jumble of people of all classes, creeds and opinions, who are ready to suffer and die for Ireland."[73] It was as a member of Sinn Fein therefore that Markievicz aimed at narrowing the gap between Labour and the nationalist movement. In her revolutionary speeches, which had irritated Griffith, she did not comment on the situation in Russia or on the Bolshevik Revolution, but concentrated on the struggle in Ireland.

At the Annual Convention of Sinn Fein there was no discussion about establishing a Labour Department even though a number of other departments were formed.[74] Even so, only a few months later, at the first meeting of the executive of Sinn Fein in December 1917, Markievicz was nominated as head of a Department of Labour together with Cathal O'Shannon, who represented the Labour movement itself.[75] Her nomination shows that her contacts with the movement were acknowledged in Sinn Fein. Unfortunately the reports of the Department give no details that shed light on its activities[76] and there is also no information on whose idea the Department was and what motives there were behind its formation.

"Life is Politics"

After her pardon Markievicz had been able to present her ideas of Irish independence to a larger and, more importantly, a more supportive audience than ever before. However, she was subject to British Government control and was concretely reminded of that when she was taken to prison. The situation had begun to become tense and in May 1918 73 leading Sinn Feiners were deported to England, among them Griffith, de Valera, and Markievicz. They were imprisoned in England without charge or trial, to be held for an indefinite

---

72   Markievicz to Eva Gore-Booth, 17.8.1919, PL, 238.
73   Markievicz to Eva Gore-Booth, 17.8.1919, PL, 238.
74   Sinn Fein Annual Convention 1917, 55-56.
75   Van Voris, 242. The records of meetings of the Sinn Fein Executive are preserved only from the beginning of 1918.
76   On 4th March 1918 it is mentioned that Markievicz had submitted a report and that it was approved, Meetings of the Sinn Fein Standing Committee, 2B/82/116, 19, National Archives of Ireland (NAI).

time[77] On July 4th Sinn Fein, the Volunteers, Cumann na mBan, and the Gaelic League were all proclaimed dangerous associations and their meetings were declared illegal.[78]

Markievicz regarded the arrests as "about the best thing that could have happened for Ireland, as there was so little to be done there, only propaganda, and our arrests carry so much further than speeches."[79] The Sinn Fein victory in the East Cavan by-election only strengthened her conviction: "Putting us away cleared the issues for us, so much better than our own speeches ever could."[80] Markievicz believed that suppression brought about sympathy for the nationalists and thus promoted the cause. In terms of independent action, her imprisonment had in her view offered a chance to activate women.[81]

Markievicz belittled the effect of the arrests by declaring that she did not believe in leaders herself.[82] Without leaders people got a chance to think and act for themselves: leaders could be "such a curse", argued Markievicz.[83] Her scepticism extended to both Labour and Nationalism: on one occasion she pessimistically speculated on how "Reds" - in Russia - would abuse power if they got it.[84] Her personal experience of the countermanding of orders for the Easter Rising perhaps enforced her doubts and on a later occasion she pointed to Connolly's mistrust of leaders.[85] Yet her critique of leaders did not cover all of them because the example of the dead Irish martyrs was a proof of continuity in the national struggle.

Markievicz was well aware that the British censor was reading her letters, and was perhaps partly trying to irritate him by her remarks. However, denying the importance of leaders is also to be seen in her thoughts after Rising, when she pointed out that there was nothing that others could not do without her. This reflects the idea that the nationalist movement was something bigger than the actions of one person; it was linked with the idea that everyone should be responsible for what was done. Distrust of leaders connected with the idea of self-help, of the moral duties that every Irishman should embrace. The situation in Ireland demanded the contribution of all, and no-one could evade his or her duty. In prison, Markievicz refused to give a promise not to talk politics with her visitors. She wrote:

---

77 In the middle of February 28 Sinn Fein prisoners were on hungerstrike to demand being treated as political prisoners in Mountjoy. In April many papers were suppressed. Macardle, 242-243, 254.
78 Macardle, 256.
79 Markievicz to Eva Gore-Booth, 8.6.1918, PL, 179. "Sending you to jail is like pulling out all the loud stops on all the speeches you ever made or words you ever wrote!", ibid.
80 Markievicz to Eva Gore-Booth, 22.6.1918, PL, 180.
81 Markievicz to Eva Gore-Booth, 22.1.1919, PL, 191.
82 Ibid.
83 Markievicz to Hanna Sheehy-Skeffington, 12.12. 1918, Hanna Sheehy-Skeffington Papers, MS 22 696, NLI.
84 Markievicz to Eva Gore-Booth, 30.1.1919, PL, 193.
85 Markievicz in a letter to Joseph McGarrity in 1924; about Connolly's concern that rank-and-file radicalism could be thwarted by corrupt or cautious leaders, English 1994, 31. It also reflects syndicalism's mistrust of party politics that would eventually create an elite which would always betray the masses, O'Connor, 67. Similarly the inter-war republicans held that leaderships, labour and republican, had frustrated the radical potential of those years, English 1994, 31.

" To-day life is 'politics.' Finance, economics, education, even the ever-popular (in England) subject of divorce is all mixed up with politics to-day. I can't invest my money, without politics; buy clothes without politics. Art is all political, music is battle tunes of hymns of hate or self-glorification, and so I simply do not know what they mean when they say we must not talk politics..."[86]

This definition that "life is politics" sums up her vision of politics and the foundation of her political action, in other words, the idea that a national ideology should be encapsulated within every action and thought and that it should not be employed only in a certain political sphere.

The First Woman Member of the British Parliament

Markievicz was recognised in a rare way for a woman when Sinn Fein asked her to be a candidate in the forthcoming general election in December 1918. Its election manifesto stood for securing the establishment of the Irish Republic by withdrawing the Irish representatives from the British parliament and it promised the establishment of a constituent assembly and an appeal to the Peace Conference as well as guaranteeing within an independent nation equal rights and equal opportunites for all its citizens.[87]

Even so, as recently as the previous year Markievicz had not only stressed that she did not want to have a vote for an English parliament, but had expressed a considerable mistrust of parliamentary action in general:

"I don't think that Parliaments are much use anyhow. All authority in a country always seems to get into the hands of a clique and permanent officials. I think I am beginning to believe in anarchy. Laws work out as injustice, legalised by red tape."[88]

Overall, mistrust of parliamentarianism and a dislike of the process of electoral politics were strong among key groups of political leaders, both republican and socialist.[89] Markievicz's words above have been referred to as an example of militarism which tended to obscure other forms of political expression.[90] The conclusion is partly correct, but the context of the citation should be noted as well. Markievicz wrote those words when she was in prison after the Rising. Her words are connected with the tradition of abstentionism from Westminster but are not directly defining a political strategy for the future. Rather, the words of Markievicz echo the ideas presented by a co-operative nationalist

---

86 Markievicz to Eva Gore-Booth, no date, PL, 208.
87 Macardle, Text of the manifesto of Sinn Fein as passed by the Dublin Castle Censor, 921.
88 Markievicz to Eva Gore-Booth, 9.6.1917, PL, 175.
89 Garvin 1993, 10. About the nonpolitical nature of Irish politics, see Eagleton, 233; about neo-Fenian distaste for politics among republicans, also English 1993, 174.
90 English 1994, 51.

Aodh de Blacam, whose book Towards the Republic was published in 1918. In a chapter entitled 'Away with Parliaments' he declared that Ireland had no use for the "corrupt, inefficient and decivilising institution called Parliament" because the country "has a different conception of the right way to conduct a state." The Irish conception was, in his opinion, that the agricultural industry, education and all other great agencies of public service would be made self-directing.[91] The message Markievicz gave in her election address had a similar tone: new Ireland had to be built in a completely new, democratic way. In her demands, which she drew from the ideas of Connolly, she, however, went further than most Sinn Feiners.

In spite of her mistrust of parliament, Markievicz said that she "wouldn't mind" standing for Parliament as an election sport[92] and in her election address she put two choices before the Irish people; either to desire complete and unlimited self-determination for Ireland - the republic of James Connolly - or to deny Ireland's nationhood by supporting Home Rule.[93] The result of the general election was a landslide victory for Sinn Fein, which had 73 succesful candidates out of a total of 105. The ultimate significance of the election was that the Irish people as a whole had decided for full self-government.[94]

Markievicz was elected for the St.Patrick's Division of Dublin with an overwhelming majority.[95] Her candidature had been supported largely by the women members of Sinn Fein with the assistance of other women's organisations such as IWFL and Cumann na mBan.[96] She had been promoted by the ICA also[97], but it is obvious that she was elected because of her nationalist views. Markievicz described her election as a "foregone conclusion" and believed that she knew most of those who voted for her.[98] She took her new task seriously, planning to read up about

"Imperialism and earlier Peace Conferences and anything about Empire building and theories about the internal construction of a State. I would buy any good books that might be useful to pass on. I want to get together a little library of Economics and Welt-Politik."[99]

Again Markievicz returned to Yeats' Cathleen ni Houlihan and the demand, "If you would help me, you must give me yourself, give me all." In the new situation the words had a different significance from previously when Markievicz had

---

91   Mitchell 1995, 45.
92   Markievicz to Eva Gore-Booth, no date, PL, 205-206.
93   Holloway Prison, Countess Markievicz, To The Director of Elections (Sinn Fein), 6 Harcourt St., Dublin, Ireland, 6.12.18, CO 904/164, page 33, PRO.
94   Mitchell 1995, 3.
95   She got 7835 votes when the cancidate who came second gained only 3752 votes, Ireland's Declaration of Independence, *Nationality*, 4.1.1919.
96   Wyse-Power, 160; Ward 1983, 136. However, not all feminists were eager to support Markievicz, see Ward 1983, ibid.
97   Fox 1943, 202.
98   Markievicz to Eva Gore-Booth, 6.2. 1919, PL, 193.
99   Markievicz to Eva Gore-Booth, 22.1.1919, PL, 191. She was going to donate the books to Connolly's college, Litton, 163.

used them merely to refer to the sacrifice of the Rising. Now they showed "what the elections meant for Ireland"[100]; they showed the willingness of the Irish to give their vote to the cause, to give it their "all." Yeats's celebrated words seem to have defined the all-sacrificing politics of Markievicz in a way she found most impressive.

Markievicz was the first and in this election the only woman to be elected to the House of Commons[101], which was a significant personal achievement. Markievicz was for long the only woman both in the Irish and British parliaments to have been elected because of her own accomplishments and not because she was relative of a notable man. Her election also gave hope to women. In her election address to the IWFL she had promised to make her constituency a rallying ground for woman and a centre for constructive work by them – she was "full of schemes and ideas."[102] She had appealed to women to vote for her and had believed that they would show that "women trust women to speak for them, to work for them and fight for them and to look after their interests in the Irish Republic."[103]

Markievicz was able to concentrate on her work again when she was released from prison on March 10th 1919. Her welcome in Dublin was even more enthusiastic than after the Rising.[104] Her homecoming was crowned with her selection as Minister of Labour in the Shadow Government of Republicans, Dáil Eireann. She had been proposed for this post by Eamon de Valera, who became the President of the Dáil. This title was rendered in Irish as Priomh Aire, in English the Prime Minister.[105] Other ministers were Arthur Griffith, Minister for Home Affairs, Cathal Brugha for Defence, Count Plunkett for Foreign Affairs, Eoin MacNeill for Industry, W.T.Cosgrave for Local Government, and Michael Collins for Finance. Three non-cabinet ministers were Robert Barton for Agriculture, Ernest Blythe for Trade and Commerce and Laurence Ginnell for Propaganda.[106] The nomination of ministers was considered very important, because de Valera was on his way to America to get recognition and money for the Republic and thus knew that he must leave

---

100   Markievicz to Eva Gore-Booth, 6.1.1919, Pl, 189. She had referred to this passage by Yeats from early on, for instance see Love of Country. Extracts from a lecture by Constance de Markievicz, *Bean na hEireann*, 20/1910 (July).
101   Of the 17 women who stood for Parliament in 1918, one was an Independent Unionist, one for the Coalition, two for Sinn Fein, five Independents, four Liberals and four Labour, Garner, 109. The other candidate for Sinn Fein was Winifred Carney, a socialist from Belfast.
102   *Irish Citizen*, January 1919.
103   Holloway Prison, Countess Markievicz, To The Director of Elections (Sinn Fein), 6 Harcourt St., Dublin, Ireland, 6.12.18, CO 904/164, pages 33-34, PRO.
104   Irish Citizen, April 1919; Lady Gregory's Journals. Volume One. Books One to Twenty-Nine. 10 October 1916 - 24 February 1925. Edited by Daniel J.Murphy, New York 1978, 55.
105   Before the summer was out he was being introduced in America as the 'President of the Irish Republic', Coogan 1993, 132
106   See Dáil Eireann, Official Report 2.4.1919, 36. The cabinet was expanded to eleven members with the addition in June 1919 of Sean Etchingham as Minister for Fisheries and J.J.O'Kelly as Minister for the National Language, and, in November, of Austin Stack as Minister for Home Affairs, replacing Griffith, who became Acting President while de Valera was in America, Mitchell 1995, 33.

matters to his colleaques.[107] Markievicz assured him that she would give all her time for Ireland.[108]

Why was she elected? It is interesting to note that a contemporary, Sean O'Faolain, only mentions her nomination without commenting it.[109] According to another contemporary, Esther Roper, her selection was natural because she had kept in touch with 'industrial matters' and was trusted by Labour.[110] Two recent biographers have also adverted to the Labour connections of Markievicz, speculating that de Valera wanted to woo Labour through her.[111] Certainly, de Valera on many occasions underlined the mutual interests of Labour and the Republic[112], and seemed thus to have a more positive view of the Labour than the previous Sinn Fein leader Griffith who had adopted a reserved attitude towards it. In creating the Department of Labour and in its relations with the Labour movement the government appeared to have progressive tendencies.[113]

However, opinions quoted above have ignored one quite obvious factor. Markievicz had already in the year of 1917 been chosen a head of the Department of Labour in Sinn Fein. Her nomination as a minister can thus be seen as a logical continuance; she was perceived as an expert on labour matters within the party and was also a reliable choice for de Valera, because she could be trusted to be first and foremost loyal to the party. On the other hand, his sympathy for her has also been questioned[114] and certainly the sympathies of other men were not self-evident. Markievicz on the other hand had no doubts about her own capabilites; she was convinced that she was just as suitable a minister as any of the men. She claimed to have bullied the leaders of Sinn Fein by threatening that if she were not made a minister she would go over to the Labour Party.[115] This may mean that the goals and programme of Labour Party were not far from her own but it also may mean that she played on the antipathy towards Labour that was present in Sinn Fein. Either way, it is obvious that she wanted to have a position in the government of Ireland and she knew that her participation in the Rising could contribute to bringing that about.

The Irish choice of a woman as minister of Labour was among the first such appointments in Europe. In Finland the Social Democrat Hilja Pärssinen had been chosen as Minister for Social Affairs in the short-lived revolutionary cabinet of 1918 but it was only in the 1920s, that left-wing governments in power in other European countries began to appoint a women to minor cabinet posts, usually those having to do with areas traditionally considered female. Early

---

107   Lyons 1973, 406.
108   Marreco, 246. A letter in the Sligo County Library.
109   O'Faolain, 179.
110   Roper, 91.
111   Norman, 198-199; Haverty, 190.
112   See for example Berresford Ellis, 245-246.
113   Mitchell 1974, 136.
114   Coxhead, 110. De Valera viewed the role of women in a more traditional way than e.g. Connolly; he had objected to having members of Cumann na mBan as combatants at his post during the Rising, Coogan, 1993, 67; He was the only commander to do so, Sebastyen, xix.
115   Litton, 170.

female cabinet ministers were usually orthodox party members who consistently put their party's needs above those of women when a conflict occurred.[116]

Markievicz, who "hated to be treated as a woman"[117], would most certainly have disliked being described as a token woman. She, who after the Rising was often portrayed as the rebellious daughter of Cathleen ni Houlihan with a tender heart, symbolized both the sacrifice of the Rising (a traditionally male arena) and social concern for the Dublin poor (a traditionally female arena) and thus united images of male and female duty in a way that evoked a response to a woman candidate in Irish electorate. She was elected in an election that her party, Sinn Fein, had won and she had gone through the Rising, and at that stage these were the most powerful arguments for having confidence in her competence. But to be a minister meant that she could carry on a policy that upheld the causes of both the workers and women inside the nationalist movement.

---

116 Anderson, Bonnie S., 213. About the political career of Hilja Pärssinen see Oikarinen, Sari, Hilja Pärssinen -Työväenliikkeen runoilja ja poliitikko, in Yksi kamari - kaksi sukupuolta. Suomen eduskunnan ensimmäiset naiset. Eduskunnan kirjaston tutkimuksia ja selvityksiä 4. Jyväskylä 1997, 126-144 and Asikainen, Sari, "Me toivomme ihannemaata." Hilja Pärssisen varhainen aatemaailma ennen kansanedustajuutta, Tampereen yliopisto. Yhteiskuntatieteiden tutkimuslaitos. Naistutkimusyksikkö. Julkaisuja - Sarja N 9/1994, Tampere 1994. In Finland Miina Sillanpää became in 1926 assistant minister for social affairs and in 1927 she was appointed a minister in her own right. In England, Margaret Bondfield became first female cabinet minister in 1929, Anderson, Bonnie S., 293.
117 Hanna Sheehy Skeffington to Eva Gore-Booth in 1920, Eva Gore-Booth Papers, MS 21 816, NLI.

■ The Minister of Labour

The policy and work of the Shadow Government

Sinn Fein had proposed to establish a constituent assembly in its election address. As expected, no members of other political parties accepted invitations to the new assembly. The new body was thus composed solely of 69 Sinn Feiners[1], of which Markievicz was the only woman. Given that the body consisted of predominantly young and urban middle-class people, she – being a 51-year-old and of the upper class – was also an exception in another way.

On 21st January 1919 the 27 free members of Dáil Eireann (the Irish Parliament) held its first public meeting in which they accepted a constitution[2] that gave the Dáil full powers of legislation and absolute control over finance and declared in the Declaration of Independence, which was committed to the legacy of the Easter Rising, that Ireland was a sovereign, democratic and independent republic. The Declaration was linked to their victory in the election:

> "...the Irish electorate has in the General Election of December, 1918, seized the first occasion to declare by an overwhelming majority its firm allegiance to the Irish Republic...we, the elected Representatives of the ancient Irish people in national Parliament assembled, do, in the name of the Irish nation, ratify the establishment of the Irish Republic... "[3]

At the same meeting, a message to the Free Nations of the World was read and the appointment of a delegation to the Paris Peace Conference was proposed. To appeal the Peace Conference for the acceptance of Ireland as an independent nation had commitment of the Sinn Fein election manifesto[4] and was also referred to in Markievicz's own election address.[5] To further the chances at the Conference Markievicz had provided evidence of British atrocities and conditions in Ireland to an American Commission that was heading for the Conference.[6] However,that Ireland would be internationally recognised at the Peace Conference was never a realistic possibility.The War had not been fought

---

1   Mitchell, Arthur, Revolutionary Government in Ireland: Dáil Eireann 1919-22, Dublin 1995, 9.
2   The constitution provided for a democratically elected single legislative body and a cabinet dependant on majority support. The instrument was provisional, subject to simple legislative amendment, and made no mention of a republic, Mitchell 1995, 13.
3   Dáil Eireann, Minutes of Proceedings of the First Parliament of the Republic of Ireland 1919-1921. Official Record, Dublin 1922, 15-16.
4   Macardle, 921.
5   Haverty, 187.
6   Phillips, 159.

on Irish soil and the leading countries were not willing to risk their relations with Britain by pressing her publicly on the Irish question.[7] After the hopes were crushed, in May 1919, republican propaganda was redirected towards mobilizing the Irish abroad in support of self-determination.[8]

The only programme presented at the meeting – the Democratic Programme[9] – included the most radical and controversial frameworks for the future. A compromise version of an even more radical draft by the Labour leader Thomas Johnson, it was founded on the Easter Week Proclamation while the ideas of Patrick Pearse were also to be found in the programme. In the spring of 1916 Pearse had written:

> "....national freedom involves control of the material things which are essential to the continued physical life and freedom of the nation...In other words, no private right to property is good against the public right of the nation..."[10]

Behind the adoption of the Democratic Programme might have been a desire to influence the Labour Party to attempt to get recognition for the republic from the International Socialist' Conference in Bern.[11] The leadership of Sinn Fein had decided to present the social and economic goals of the new state in order to get support of the people, and it had asked Labour for help. Nonetheless, the suggestions of Johnson aroused considerable opposition in Sinn Fein; they were even described by some opponents as 'communistic'. The arguments against his programme's radicalism were based on the greater priority of the national struggle. Despite criticism, the programme in the end was not entirely rejected, but was certainly modified.[12] However, it has been pointed out recently that the Democratic Programme was in fact following the political fashion of the day in pledging to an extension of state responsibility for social and economic conditions. At the time there was great enthusiasm for a Gaelic Communist Society in Ireland, where was to be "no more poverty, no more social conflict, no more hatred, no more ugliness."[13]

The efforts of the Dáil were made more difficult in September 1919, when nationalist organisations were suppressed and the Dáil itself was declared an illegal assembly. The encounters between the British police force situated in Ireland, the RIC, and the Volunteers had led to violence.[14] In response, the

---

7   Hopkinson, Michael, Green Against Green: The Irish Civil War, Dublin 1988, 6; Lee, J.J., 41.
8   Fitzpatrick 1989, 203-204
9   See Dáil Eireann, Minutes of Proceedings of the First Parliament of the Republic of Ireland 1919-1921. Official Record, Dublin 1922, 22-23.
10   Cronin, 110.
11   Mitchell 1974, 110. The Second International supported the demands of Ireland, also Litvinov promised the full support of Russia, Berresford Ellis, 247.
12   Valiulis, M.G., quoted in English 1994, 43; see also Rumpf & Hepburn, 24; Mitchell 1995, 15.
13   Mitchell 1995, 15-16, 43. He quotes Liam O'Flaherty's Life of Tim Healy from year 1927; about idealism in Ireland at that time, see e.g. Garvin, Tom, 1922. The Birth of Irish Democracy, Dublin 1996, 61.
14   Lyons 1973, 412.

round of arrests started again. In June 1919 Markievicz was sentenced to four months in prison for supposedly talking sedition at a meeting in Cork - she had talked about ostracizing the police, a measure which had been accepted by the Dáil.[15] The situation in Ireland deteriorated into terror in the year 1920. In March the notorious Black and Tans were sent to Ireland and in August martial law came into force. In the autumn of 1920 the full effect of the British military response was felt throughout Ireland. At the same time the Irish were shocked when Terence MacSwiney, Lord Mayor of Cork, who had been arrested in August, went on a hunger-strike leading to his death .[16]

Even though the Dáil had been declared illegal, it continued to meet and the departments tried to maintain on their work on the run in disguided offices throughout the city. De Valera toured America collecting money and support for the Irish cause. In Ireland funds were collected succesfully under the guidance of Michael Collins[17], one of the key figures in the fight. Eventually the Dáil secured the financial basis it needed to create an alternative administration.[18] The 'constructive programme' presented to the Dáil in June 1919 proposed to create a consular service, to stimulate fishing and forestry, to provide for land redistribution, to establish a system of arbitration courts, and to launch a commission of inquiry into the nation's resources. They were very general measures; how they would be implemented was not revealed.[19]

While on the run the number of Dáil meetings declined; in the year 1919 there were six meetings, and in 1920 and 1921 only three meetings each year. Ordinary parliamentary work was impossible. The work of the ministries remained unexamined inspection and most of them got very little done.[20] However, the Dáil was quite succesful in taking control of the local government and in supplanting the British machinery of justice with Dáil Courts.[21] Although the British government and military were technically in power, in the summer of 1920 Dáil Eireann was seen by many people as if not the *de facto* government of the country, then at least one of the governing forces in Ireland. Its successes with the courts, police, army, and local government created a public demand for its services far beyond these areas of administration.[22]

---

15   Ward 1983, 137-138; Dáil, Official Report, 10.4.1919, 67; this was a tactic of Parnell, see Moynahan 1995, 139; Also Cumann na mBan was active on boycotting the police, see Phillips, 167; Laffan 1982, 161.
16   Mitchell 1995, 213.
17   Michael Collins (1890-1922) had participated in the Easter Rising and was by now a central figure in the Volunteers and the IRB.
18   See Mitchell 1995, 57-65.
19   Mitchell 1995, 49.
20   Lyons 1973, 406-407.
21   Lyons 1973, 406-408. At the local elections in 1920 Sinn Fein won a sweeping victory after which the Dáil recommended that councils should break off their connection with the existing Local Government Board. By October, practically all of them outside northeast Ulster had done so, ibid.
22   Laffan 1982, 162-163; Mitchell 1995, 154.

"A State run by the Irish people for the people"

The real commitment to social reform on the part of the members of the shadow government is arguable. On the one hand the Sinn Feiners wanted to portray themselves as having real solutions to acute social problems. On the other hand the discussion was to be kept to a minimum: de Valera argued that the immediate question was to get possession of the country. [23] For some of them, however, the Democratic programme contained essential goals. One of them — Markievicz—gave an address in which she linked together the ideas of two leaders of the Rising, Pearse and Connolly. The future would be found in a

> "Republic of Ireland...a state run by the Irish people for the people. That means a Government that looks after the rights of the people before the rights of property. My idea is the Workers' Republic for which Connolly died." [24]

A republican form of government was certainly the goal of Sinn Fein. Markievicz, who sought to establish a workers' republic, made that clear at a Sinn Fein meeting as early as the spring of 1919[25], and she was devoted to Connolly's goals. She defined the republic explicitly as the republic of the workers, a concept that in her thought actually widened to incorporate the poor, the workers and the landless, in fact the "men of no property" who would be granted a better life. On the other hand, it was clear that "a state run by the people" implied that the people should depend on the republicans, who best represented their interests.

Markievicz was not satisfied with a republic without reforms: she criticised the Irish rebels of 1848 for their lack of policy and organisation. She contrasted the situation with that of the Easter Rising, where Tom Clarke and Sean McDermott had provided the organisation, and "Connolly had the brain." In Markievicz's view, Pearse was a beautiful orator, but rather like the '48 men. Nevertheless, Pearse and Connolly complemented to each other.[26] Hence, only the ideas brought out in the Easter Rising – especially by Connolly – offered a coherent programme for a future society.

The policy that she pursued had two bases, history and economics. According to Markievicz, they spelled politics.[27] Irish history justified the struggle. Markievicz had embraced the rigid nationalist view that on the one hand emphasised the terrible wrongs committed by the alien invader, and on the other hand celebrated the high cultural achievements of the Irish nation. This general view of history was that of the republicans and Connolly in particular.

---

23   Coogan 1993, 132
24   *Watchword of Labour*, 15.11.1919(At a meeting in the Trades Hall held under Socialist party auspices to mark the second anniversary of the Bolshevik Revolution)
25   See Cahill, 143.
26   Markievicz to Eva Gore-Booth, 9.7.1919, PL, 226-227.
27   Markievicz to Nellie Gifford, quoted in Marreco, 248.

However, Markievicz did not ponder the coming economic programmes in very great detail; she only asserted that there were "endless possibilities" and that a lot would be done after they had got the Republic into working order.[28] In the meantime she, in the tradition of Sinn Fein, supported the development of Irish industries. She was worried about their prospects, but believed that the problems would partly be solved by the increased advertising of Irish goods, and on the other hand by Dáil members themselves: she asked them to speak on behalf of Irish goods, because for instance in Dublin over 400 girls had become unemployed "owing to a decrease in the smoking of Irish cigarettes alone."[29] She also urged the women of the Cumann to purchase Irish goods, because to support Irish industries was as important in winning the war as was fighting.[30] The methods which Markievicz had proposed during her active political career, were permanently valuable. The struggle was not about mere political independence, but to an important extent about making a self-sufficent Irish economy possible.

In the economic struggle, Markievicz believed more in raising the consciousness of individuals than on forcing them to take certain measures. She criticised the decree that ordered citizens to purchase products from a schedule of Irish goods, pointing out that customers would purchase the goods by post from London if they did not get them from local retailers. On the other hand she admitted that many retailers would not stock Irish-made goods unless they were forced to do so.[31] Hence, Markievicz was ambivalent as to the methods that should be used, but agreed that a virtuous Irish citizen would have to do his or her duty in order to be a worthy citizen of the republic. In economics, that meant supporting the co-operative movement, which in her view derived from the ancient past.

Organising the future: Markievicz and the co-operative movement

A few years after Markievicz's period as a Minister, in time when the Civil War being fought between former comrades had changed the situation, she praised the co-operative movement, partly to condemn the policy the opposite side was pursuing. She stressed that

> "...Sir Horace Plunkett had pointed the way along which Ireland must go if we desired to work out her salvation on Gaelic lines and to avoid becoming a miniature Britain...

---

28 Markievicz to Eva Gore-Booth, 2.8.1919, PL, 234-235.
29 Dáil Eireann, Official report, 6.8.1920, 197-198; Ministry of Labour, 29.6.1920, DE 4/2/6, NAI.
30 Cumann na mBan: Annual Convention. October 22nd and 23rd 1921. Report. NLI, 1-2.
31 Dáil Eireann, Official report, 229-231. Markievicz bought Irish goods herself, Marreco, 277.

[he] declared that the movement was non-political...it was perhaps the greatest political movement of the time...he had struck a vital note that would help bring the country back to the ideals of a Gaelic state. "[32]

Markievicz had employed a quite similar vocabulary in describing the significance of Connolly's ideas. In fact, the two approaches could be pursued simultaneously: both Larkin and Connolly had unofficially defined their goal as a co-operative commonwealth.[33] In addition to that, Connolly had, together with Helena Moloney, established a Workers' Co-operative for the women workers who were unemployed.[34] Markievicz had supported the co-operative movement from the start of her political career.[35] During her ministry, she also paid attention to it. In the autumn of 1919 Markievicz wondered if the time was ripe to push forward a scheme for co-operative farming.[36] In October 1921, she again proposed the establishment of co-operatives [37] She also seconded the motion for establishing co-operatives in the fishing industry. However, despite the general acceptance of co-operative ideals, she, together with Sean Etchingham, the Minister responsible for the fishing industry, faced a confrontation on this issue with the other members of the Dáil Cabinet[38].

The Democratic Programme had recommended the organisation of the economy along co-operative lines. In spring 1919 Sinn Fein urged its *cumainn* to form co-operative societies. Griffith also produced a pamphlet urging the formation of distributive co-operatives. Many of the leaders of Sinn Fein — like Ernest Blythe and Eoin MacNeill- -lent their support to the idea that the economy should be shaped by co-operative organisation, which was seen as the way to combat foreign trusts. In August 1919 de Valera made it clear that he regarded the principle of the co-operative commonwealth as the best social and economic framework for the nation. On 26th September 1919 the Dáil cabinet went on record as favouring co-operative production. According to a recent study, however, Sinn Fein's interest in co-operatives was not sustained, perhaps because it was seen as diverting the movement from the task of destroying and supplanting the British administration to the pursuit of social and economic causes.[39]

Among Sinn Fein there were some – Darrell Figgis, Aodh de Blacam, AE – who in their support for co-operative methods were, like Markievicz, inspired by their view of a Gaelic social organisation in the ancient past.[40] AE, whom Markievicz had befriended after moving to Dublin, was one of the most

---

32   Markievicz, Constance de, Memories, Mr. Griffith, *Eire*, 25.8.1923,
33   Mitchell 1974, 135. The programme of the ITGWU endorsed the co-operative commonwealth in 1909, Mitchell 1974, 225.
34   The co-operative specialised in a man's working shirt called "The Red Hand", Jones, Mary, 16.
35   See chapter "Raising the Generation of the Future..."
36   Connolly, Nora, In Jail With Madame de Markievicz, *Irish Citizen*, September 1919.
37   Mitchell 1974, 141-142.
38   See O'Connor, 106. The reluctance of the Cabinet was possibly due to mismanagement relating to fishery co-operatives, Mitchell 1995, 90-92.
39   Mitchell 1995,45,47-48; Mitchell 1974,136.
40   Mitchell 1995, 45.

prominent representatives of co-operative ideas. He strove to weld country people and townspeople into one single movement. However, he did not want the State to participate in economic reform. Essential to his ideas was the perception of the co-operative movement as an articulation of the national instinct. According to him, the co-operative movement would also bring about economic freedom of workers. The workers of Ireland should first establish co-operative shops, then producers' co-operatives.[41] In Ireland, as elsewhere, there were different ways of understanding the importance and the background of these co-operative ideas. The nationalists often saw them as something exclusively Irish, in spite of their development in other countries. On the other hand, according to the founder of the co-operative movement in Ireland, Horace Plunkett, the root of the Irish problem lay in a deficiency of character, which the self-reliance induced by co-operatives might cure.[42]

The idea of the co-operative movement appealed at that time not only to Sinn Feiners but also to many different groups in Irish society; to cultural nationalists and Catholic priests as well as to Labour.[43] However, in fact the Labour movement was not focusing on the issue[44] even if some members of the Labour movement suggested democracy would gain power in society by means of both the co-operative and the union movement.[45] In other parts of Europe and in America, the co-operative movement had spread widely. In Finland, it was seen as a way of raising the morals and educational level of the poorer classes of the society.[46]

However, Markievicz noted that while the co-operative movement was good, it was by no means a panacea:"The old problem always remains: how to prevent all the money and power, etc. getting into the hands of a few, and they establishing themselves as a ruling tyrant class."[47] The co-operative movement had thus neither spread to the necessary extent nor fulfilled the hopes that Markievicz entertained for a future society.

Arbitrator and Mediator

As a Minister in the Dáil Markievicz was chiefly concerned with motions aimed settling a disputes. She planned to setting up of Conciliation Boards to settle

---

41   AE, The National Being, Dublin 1918, 85–129.
42   Eagleton, 100.
43   See Hutchinson, 146; Garvin 1987, 133.
44   Mitchell 1974, 225. The objective of a co-operative commonwealth is also found in the programme of the Labour Party in 1918, ibid.
45   See e.g. O'Shannon, Cathal, Our Outlook, Voice of Labour, 1.12.1917; Towards the Co-operative Commonwealth, Voice of Ireland,19.4.1919.
46   Mauranen, Tapani, Osuustoiminta - kansanliikettä aatteen ja rahan vuoksi, in Alapuro, Risto, Liikanen, Ilkka, Smeds, Kerstin, Stenius, Henrik, Kansa Liikkeessä, Helsinki 1987, 176.
47   Markievicz to Eva Gore-Booth, 11.12.1920, PL, 259.

disputes between local councils and their employees [48] and tried to find arbitrators.[49] To prevent lock-outs and strikes, she urged co-operation between workers and employers and the promotion of negotiations.[50]

Markievicz herself acted as an arbitrator in disputes between the trade unions[51] and during strikes [52], things which kept her "very busy".[53] Between July and September 1920 the Ministry had intervened in thirty-one disputes.[54] When Markievicz was in prison, in August 1919, the Ministry of Labour founded a National Conciliation Board for the settlement of Trade Disputes.[55] It is worth noting that at the same time an arbitration tribunal ("Industrial Court") to which disputes could be taken was established in Britain.[56] The Irish Ministry of Labour was more successful in the arbitration of disputes than any existing British Board or Commission in Ireland.[57]

In Sinn Fein circles the importance of settling industrial disputes had already been noted by Griffith in 1908[58]. The programme for the year 1917 also envisaged a Labour Arbitration Tribunal. At the time that Markievicz was a Minister, the settling of disputes was a much more acute issue. In the years 1918-20 the workers were particularly given to striking, although their activities were not coherent and were not backed by an efficient policy. The early months of 1919 was a period of unusual labour strife, with a large number of strikes taking place throughout the country.[59] Markievicz's role as an arbitrator reflected her concern with the unity of the Irish nation. They should not be involved in mutual strife when they, in Markievicz's understanding, had one common enemy, the British government. On the other hand, strikes were accepted by nationalists if they were aimed at the British regime and would further the cause of Irish

48 Dáil Eireann, Official Report, 6.8.1920, 197; See Appendix A on Conciliation Boards, Interim Report, Dáil Eireann, Official Report, 30-31. She did not believe that it was possible to obtain fees for covering the expenses of labour arbitration in cities and towns, Dáil Eireann, Official report, 17.9.1920, 218. Conciliation Boards were discussed in Cabinet, Copy Minutes of Dáil.., 17.7.1920, DE 1/2, 134. A list of agreed arbitrators, see Dáil Eireann. Ministry and Cabinet Meetings, DE 1/2, 22.7.1920, 138.

49 She asked the Deputies to name persons for chairmen of Conciliation Boards or arbitrators in ordinary labour disputes Dáil Eireann, Official Report, 6.8.1920, 197; See Appendix A on Conciliation Boards, Interim Report, Dáil Eireann, Official Report, 30-31. When the situation in 1921 deteriorated, Markievicz also asked a non-violent person, whom she thought would be trusted by both parties, to arbitrate in a dispute, see her letter to Edward M.Stephens, 29.11.1921, in Coxhead, 109.

50 Markievicz's letter to the *Irish Opinion: Voice of Labour*, 19.11.1921, DE 2/5, NAI.

51 The Dáil gave the Minister of Labour authority to consult on disputes between employers and employees, to call them to negotiation and to name umpires. According to Louie Bennett Markievicz once arranged an agreement quickly by bluffing the employer into believing that the army was coming, Fox 1958, 75-76.

52 Eg. on the Cork Rail Dispute, 25.11.1921, DE 1/3, 164, NAI.

53 Markievicz to Joseph McGarrity, no date, Joseph McGarrity Papers, MS 17 627, NLI.

54 Interim report, Dáil Eireann, Official Report, 29.

55 Interim report, Dáil Eireann, Official Report, 28; Dáil Eireann, Official Report, 27.10.1919, 164.

56 See Pelling, Henry, A History of British Trade Unionism, Harmondsworth 1992, 149.

57 Macardle, 387.

58 He recommended the settlement of industrial disputes by conciliation and arbitration in the manner of countries like New Zealand, Ó Luing, Sean, Arthur Griffith and Sinn Fein, in Martin 1967, 61.

59 Mitchell 1995, 44; Robbins, 105, 217; Mitchell 1974, 104.

self-government.[60] The Labour movement initiated several strikes which helped to weaken British control.[61] In 1919 the power of Labour, as demonstrated in the strikes, seemed to be as great as that of militant nationalism.[62]

Markievicz had expressed her concern at the influence of English Trade Unions in 1917 and kept on emphasizing it as a Minister. According to her, the Irish trade union movement should be centralised. In addition to that, the ministry of Labour was going to study foreign labour legislation so that it could either be adopted or consciously rejected.[63] However, to improve the situation in Ireland, the conditions under which the workers lived had also to be examined. Thus, the ministry decided to collect statistics relating to the price of agricultural produce used for food, and the wages and hours of employees in agriculture, industry and commerce.[64] Nonetheless, there seemed to be no great interest "to seek the co-operation of the governments of other countries in determining a standard of social and industrial legislation" as the Democratic Programme had promised.[65]

Together with arbitration and the attempts to found an Irish version of labour legislation, the reduction of unemployment was also seen as important. At that time there were about 100 000 persons without jobs.[66] The Ministry of Labour's efforts to find work were an integral part of the effort to overthrow British government. The Ministry opened an employment agency for those men who had resigned form the RIC (Royal Irish Constabulary) from "patriotic motives"; and tried to find work for members of the IRA and Cumann na mBan. Markievicz organised a circular to be sent to members of the RIC, pleading with them resign from their jobs and join the Irish struggle. In another circular she asked for help in getting employment for those who had left the RIC.[67] Shattering the force of this body was considered important, because they, along with the soldiers, were seen as the chief visible representatives of British government in Ireland. In June 1920 the Dáil ministry asked Sinn Fein to undertake a systematic campaign for obtaining the resignation of policemen.[68] Otherwise, it was decided not to establish republican labour exchanges, since workers preferred to find jobs through the unions[69], although the Irish Labour

---

60   Mitchell 1995, 179.
61   For instance a munitions transport stike, Mitchell 1974, 117.
62   Mitchell 1995, 178.
63   Ministry of Labour, 29.6.1920, DE 4/2/6, NAI. At that time probably over seventy persent of Irish trade unionists were members of British trade unions, Cahill, 138.
64   Interim report, Dáil Eireann, Official Report, 17.8.1921, 28; Dáil Eireann, Official Report, 27.10.1919, 164.
65   See Democratic Programme, Dáil Eireann. Official Report, 22-23.
66   Mitchell 1974, 117.
67   See memoirs of Jeremiah Mee, Marreco 255-257; Markievicz to Joseph McGarrity, no date, Joseph McGarrity Papers, MS 17 627, NLI. Markievicz had promised to ask the ITGWU about an agreement of getting jobs for the "on the run"-men, even if they were not members of the unions, Dáil, Official Report, 17.9.1920, 218.
68   About 1590 RIC men applied to resign during 1920 and 1428 during 1921, Fitzpatrick, David, Politics and Irish Life 1913-1921: Provincial Experience of War and Revolution, Dublin 1977, 40.
69   Ministry of Labour 29.6.1920, DE 4/2/6, NAI.

Party did promise to help the Department of Labour to organise the relief of unemployment.[70]

In October 1921, to meet the danger of an upheaval in the countryside, something of concern also to the Labour[71], Markievicz proposed that the government should investigate farm profits, establish co-operatives and take over the Irish Packing Company "to show the workers that we [have] their interests at heart." However, the Cabinet rejected her proposal.[72] The unrest in the countryside remained a problem for Markievicz. On the one hand she feared that it would disrupt the nationalist struggle, on the other hand she wanted to push Dáil Eireann in a more socially radical direction. Certainly it was important to her that the disputes should be solved peacefully so that division into two different Irish parties could be prevented. Even though Markievicz declared herself to be a follower of the programme of Connolly and even though she urged the workers to organise "politically and economically" to be ready to take their stand for Connolly's Commonwealth, she simultaneously advised them to put their trust "in God and the spirit of Republican Ireland."[73]

In her attempts, Markievicz was by no means the only important link between Labour and Sinn Fein. The relationship between organised Irish labour and the Dáil was at a general level unproblematic. According to Mitchell, both the key leaders of Labour, O'Brien and Johnson, could be trusted absolutely by the Dáil leaders. A close working relationship existed between their two organisations at all levels. This happened also because most of the members of Irish unions strongly supported Irish independence.[74] Irish unions employed the conciliation and arbitration schemes set up by the Department of Labour, although they simultaneously continued to take advantage of British labour legislation.[75] The Dáil was seen as a potential tool in furthering the cause of the workers.[76] Markievicz, who had supported the ICA before and after the Rising, was, – though her support for the Connollyian workers' republic –, in fact in the same camp as the minority in the Labour movement. Her goals also made her part of the minority in Sinn Fein.

Land for the Landless

The role of Markievicz as an arbitrator between the disputes in industry extended to disputes in agriculture. In June 1919 the Dáil approved a decree that aimed

---

70   Interim Report, Dáil Eireann, Official Report, 31.
71   In April 1921 the ILPTUC had issued a manifesto in which it warned that growing unemployment would lead to a violent response by hungry workers, pointing to farmers who were reducing tillage and labourers' wages, Mitchell 1995,244.
72   Mitchell 1974, 141-142. After the truce there had been new takeovers of farms and violent conflicts between farmers and workers in the countryside, ibid.
73   Message to the Workers of Ireland, C.de Markievicz, *Irish Opinion: Voice of Labour*, 22.3.1919.
74   Mitchell 1974, 104-105.
75   Mitchell 1995, 183.
76   For instance Peadar O'Donnell saw that workers should support the existing Dàil republic and attempt to utilize it for the advancement of the workers, Mitchell 1974, 113.

at the provision of land for those sections of the agricultural population which was deprived of it. The land agitation in 1920, which had taken on aggressive forms, was felt throughout the country. Previously, the Sinn Fein leadership had discouraged such agitation.[77]

Markievicz had expressed her commitment to a Government that placed the rights of the people before those of property. [78] She was involved in settling down the land dispute in Co. Kerry and on her initiative the possibility of Labour Unions taking some active part in the acquisition, management and control of Co-operative farms to be worked by labourers was discussed. A manifesto appealing to the patriotism of all parties and to asking them to end their strife, according to one report, " finally calmed the trouble."[79] In addition to that, Markievicz had also been succesful in settling serious disputes in Kildare and Meath.[80]

Markievicz took seriously and quite concretely the statement of both the declaration of the Easter Rising and the Democratic Programme on the ownership of Irish soil by the Irish people. At this period the left-wing republicans – a description that suits Markievicz too – justified land seizures by the landless poor and their expressing their economic grievances in terms of loyalty to the Republic and hostility to the ruling circles, whose interests led them to pursue a policy of close co-operation and intergration with the British economy. [81]

In the Dáil Markievicz seconded a proposal about the distribution of vacant land and farms to the unemployed and landless.[82] The proposal did not gain support; possibly because Sinn Fein was conscious of its dependance on 'big farmers'.[83] Markievicz seemed to entertain a hope that simply giving the Irish soil to the Irish people would partly solve problems experienced under foreign rule. To advocate the idea of giving land to the unemployed implied that she considered the establishment of small farms, which would enable people to live in the countryside, as an ideal for the future. It was an ideal that derived from the republican tradition: in the 1840s Lalor had argued the importance of a "secure and independent agricultural peasantry", one that owned property and determined its use.[84]

To solve the land question was important to all republicans. In July 1920 Griffith expressed the view that perhaps the greatest achievement of the work of Dáil was the establishment of the Land Bank, which enabled them to settle the land crisis that arose in the West of Ireland, and the establishment of the Land Arbitration Courts, which prevented the land question being used to divert

---

77   Mitchell 1995, 85, 131-134.
78   *Watchword of Labour, 15.11.1919*(At a meeting in the Trades Hall held under Socialist party auspices to mark the second anniversary of the Bolshevik Revolution)
79   Dáil Eireann, Official report, 17.8.1921, 56.
80   Interim report, Dáil Eireann, Official Report, 29.
81   Dunphy, 33.
82   Dáil, Official report, 4.4.1919, 42.
83   Patterson, 12.
84   Cited in Hall, 4.

the energies of the people from the national issue.[85] In a similar tone, the Dáil decreed that when the Irish people were 'locked in a life and death struggle with their traditional enemy', there should be no stirring up of strife amongst fellow-countrymen; and that all energies must be directed towards clearing out – not the occupier of this or that piece of land - but the foreign invader.[86] Markievicz, who at the time of the land war wrote to her brother reminding him that he, whose farm workers were now on a strike, also came from a family of tyrants and usurpers[87], did not raise her voice against the decree of the Dáil. Even though she had seconded the motion concerning the distribution of vacant lands the previous year, she considered it best to stand behind the decisions of the Dáil. And despite her reformist willingness, she yielded to the nationalist consensus.

Markievicz had worked for the settling of disputes between employees and employers in order to avoid a possiblity of labour disturbances, which might hamper the ongoing nationalist struggle. She did not want to divide Ireland and against that background it seems logical that she opposed the Belfast boycott, when it was first suggested in the Dáil. The question arose in summer 1920 when large pogroms against thousands of Catholics were started in Belfast. Then, the representatives from Belfast wanted Sinn Fein to strike back with a commercial boycott. Markievicz did not believe that a blockade could be effective; it would only "be playing into the hands of the enemy and giving them a good execuse for partition." She even suspected that the British Government was trying to cut off trade with Belfast and so make the two parts of Ireland into separate trading centres.However, she seconded the amendment proposing that action could be taken against the individuals responsible for inciting the pogroms. In the discussion that followed the boycott was rejected[88], but it was nonetheless started unofficially and the next month the Dáil nominated a person to take charge of it.[89] In this respect, the policy of Sinn Fein contradicted its own theory of one nation.[90] The Ministry of Labour also was later actively connected with the boycott, but by that time Markievicz was in prison. She nevertheless made it clear, writing to Catholic quarrymen, that no intimidation in Ulster should be acceptable on either side.[91]

Helping working class mothers

In the shadow government, the furthering of the cause of women was left to Markievicz. Her political contribution had been eagerly waited by the members

---

85   Dáil, Official report, 29.7.1920, 170-171.
86   Dáil,Official report, ibid., 179. Sinn Fein established land courts to punish the seizure of land by landless elements, Dunphy, 35.
87   Marreco, 253.
88   Dáil, Official report, 6.8.1920, 191-194.
89   Dáil, Official report, 17.9.1920, 233.
90   Lee 1989, 59. Criticism to the boycott, see e.g., P.S. O'Hegarty, Should Ulster Be Boycotted Economically, *Old Ireland*, 21.2.1920.
91   C de M, To The Catholic Quarrymen, Carrigmore Quarry, Co.Tyrone, *Irish Bulletin*, 24.11.1921.

of the IWFL after she had been elected to Parliament.[92] Her desire to push women to the forefront of public life was also demonstrated during her period as a minister; she employed them in her ministry and said that she liked "to set women on to these jobs."[93] She most certainly preferred the way in which Cumann na mBan aimed at developing military activities in conjunction with the Volunteers and tried to organise the women of Ireland to carry out the decrees of Dáil Eireann and to assist in its schemes of national reconstruction.[94] Markievicz, who always encouraged women to take part in the public life, found to her dismay that it was hard to get them to stand in the municipal elections of 1920. On the other hand, she was glad that women had "done well in Corporation", at the local elections.[95] She was confident that her getting locked up had done more to bring women out into the open than anything else; even the shyest were ready to do her work when she was not there.[96]

Her second initiative in bringing women forward clearly reflected the discussion in Britain concerning male bias of the justice system, which produced the struggles to gain the appointment of women magistrates, women police and women doctors to deal with abused girls.[97] Such idea were shared with the Irish suffragists, who also seemed to suppose that women operating within the legal system or in parliament would act differently from men.[98] In her writings, Markievicz explained that she had been involved with most of the criminal assault cases on children that came in the Dublin police courts and claimed that it was impossible for men to adapt themselves to "a child's small understanding." She urged women to start campaigning against assaults on children and regarded women as the best choice for the jobs involved.[99]

Another group of women that she focused on, in addition to the able women who could be employed in different jobs in the republic, were those who were less fortunate. Markievicz was very concerned about the desperate situation of working class mothers. Writing in prison, she lamented that

> " The whole economic position of Ireland has reduced our workers to such a terrible state of poverty and uncertainty that one bows in admiration to the splendid mothers of the lovely children that they have given to Ireland with such unthinkable suffering & self denial...If ever I am free...I will see you & consult with Labour as to what I can best do to help Ireland to do justice to her mothers in their great work."[100]

---

92   Activities, *Irish Citizen*, April 1919.
93   Markievicz to Joseph McGarrity, no date, Joseph McGarrity Papers, MS 17 627, NLI.
94   Cumann na mBan, The Policy for 1919-1920, in Conlon, 300-301.
95   Markievicz to Eva Gore-Booth, no date, PL, 218. The women, who had done well, were Hanna Sheehy-Skeffington, who was the President of the Court of Conscience, Mrs. Clark of the Children's Court and Mrs. Wyse Power, the Chairman of the Public Health Board, ibid.
96   Markievicz to Eva Gore-Booth, 16.7.1919, PL, 232.
97   Jeffreys, Sheila, The Spinster and Her Enemies: Feminism and Sexuality 1880-1930, London 1985, 54-60.
98   Ryan, Louise, Irish Feminism and the Vote. An anthology of the Irish Citizen Newspaper 1912–1920, Dublin 1996, 55.
99   C.M., Something wrong Somewhere, *Irish Citizen*, January 1920.
100 Markievicz to J.P Dunne 5.12.1918, Markievicz Papers, MS 13 778, NLI

The situation was partly linked to the nationalist struggle. Markievicz noted in particular how the mothers faced many hardships while the fathers were on the run.[101] She asked her friends to help these women by giving them the food that they had intended to send to her in prison. The suffering of little children especially worried her.[102] On a wider level, Markievicz was trying to solve the problem with the idea of a co-operative dairy in her own constituency and was confident that help would be got for such a scheme to help "our poor mothers."[103] She outlined her plans for social reforms, such as the distribution of milk and a solution of the housing question at a meeting of the IWFL.[104]

Markievicz's concern was felt within the women's movements, which in general turned their attention to motherhood at that period.[105] Ideas for helping the situation were not, however, found only in Ireland: for instance a few years earlier Sylvia Pankhurst, Eva Gore-Booth's friend, had established milk centres in London East End.[106] More directly the issue concerned women among her own near circle: for instance her sister Eva Gore-Booth and her friend Kathleen Lynn. It is important to note that Markievicz was not, however, trying to bring comfort the lives of mothers and children in every aspect: there is no indication, for example, that she was interested in developing the local maternity clinics and services, the establishment of which was encouraged by the British Maternity and Child Welfare Act of 1918, or to create birth-control clinics.[107] Those areas related to sexuality would continue to be ignored by the women in the Irish Parliament in the years to come, something that has been attributed to an accommodation of Catholic opinion.[108]

Focusing on working class mothers resulted partly from Markievicz's personal experiences in prison. In the spring of the year 1919 she noted that

> " ..It is a rare thing for a rich and educated woman to get to jail...A rich woman has no temptation to steal, shop-lift or pick pockets... her little children are not hungry and cold, so she is never driven to desperate acts...I

---

101 Markievicz to Eva Gore-Booth, 1.1.1921, PL, 266.
102 Marreco, 258.
103 From Ireland's First Woman M.P., *Irish Opinion: Voice of Labour*, 11.1.1919. (Letter to IWWU) About the concern of the conditions in which working-class women lived, see also letter from AE to Mrs. Hobson 1.9.1917, quoted in Sawyer, 98-99.
104 Activities, *Irish Citizen*, April 1919.
105 Editor's Introduction, in Maternity and Gender Policies. Women and the Rise of the European Welfare States, 1880s -1950s, Bock, Gisela and Thane, Pat (eds.), London 1991,1, 14. At that time, throughout Western Europe, women had a higher propensity than men to suffer deprivation.Their poverty often resulted above all from economies which had not been structured as to enable them to support themselves and children at an adequate level, ibid, 1.
106 Garner, 90. Sylvia Pankhurst had shown sympathy towards Irish workers during the lock-out, Romero, 66, and had also supported the Easter Rising against the actions of the British, see Pankhurst, Sylvia, Thoughts on the Easter Week Rebellion, pamphlet, n.d.,NLI; According to Romero, Sylvia's friends provided money to buy milk and eggs for hungry babies and small children in 1914, Romero, 98.
107 The local maternity clinics and services were encouraged in the British Maternity and Child Welfare Act of 1918, Editors Introduction, in Bock, Gisela and Thane, Pat (eds.), 4; Holton 1986,152.
108 Clancy, Mary, Aspects of Women's Contribution to the Oireachtas Debate in the Irish Free State,1922-1937, in Women Surviving. Studies in Irish Women's History in the 19th & 20th centuries, edited by Maria Luddy and Cliona Murphy, Dublin 1990, 210.

worked with a gang of murderesses in Aylesbury...most were foolish working girls who had got into trouble and had killed their little babies because life with them was impossible because they had no way of earning a living, nowhere to go and nothing to eat..."[109]

Markievicz's concern for working class mothers touched on a very serious problem in Dublin, and was shared in labour circles.[110] But although she was touched by the living reality in Dublin, in writing about the situation she was also using the image of suffering, in all her poverty and despair of a saint-like pure mother. That image of suffering mothers was common in other countries at that time as well.[111]

To take care of mothers was also to take care of the next generation. To a friend in the Labour movement Markievicz wrote:

> "I entirely agree with you when you state that the child belongs not only to the parents but to the community, & believe all thinking Irish people to be of the same mind. It was owing to the subjections of our nation that the terrible workhouse system, that you also condemn, was ever introduced: It is up to us to get rid of it."[112]

The thought that a child belonged to his or her community, to his or her nation is linked to the idea of a duty to raise children in the Irish spirit, which was the objective of the Fianna. It was also a way to take the burden off women's shoulders and to put on the state. However, Markievicz did not directly demand state welfare at that time, even though on many occasions in Europe there were close links between the women's demand for political rights and for state welfare, which was understood as their social right.[113] Nor was Markievicz simply waiting for any action the Dáil might take. To help the children, she organised a Connolly Memorial Children's Treat at Christmas[114], an arrangement that on the other hand reflected her upper-class way of doing things.

---

109   Break down the Bastilles, By Countess Markievicz, *Irish Opinion:Voice of Labour*, 1.5.1919. Her experiences were shared by Maud Gonne, who felt the prison conditions as horribly as Markievicz did, see My Experiences In Prison, by Maud Gonne MacBride (Read at the I.W.F.L.), *Irish Citizen*, June-July 1919, in Ryan 1996, 174-177.

110   About 30 per cent of the Dublin population lived in the worst slums in Western Europe, Larkin 1965, 42; The infant mortality rate was abnormally high in Dublin. Nationalist activists, doctor Kathleen Lynn and Miss ffrench-Mullen started a little children's hospital in the heart of Dublin in Spring 1919, Levenson, 130; about concern see Murder in Milk, *Irish Opinion: Voice of Labour*, 9.3.1918; Kathleen Lynn, The Milk and the Murder of Babies, *Old Ireland*,21.8.1920.

111   For instance, Afrikaner motherhood was at the beginning of 20th century perceived as saintly in suffering, Gaitskell, Deborah & Unterhalter, Elaine, Mothers of the Nation: a Comparative Analysis of Nation, Race and Motherhood in Afrikaner Nationalism and the African National Congress, in Yuval-Davis, Nira and Anthias, Floya (ed.), Woman - Nation-State, New York 1989,60.

112   Markievicz to J.P Dunne 5.12.1918, Markievicz Papers, MS 13 778, NLI

113   Editors Introduction, in Bock, Gisela and Thane, Pat (eds.), 7.

114   See correspondence of Countess Markievicz, Holloway Prison, CO 904/164, page 32, PRO.

A good home – a miniature nation

During her ministry, Markievicz produced an ideal of the possible future of women in the Irish republic. She pointed out the need for a good home and urged women to vote in the municipal elections with the object of getting good workers' houses built at once. In order to better the living environment the rents and rates outside the city had to be cheaper, and reduced tram rates would be provided where possible.[115] Furthermore, cottages should not be too expensive.[116] Her concern with the housing question reflected part of the programme of both Labour and Sinn Fein. The Labour party had developed a comprehensive programme of municipal reform emphasizing public housing and education. In the elections for county councils in June 1920, the Sinn Fein candidates and allies advocated an expansion of public housing, health services and education.[117]

Despite her sincere concern the suggestions of Markievicz were not always realistic in relation to the possibilities of working class families. Rather, they seemed to be directed at the middle class. For instance, she advised women to demand a type of a home that must have seemed quite luxurious to many women with a good living-room, a boiler, gas cooker, two or three bedrooms, a coal cellar and a larder etc. She was also convinced that living outside the city was a great advantage because one could grow vegetables and children would have room to play and grow strong.[118] Safety and happiness were on a totally different level in such an environment:

> "Crime and cruelty is found far less in these beautiful suburbs, where every housewife wears a dignified air of being mistress to a real good home with a lovely garden, where she can grow fruit, vegetables and flowers."[119]

Undoubtedly living outside the slums in a roomy house would be a change for the better, but the beautiful picture she painted was always to be difficult to realize. Obviously, Markievicz was preparing women to a coming time, when an independent Ireland would have as its basis families living in their own houses, growing their own food and raising healthy children for the Ireland of the future. Similarly with her fellow nationalists, she seemed to vision an Ireland which would not be based on cities, but on the countryside: " We did not want a black country with all its slums, misery and crime to be built among the "fair hills of Holy Ireland."[120] Hostility to the city was not unique to Ireland.

---

115 Vote for Decent Homes by C.M. *Irish Citizen*, January 1920.
116 She wanted to make sure that the plans of the Dàil concerning the purchase of labourers' cottages by the occupiers would not result in the placing of a large number of families on uneconomic holdings. Dàil, Official report, 17.9.1920, 219; see discussion in Dàil and Sinn Fein on housing question, Copy Minutes of Sinn Fein Standing Committee, 3.7.1919, 999/ 40,12, NAI.
117 Mitchell 1995, 122,125-126.
118 Vote for Decent Homes by C.M., *Irish Citizen*, January 1920.
119 C.M., Smiling and Frowning Homes, *Irish Citizen*, July-August 1920.
120 Markievicz, Constance de, Memories, Mr. Griffith, *Eire*, 25.8.1923.

Similar sentiments were found for instance among nineteenth-century German intellectuals and in Victorian England. [121] That the family would be self-sufficent, reflected the general idea of self-sufficiency promoted by Sinn Fein.

In addition to that, Markievicz's suggestion reflected the views that were being expressed in Britain during the late nineteenth and early twentieth centuries, when poor families were treated on the basis of middle-class male breadwinner model. The working-class wife's job was seen to be that of a household manager, who determined a family's level of comfort.[122] Following that idea, Markievicz wanted women to take responsibility into their own hands. The home should be kept clean and tidy, "no matter however simple and poor it might be." She also gave tips on furnishing a home.[123] These writings bring forth the Markievicz who was quick to employ material - in this case various English papers - for her own purposes without always bearing in mind all the possible connotations.

Her suggestions were not accepted without criticism. It was considered appalling that women should be classified by their ability to "keep a living room nice" at a time when women were being taught self-respect and -reliance. Her basis for writing was seen as an English one.[124] However, Markievicz's "home chat" did also get supporters.[125]

Markievicz regretted the criticism and argued that the state was but a larger edition of the home. Therefore, women should not consider the management of the home to be beneath them. Markievicz promised to do her utmost in urging better homes and better town planning for all of them. She advised all women of every class to "arouse themselves and take the keenest interest to abolish all slums and to see in Dublin a city built worth of the lovely mountains and the surrounding country and sea."[126]

To see the nation-state as a large home has been a global metaphor.[127] The conception of home as an important arena in forming the nation state emerged in many European countries after the Great War. For instance in Sweden, the clear focus of the Social Democratic welfare policy for a "national home" was upon women as mothers.[128] It seems that Markievicz was fascinated by the

---

121 Daly 1994, 86; Lyons 1979, 81.In Finland, a similar vision prevailed after independence, see for instance Oikarinen, Sari, Hilja Pärssinen -Työväenliikkeen runoilja ja poliitikko, in Yksi kamari – kaksi sukupuolta. Suomen eduskunnan ensimmäiset naiset, Eduskunnan kirjaston tutkimuksia ja selvityksiä 4, Jyväskylä 1997, 141.

122 Lewis, Jane, Models of equality for women:the case of state support for children in twentieth-century Britain, in Bock, Gisela and Thane, Pat (eds.), 76.

123 A Smiling or a Frowning Home?, *Irish Citizen* April-May 1920; C.M., Smiling and Frowning Homes, *Irish Citizen*, July-August 1920. The first article does not have a name on it, but that it was written by Markievicz can be concluded from the following article and from her response to the criticism.

124 M.K. O'Connery, *Irish Citizen*, May-June 1920. However, there had been interest towards other subjects than politics on rebellious women's paper before: *Bean na hEireann* also included tips for interior desing and food recipes etc.

125 For example Helena Moloney and Kathleen Nicholls, see *Irish Citizen*, June-July 1920.

126 *Irish Citizen*, June-July 1920.

127 Blom, Ida, World History as Gender History. The Case of the Nation State, in Tonnesson, Stein, Koponen, Juhani, Steensgaard, Niels and Svensson, Thommy (eds.), Between National Histories and Global History, Historiallinen Arkisto 110:4, Helsinki 1997, 80.

128 Meyer, Donald, Sex and Power: The Rise of Women in America, Russia, Sweden, and Italy, Second Edition, with a New Introduction, Connecticut 1989, 63.

idea of the home and women's role in the building of ideal homes in an ideal Ireland. Thus, while she was doing her best to extricate women from the private sphere, she was at the same time – at least the working class women living in the Dublin slums – placing them back there. This was happening concurrently when in 1920s women's equal rights organizations and feminist socialist groups in Europe often turned to welfare work, to causes associated with women's traditional roles as housekeeper and carer for the family.[129]

The question of Bolsheviks

The establishment of Dáil Eireann and the support of the Irish people for independence were not the sole factors that encouraged Markievicz and other nationalists in their work. The Bolshevik revolution in Russia and the troubles in Britain gave hope for them as well. In the summer of 1919 Markievicz assumed "England" to be in an "awful state, much worse than Ireland." She went on by asserting that if a revolution were to come there, it would be much worse than in Russia, for people were so congested. Completely separating the situation in England from that in Ireland, she declared that she did not "...fear a revolution here as many are so disciplined -not that silly compulsory thing which is automatic and breaks down - but disciplined voluntarily, which is quite a different thing."[130]

It is interesting to note that Markievicz chose to say that she did not "fear" revolution in Ireland. It implies that already in 1919 she did not want the situation to get out of the hands of the republicans who were now trying to establish their own government. Her aim was expressed more clearly in October 1921, when alarmed by the situation in Ireland, Markievicz submitted a memorandum to the cabinet warning of the imminence of social revolution. She feared a sequence of events, beginning with "small outbreaks growing more and more frequent and violent, the immediate result of which will tend to disrupt the Republican cause." The only missing ingredient so far was the emergence of a "violent popular leader." [131] Thus a spontaneous turmoil, born without a programme only when living conditions deteriorated, was far from ideal for her, whether in Ireland or elsewhere.

Yet the economic situation in Britain was not at its worst.[132] In addition, compared to that of other belligerents in the First World War, Britain's political system emerged relatively unscathed from the war, in spite of the huge series

---

129 Anderson, Bonnie S., 397.
130 Markievicz to Eva Gore-Booth, 22.7.1919, PL, 232; about troubles in England and anticipation of revolution, see also Markievicz to Eva Gore-Booth, 23.8.1919, PL, 241; Markievicz to Eva Gore-Booth, 20.12.1920, PL, 262.
131 Mitchell 1974, 141-142.
132 The postwar boom lasted from approximately April 1919 to May 1920, Lawrence, Jon, The First World War and its Aftermath, in Johnson, Paul (ed.), Twentieth-Century Britain: Economic, Social and Cultural Change, London 1994, 163; also Phillips, Gordon, The Social Impact, in Constantine etc. 1995, 112.

of strikes from 1917 to 1920, and the appearance of 'soviets.'[133] Nonetheless, the upheaval together with the example of the Bolshevik revolution in Russia, gave encouragement to some of the radical British socialists. Sylvia Pankhurst, whose *Dreadnought* Markievicz read in prison, and whose ideas obviously contributed to her view of the British situation, took a radical line. In her paper, she did everything to compare Russia favourably to England.[134] The *Dreadnought* carried political columns and propaganda from Russia, including translations of Lenin and Trotsky.[135]

Concurrently with the strikes, the fear of Bolshevism was being expressed in Britain and in Ireland. In January 1919 *the Irish Times* warned that the republicans might be moving towards a liaison with Bolshevism. During the early months of 1919 there was considerable alarm among the Catholic Church about Sinn Fein and Bolshevism. Bishop Kelly of Ross criticised the leaders of the Dáil, particularly Constance Markievicz, for their extremist tendencies. [136] But in fact how extreme was Markievicz in this respect?

In spring 1919 she had declared that if Wilson failed, they had another solution – the Bolsehevik revolution in Russia.[137] A bit surprisingly, she did not champion the Bolshevik cause in this way in front of a Labour audience, but at a Sinn Fein meeting. Her proposal for "another solution" did not mean that she anticipated or expected a sudden revolution in Ireland. Rather, it was connected with the fact that the new government of Russia had been consistently supportive of the cause of Irish national freedom. Both the *Voice of Labour* and the left-wing Sinn Fein paper *New Ireland* gave considerable and favourable attention to developments in the communist state.[138] At that stage, the republicans were friendly towards the Bolsheviks and were trying to establish relations with them.[139] The news of atrocities and brutality on the part of Bolsheviks were received with suspicion.[140] Simultaneously, the hopes that the republicans had placed in Wilson were vanishing. Together with this, both de Valera and Markievicz expressed their fears about the League of Nations, which might not after all be based on equality between big and small nations.[141]

---

133   Pugh, Martin, Domestic Politics, in Constantine etc. 1995, 10.
134   Romero, 124. When police in London went on strike, an overjoyed Sylvia Pankhurst declared it to be the 'spirit of Petrograd!...After that anything may happen!" Garner, 101, Pankhurst in *Workers' Dreadnought*, September 7, 1918.
135   Romero, 128.
136   Mitchell 1995, 44; also the United Irish League and the Irish Unionist Alliance showed concern, ibid.
137   Cahill, 143.
138   Mitchell 1995, 189-190.
139   For instance de Valera emphasized the sympathy for them at that time, *Irish Opinion: Voice of Labour*, 30.8.1919; A Draft for Russo-Irish agreement, Circulars Issued by Dàil 1919-1921, Count Plunkett Papers, MS 11 404, NLI.
140   Eg. AE, On the New Order, *Irish Opinion:Voice of Labour*,23.11.1919.
141   de Valera in Dàil 11.4.1919, Macardle, 288; Markievicz criticised the League of Nations of talking "pompous rubbish about the reduction of armaments" while the different countries at the same time only wanted to know what their neighbours were going to do, Markievicz to Eva Gore-Booth, PL, 15.12.1920, 261. In summer 1919 she had still trusted in Wilson, Connolly, Nora, In Jail With Madame Markievicz, *Irish Citizen*, September 1919.

Obviously Markievicz had read about Lenin in *Dreadnought* and other papers. She agreed with him about the preconditions for revolution: "if the conditions are not there, no sort of propaganda will hasten or impede it."[142] Her other remarks on Lenin show neither a particular interest in his ideas nor familiarity with them; she wished him "God speed" and hoped that he would not be treated like the French treated Danton.[143] However, she believed that the Bolsheviks would greatly improve conditions for the world. Markievicz disliked autocracy of any class, but was optimistic:

> "...surely if they have sense to organise education, they can abolish class. While they are menaced by the moneyed classes of the whole world their only hope lies in the success of a strong central government: a tyranny in fact, but once the pressure is relieved, Lenin survives, and he has not lost his original ideals, we may hope. Of course, they may go mad with the idea of Empire, and go out with their armies to force the world to come under their ideas and do awful things in the name of freedom, small nationalities, etc., but even so, they have done something. The French Revolution gave France new life, though all their fine ideas ended in horrors and bloodshed and wars. The world, too, gained. Nothing else would have given courage to the underdog and put fear into the heart of the oppressor in the way it did. I believe all the reforms at the beginning of the nineteenth century had their roots in the Terror."[144]

Markievicz's view of the French Revolution reflected that of Carlyle. He was the first apologist among historians for the Terror, arguing that it had been at the heart of the French Revolution, and bore the hopes of future ages.[145] Markievicz wanted to believe that the time of terror was a prelude to reforms and a better society, even though she does not seem to be wholly convinced about the pure motives of Lenin and Bolsheviks. To see violence as justified and necessary in order to discard the old regime was a part of the tradition of the French revolution and romantic nationalism, but it was blended also with the idea of freedom attained by the ultimate sacrifice, which was an essential part of radical Irish nationalism.

Markievicz cast a keen eye on the development of Russia. From James Connolly's daughter Nora she had heard accounts of the organisation of railways and industries, "in face of almost insuperable difficulties" but also of terrible ruthlessness to everyone who is "an enemy of the Republic."[146] Later she noted the "wonderful constructive work" in Russia. Although admitting that the workers were horrified by the number of executions which they thought cruel and drastic, she insisted that in comparing them to the French Terror they were

---

142   Markievicz to Eva Gore-Booth, 9.6.1919, PL, 226.
143   Markievicz to Eva Gore-Booth, 30.8.1919, PL, 242; Markievicz to Eva Gore-Booth, 8.12.1920, PL, 257.
144   Markievicz to Eva Gore-Booth, 6.12.1920, PL, 255-256.
145   Holton 1990, 13.
146   Markievicz to Eva Gore-Booth, 8.12.1920, PL, 257.

just and the accusations made against the executed were proved "quite honestly."[147]

A few years later she remarked that she knew very little about the Bolsheviks,[148] but at that time the situation was somewhat different; it is clear that she perceived Bolsheviks to be rather alike the ancient Irish. Looking at Irish history, she detected "...a sort of feeling for 'decentralization' (modern soviets)."[149] And again, while reading about the early days of parliament in England, when much land was common and when religious communites looked after education, the sick and the poor, she described the period as "England's high road to Bolshevism."[150] Thus, the old communities as well as the Bolsheviks then served as an inspiration and example for the future. It is interesting to note, that Markievicz did not stress the different characteristics of the Irish and the English race in this connection. On the contrary, she implicitly seemed to assume that it was only later, when Britain had become an Imperium and after it had conquered Ireland, that the differences had sharpened.

Markievicz considered the Bolshevik revolution equal to the French Revolution. Both overthrew an undemocratic autocracy and strove to establish a new society based on equality. In other words, for her the Russian revolution was not so much a socialist revolution as a successor to the events in France. Viewing the situation in Russia she returned over and over again to it, even describing the terror in Russia as action against enemies of the "Republic", thus implying that the Bolshevik revolution simply involved overthrowing a monarchy. In the Irish context, Markievicz regarded it as misleading to claim that Sinn Fein was Bolshevik,[151] and she does not seem to have lent her support to the spontaneously born soviets in Ireland.[152]

Markievicz as a Minister

In the Dáil or in the Cabinet there was no great interest in the problems of the workers. Obviously to a majority of the nationalists the most important thing was to make sure that Labour would not compete with Sinn Fein or that it would not try to institute reforms that were too radical during the time of struggle with the British. Obviously, the post of Minister of Labour was seen as a link between both groups. Markievicz filled that role well even though her

---

147 Markievicz to Eva Gore-Booth, 15.12.1920, PL, 260. Her interest in Russia propably led her to read the life of Tolstoi, whose "compromises with all his principles" she did not approve of, Markievicz to Eva Gore-Booth, 11.12.1920, PL, 259.
148 Markievicz to Stanislaus Dunin-Markievicz, May 1922, Markievicz Papers, MS 13 778, NLI.
149 Markievicz to Eva Gore-Booth, 18.10.1919, PL, 246.
150 Markievicz to Eva Gore-Booth, 5.7.1919, PL, 230.
151 Markievicz to Eva Gore-Booth, 17.8.1919, PL, 238.
152 About soviets, see e.g. O'Connor, 99-100.

remarks on James Connolly's workers' republic must have sounded annoying to some Sinn Feiners.

The realisation of the Democratic Programme was for most of the nationalists not an immediate task, and they preferred it to be forgotten. To some extent that created problems for Markievicz, whose idea of linking social reforms to political independence had been formed before the Easter Rising, when the real chances for realizing the reforms were minimal. In the new situation the tactic of Markievicz was once more to propose reforms. Nonetheless, the most important thing for her was to follow the decisions of the Dáil, even if they postponed such reforms.

Markievicz was out of step with many of her fellow members of the Dáil in supporting the cause of the workers, in urging co-operative methods, being sympathetic to bolsheviks - or even placing the women in the forefront of politics. To some Sinn Feiners her arrest was a relief, because they considered her "a firebrand and dangerous, even to them."[153] She was described by the enemies of republicanism as "a thorn in the flesh of Sinn Fein, so it may be a pity to take her away from them."[154]

Markievicz's time as a minister did not impress her first biographer, Sean O'Faolain, who did not consider her a particularly useful member of the Cabinet, although he remarked that she evidently was not "generally popular with men in revolutionary circles", in addition to being the only woman in the Cabinet. Furthermore, recounting examples of how Markievicz had irritated the other members of the Cabinet by her seemingly illogical speeches and interruptions, he maintained that the meetings of Dáil from August 1921 to June 1922 show that she was received with scant courtesy.[155] It should be noted, however, that those minutes dealt mainly with the Treaty between Britain and Ireland and that it is therefore not surprsing that Markievicz, who bitterly opposed the Treaty, faced criticism. It is true, however, that the suggestions of Markievicz and her memoranda were constantly transmitted from one meeting to another and were finally abandoned without action.[156] When money was given to different departments in the Dáil, the Department of Labour got the least of - and Markievicz did not demand more.[157] It is clear that there was no great eagerness to invest in the Department of Labour, which reflected attitude towards labour issues in the Dáil overall.

That she was not regarded as an important minister, was demonstrated after she was released in July 1921, when the truce was declared. In August the Dáil

---

153   The words of a British official in Dublin Castle, Records of Department of State. Relating to Internal Affairs of Great Britain, 1910-1929, American Consulate, Dublin, Ireland, November 12, 1920, 841d.00/259, National Archives, Washington d.c.
154   Mitchell 1995, 162.
155   O'Faolain, 188-189. Hanna Sheehy-Skeffington remarked that Collins "had the usual soldiers' contempt for civilians, particularly for women.", Levenson, 112.
156   See Dáil Eireann, Ministry & Cabinet Minutes 1919, 7.11.1919, DE 1/2; 14.11.1919; 28.11.1919, 20-24.
157   Dáil Eireann, Official Report, 29.7.1920, 184. Whereas Department of Labour got £450, Irish got £5000 and propaganda £950 - not to speak of the other departments. Later Markievicz was given £500 for the costs of the Labour Arbitration Tribunal, Dáil, Official Report, 17.9.1920, 232.

Cabinet was restructured. On grounds of efficiency and the speeding up of decision-making, a smaller Executive, the inner Cabinet, consisting of the President and six Secretaries of State, was created with a number of other ministries becoming extra-Cabinet. Markievicz was one of those moved out of the Executive, a move later considered to give an accurate foretaste of de Valera's subsequent policy regarding women's place in public life.[158] Later Markievicz simply noted the change[159] and her personal highly sympathetic view of de Valera remained intact.[160]

According to Arthur Mitchell, who has written the most recent and comprehensive study of Dáil Eireann, the Labour Department initially had little to do.[161] It is interesting to note, that while he argues that Markievicz made no effort to establish standards for employment or anything of the sort, he, writing about the Department of Trade and Commerce whose director was Ernest Blythe, reminds his readers of the conditions under which the Dáil government operated, and thus does not find it surprising that Blythe's department achieved little.[162] Yet Markievicz worked under the same conditions. It seems, that in that case there are two different standards, one for Markievicz and another for the rest. On the other hand, a more sympathetic biographer seeks to give an impression that she did a great deal more than the evidence suggests.[163] There is relatively little material concerning the Ministry of Labour at that time. The only surviving document summarizes work from August 1919 to October 1919 and from July 1920 onwards. In the official reports of the Dáil debates the reports of her Ministry are simply mentioned as having been noted. In the autumn of 1919 it was remarked that the department had, "in its brief

---

158 Coogan 1993, 245-246. The other Ministries outside the Cabinet were Fine Arts, Publicity, Education, Trade and Commerce, Agriculture and Fisheries.
159 Private Sessions of Second Dáil. Minutes of Proceedings 18 August 1921 to 14 September 1921 and Report of Debates 14 December 1921 to 6 January 1922, Dublin 1972, 16.12.1921, 189.
160 According to her, de Valera had done wonders on his tour in America, Marreco, 252. However, Markievicz criticised de Valera once, when he had in his tour in America stated that Britain's concerns over defence could be met by guaranteeing Ireland's permanent neutrality; an idea he defined such as the Monroe doctrine. See eg. Coogan 1993, 223; Comerford, Maire, The First Dàil, Dublin 1971, 84; Lyons 1973, 403-404, 422.
161 Mitchell 1995, 161.
162 Mitchell 1995, 162.
163 Norman argues that before her imprisonment that was to happen in June 1919 Markievicz had instituted a system of Conciliation Boards for industrial arbitration, had had surveys made with a view to establishing guidelines for wages and food prices, had set up a general employment agency to find work for jobless Volunteers and Cumann na mBan, had arranged for a boycott of British goods, had initiated a campaign in support of Irish industrial development and begun a fund to establish a James Connolly Memorial Workers' College. Norman, 203-204. However, the report included in Dàil papers clearly indicates that most of those measures were taken only in late summer 1919, when she was already in prison, InterimReport Dáil Eireann, Official Report, 28-33.Furthermore, to base one's assumption of Markievicz's efficency as a minister on Colllins, who bluntly described the Ministry of Justice as "a bloody joke", and did not use the same kind of a language regarding the ministry of Markievicz's, seems to be a bit far fetched, ibid. About Collins on Stack, see e.g. Mitchell 1995, 230.

existence, a good record to show."[164] In December 1920, only the Labour and Defence departments were able to carry on in a generally effective manner.[165]

Working in a wartime cabinet and parliament entailed undeniable limits to what could be achieved. Markievicz was in prison from the middle of June till the middle of October 1919 and from September 26th 1920 to July 1921. Being locked up in prison bored her, because there was so much to be done.[166] She did not miss a meeting of Dáil Eireann or the Cabinet when she was free and was also an active participant in the meetings of the Sinn Fein Standing Committee.[167] Like other republicans, she joined meetings even when they were declared illegal.[168] Her life was not easy. She had no permanent address. Due to the possibility of arrest it was unwise to stay in one place for a long period of time.[169]

What Markievicz actually accomplished in her fragmentary period as a minister was to arbitrate in disputes between workers and employers as well as to promote social reforms amongst the Dublin poor. She felt it necessary to try and to sever the connections between the Irish and the British trade unions in order to establish a nationally organised Labour movement. It can be indeed argued that Markievicz was mainly concerned in keeping the Irish firmly together. She wanted to act as an arbitrator not only in the case of concrete disputes, but in a more subtle way, to try to ease tensions between nationalists and socialists. It is obvious that she also wanted to get the Dáil to back more radical reforms, including the establishment of co-operatives. She envisaged an Ireland where the sexes would be equal, where the land would provide a living for every family and where all the different sections of the population would solve their problems together. Her aims were difficult to achieve in time of peace and almost impossible to further in time of war.

---

164   Dáil Eireann, Official Report, 27.10.1919, 160.
165   Mitchell 1995, 227. After Markievicz had been arrested, her replacement was Joseph McGrath, and after he had been arrested on 2nd December 1920, he was replaced by Joseph McDonagh at the end of January 1921.
166   Markievicz to Eva Gore-Booth, 11.12.1920, PL, 259.
167   O'Faolain, 188; See Copy Minutes of Sinn Fein Standing Committee, October-December 1919, 999/40, NAI, 34-46.
168   For instance before the Christmas 1919, see Markievicz to Joseph McCarrity, no date, Joseph McGarrity Papers, MS 17 463, NLI; Marreco, 249-250; see also memories of Maire Comerford in Mitchell 1995, 161.
169   O'Faolain, 186; Robbins, 218; Markievicz to Joseph McGarrity, no date, Joseph McGarrity Papers, MS 17 463, NLI.

■ Against the Free State

Markievicz's vision of Irishness

The time on the run and the situation in which Markievicz had acted in general after getting out of prison in the summer of 1917, meant a busy life for her. A practical politician, always in demand for speeches and meetings, she only found time to ponder the different aspects of Irishness and the Irish situation in prison. In the light of her writings, not much had changed since the beginning of her career. That Irish history was an important tool and that it was possible to draw lessons and examples from it for contemporary politics was an essential part of her ideology, as it was for other nationalists. In prison, she had been reading histories in order to find things "we have thought and done differently from other nations" and had found out that

> "...we never produced a tyrant. There was something that prevented any man or woman ever desiring to conquer all Ireland – a sort of feeling for 'decentralization'..."[1]

That distinctive feature had first prevented an English conquest, but had at the same time prevented the Irish from getting together under one head for long enough to do more than win a battle, lamented Markievicz. On the other hand, she appeared to presume that it was possible to create a united front; according to her, history showed that there was no need to be worried about Northern Ireland , because "it held out much longer than the South...and it's only a bit behind the times."[2] Thus, she chose to close her eyes to the uncompromising attitude of the Ulster Unionists and preferred the idea of the unchangeable soul of a nation, which according to her had in history helped the North to hold out against a conquest by England. However, a year later, writing in time of war, she admitted that "Belfast is different", while the rest of the country was 'wonderfully self-controlled, patient and heroic."[3] Ignoring Ulster unionism was a common feature of many republicans.[4]

---

1   Markievicz to Eva Gore-Booth, 18.10.1919, PL, 246. One of the books relating to Irish history was P.S. O'Hegarty's The Indestructible Nation: A Survey of Irish History from the English Invasion. Dublin 1918. It emphasized the unbroken struggle of Ireland as well as spirituality and striving for liberty. Markievicz herself claimed to be reading a book by the name of The Unconquerable Nation, but the book was most likely the one above, Markievicz to Eva Gore-Booth, 21.10.1918, PL, 188.
2   Markievicz to Eva Gore-Booths, 18.10.1919, PL, 247. Markievicz, who was reading history books, might have come across the book by Alice Stopford Green, where she remarked that a country divided in government was weakened for purposes of defence, or for joint action in military matters, Green 1911, 22.
3   Markievicz to Eva Gore-Booth, 6.12. 1920, PL, 256.
4   English, Richard, Green on red; Two case studies in early twentieth-century Irish republican thought, in Boyce, George D. et al 1993, 163-64.

Nationalist Irish history provided Markievicz with examples for tracing the dissimilarities between the English and the Irish. The ancient, "decentralized" society was one thing that made them different and the powerful women in Irish history was another.[5] The way in which history was transmitted from one generation to another also differed from the English method, because in Ireland "local and family history educated the children."[6]

An essential feature of Irishness was the Irish language. Markievicz concentrated on studying it in prison, even though she found it difficult without a teacher.[7] She wondered how much of its history of a race lay in the language[8] and believed that national character was revealed in it; therefore the fact that Irish did not have the verb "to have" proved that "we are not a covetous and aggressive race." Romanticizing the language, Markievicz declared that the Irish language could give a very definite and subtle expression to shades of thought.[9] Furthermore, she liked its freedom because in English one had to speak and spell in the same way as those who belonged to the "ruling clique", whereas in Irish local expressions could add colour and beauty.[10] Thus, language not only confirmed that the Irish were a separate people, it also expressed the democratic nature of that people. However, Markievicz was not convinced of the case of reviving Irish by law; force was not a good way to put things through.[11]

Irish history and language were, howevwe, not the sole indicators of specific Irishness. Markievicz described the Irish way of thinking as one that relied on instinct: for example she held that the Irish "never philosophize about how to run a movement, we do it by faith or luck or instinct."[12] She claimed that in Ireland there never was a philosophy, because the annals and histories seemed neither to have discussed abstract things much nor to have indulged in speculation, thoughts or theories.[13] Again, she maintained that the Irish liked adjectives and symbolic things and that their speeches were often "rather rhetorical"[14] The essence of Irishness was thus identified with inborn instincts and it seems that for Markievicz the idea of a nonspeculative race, which had somehow been preserved in its natural state, seemed to shed light on the Irish way of thinking. Of course, these characteristics confirmed the image of the Irish as a sincere and innocent people in contrast with the corrupt, theorizing and calculating British.

---

5 Markievicz to Eva Gore-Booth, 18.10.1919, PL, 247.

6 Markievicz to Eva Gore-Booth, 11.12. 1920, PL, 259.

7 Markievicz to "M," 20.10.1920, PL, 253. Her decision to study the language had possibly been influenced by the view of Sinn Fein which emphasized that learning of the language was for everyone, see The Ethics of Sinn Fein, pamphlet, September 1917, NLI.

8 Markievicz to Eva Gore-Booth, 8.12.1920, PL, 258.

9 Markievicz to Eva Gore-Booth, 30.12.1920, PL, 264.

10 Markievicz to Eva Gore-Booth, 7.1.1921, PL, 267. However, Markievicz was also frustrated by her need of a good grammar and a dictionary, see letters to Eva Gore-Booth, 1.4.1921, PL, 269; 8.6.1921, PL, 274; 3.5.1921, PL, 271.

11 See Dàil Eireann, Official report, 1.3.1922, 164.

12 Markievicz to Eva Gore-Booth, 23.8.1919, PL, 240-241.

13 Markievicz to Eva Gore-Booth, Undated (presumably after June 8th 1921), PL, 275.

14 Markievicz to Eva Gore-Booth, 5.7.1919, 229.

According to Markievicz, the dichotomy between the British and the Irish was, then, invariably based on former's complete lack of ideas and idealism as opposed to the non-materialist nature of the latter.[15] In general, Irish republican idealism at that period relied on the supposed dichotomy between the spiritual and the material, a contrast complemented by an Irish attachment to the interwoven notions of sacrifice, suffering, the soul, and religious sensibility.[16] The goal of the republicans was to conquer "strong" physical force by the will-power of the "weak." According to Terence MacSwiney, who was to die on hunger-strike, victory belonged to the one who endured most suffering.[17]

For Markievicz also victory could , she felt, be achieved by sacrifice. In a poem dedicated to the executed ex-Fianna boy Kevin Barry she compared the sacrifice of a republican life with that of the ultimate sacrifice, that of the Christ.[18] And, after Terence MacSwiney had died on hunger-strike, Markievicz declared that

> "...[t]here is exaltation & joy in the fighter's death, with the passion & glory of the battlefield, but to lie in a prison cell...requires a a courage & strength that is God like... "[19]

The words of Markievicz recalled the words she wrote on Larkin during the Dublin Lock-Out in 1913. Then she had merged his image with that of a suffering Christ. Seven years later, during another lock-out she accused the employers of sticking business ethics when they should have replaced them with Christian ethics.[20]

At the time of the gravest trouble between the Irish and the British during the Anglo-Irish War Markievicz idealistically emphasized an Irish understanding of ultimate suffering and its unifying impact:

> " ...everyone realises too that it is by suffering, dying and sticking out that we will win. Great attempts have been made to divide us, but nobody differs about fundamentals, and everybody has their own ideas about details of policy, which they discuss quite amiably and openly. There is no jealousy, and no one is out for self."[21]

Not only the leaders but ordinary people were capable of doing brave things:

---

15   Markievicz to Eva Gore-Booth, 17.1.1919, PL, 190; Markievicz to Eva Gore-Booth, PL, 188-189; Markievicz to Eva Gore-Booth, 14.2.1919, PL, 195.

16   See English 1994, 46, 62-63.

17   Garvin 1987, 157; see de Valera's statement issued in America, 31 October 1920, in Moynihan, 47.

18   " .../His end! No end to lives like his!/With us he lives away,/Bright through our night, a shining star/ e lights for us the way/And Christ who died for love of us/Tortured and bruised and shamed,/Gives courage to such hero souls,/Unbending and untamed.", C de M, Kevin, *Catholic Bulletin*, September 1921.

19   Markievicz to Joseph McGarrity, no date, Joseph McGarrity Papers, MS 17 627, NLI.

20   C de M, Noted in Jail By the Countess. The Heathen Ethics of the Dublin Tramway Co.,*Watchword of Labour*, 3.1.1920.

21   Markievicz to Eva Gore-Booth, 24.12.1920, PL, 262-263.

"The present persecutions seem to have brought the living and the dead into such close touch, it is almost uncanny. It all makes one feel that they must win. The spiritual must prevail over the material in the end. We suffer, and suffering teaches us to unite and stand by each other. It also makes for us friends everywhere, while the policy of our enemies is leaving them friendless."[22]

Furthermore, the situation had positive effects on people in a political context; according to Markievicz everyone – especially the young – wanted to know, read, think and talk. It was her own policy, she claimed, always to have used her influence in making people think and act independently.[23]

For a Workers' Republic and Co-operative Commonwealth

Markievicz was always ready to compromise in relation to Irish domestic politics, but was never willing to make any concessions to British. She demonstrated this when the republicans opposed the Government of Ireland Bill introduced in December 1920. According to Markievicz, the Bill offered no real autonomy and the people would never accept it.[24] Under the new bill both Ulster and Southern Ireland were each to have their own parliament. This local autonomy was not enough for Sinn Fein, because Westminster would still be responsible for defence, foreign policy and finance and monetary politics.[25]

Sinn Fein used the elections for the Southern Irish Parliament under the new Government of Ireland Act as a poll for the second Dáil Eireann. The fact that in every single one of the 128 constituencies Sinn Feiners were returned unopposed, convinced Britain that the majority of the Irish in the South were behind the Republicans. Markievicz was re-elected to the Dáil where she was no longer the only woman; five other women were elected, four of them relatives of men killed since 1916.[26]

The result of the elections , the pressures in Britain against the war,the speech of King George V appealing for peace and the return of de Valera, who was shocked by the situation in Ireland, together led to the cease-fire of 11 July of 1921. There was great joy in Ireland, because this truce was perceived as a recognition of the republic; now Britain was willing to meet the Irish representatives on an equal basis.[27] This happiness was shared by Markievicz, who was released on 24th July after being locked up for over 10 months.[28]

---

22   Markievicz to Eva Gore-Booth, 1.4.1921, PL, 269-270.
23   Markievicz to Eva Gore-Booth, 6.12. 1920, PL, 256.
24   Markievicz to W.J.Maloney, in Van Voris,284.
25   Lee 1989, 43-44; Lyons, 1973, 413-414.
26   Norman, 220.
27   Lee, 1989, 47; Lyons 1973, 423-427. Hopkinson, 14-15. During the conference leading to the truce the crowds in the Dublin streets outside the Mansion House were saying the Rosary, praying for peace, Murphy, Daniel J. (ed.), Lady Gregory's Journals, 276.
28   "It is so heavenly to be out again...It is almost worth while being locked up, for the great joy release brings", Markievicz to Eva Gore-Booth, undated, 1921, PL,300.

However, in speaking at the Annual Convention of Cumann na mBan, which was the biggest ever in the history of the organisation, she was quick to point out that now was the time for action, not talk. She maintained that their strength lay in the fact that they were ready to fight, and it was important that the enemy saw no weakening.[29] Both Cumann na mBan and the Volunteers continued to train and drill, in order to be ready for the time when their services might be necessary.[30]

After the Dáil rejected the first proposal of Lloyd George,[31] new negotiations were started on London in October 11th 1921. The negotiators on the Irish side were Griffith, Collins, Robert Barton, E.J.Duggan and George Gavan Duffy, with Griffith and Collins as the main negotiatiors.On the British side were Lloyd George, Winston Churchill, Austen Chamberlain and others. The Irish negotiators were given full powers to negotiate, but the decisions and agreement had eventually be approved in Cabinet. The negotiations proved to be extremely difficult.The Irish delegation was disjointed and their powers were not clearly framed.[32] During the negotiations it became obvious that the recognition of an Irish Republic was out of the question. The proposal for "External Association" by de Valera was rejected not only by the British but also by radical republicans. According to it, Ireland would have been a member of the Commonwealth and the British crown would have controlled foreign policy, but Ireland would have been sovereign in domestic politics and would have maintained the status of a Republic. When the Treaty was signed on 6 December 1921 after Lloyd George had threatened the delegation with imminent war, de Valera could not, however, agree with the conditions. He hoped that the Dáil would reject the treaty and that this would make new negotiations possible.[33]

The Anglo-Irish Treaty, which established a Free State, did not fundamentally differ from the proposals that the British had made in the summer. It gave a Dominion status to the 26 Southern counties, but the British were to continue their military presence in Ireland and the members of the Free State Parliament were to take an oath of allegiance to the King. Furthermore, should the Northern Ireland Parliament reject incorporation into the Free State – which was practically certain – there should be a Boundary Commission to discuss the border between Northern Ireland and the Free State.[34]

The majority of the Irish people, businessmen, the bigger farmers, the press, the Labour movement and the Church accepted the Treaty.[35] Nevertheless, it

---

29   Cumann na mBan: Annual Convention. October 22nd and 23rd 1921. Report. NLI, 1-2.
30   Ward 1983, 154-155.
31   See Proposals of the British Government for an Irish Settlement July 20, 1921, in Correspondence relating..., 2-3. Ireland was offered a Dominion status on condition that the British controlled the seas, that the RAF would be given bases, that Ireland would contribute to War Reparations and that the forthcoming solution would acknowledge the Northern Ireland Parliament, Dáil Eireann. Official Report, 26.8. 1921, 81-82.
32   See Lyons 1973, 430-431.
33   Hopkinson, 19–35; Foster, R.F., Modern Ireland 1600-1972, London 1985, 505.
34   Treaty between Great Britain and Irish representatives, 6 December 1921, in Irish Historical Documents since 1800, 174-179.
35   Hopkinson, 35; Foster 1985, 509; Coogan 1993,295.

divided the republicans of Dáil Eireann. De Valera asserted that the Treaty was in conflict with the opinion of the majority of the Irish people, who had expressed their view in the elections.[36] Those who were for the Agreement shared the view of Collins; that even though the Treaty did not give Ireland ultimate freedom, it gave her the freedom to achieve it.[37] He felt that the non-acceptance of the Treaty would be a gamble as England could then arrange a further war in Ireland.[38]

When the Dáil assembled to discuss the Treaty on 14 December 1921, the division into two parties was obvious. First there was discussion of "Document no 2", which de Valera had compiled as a possible replacement for the Treaty. The main difference between the two was that de Valera's proposal excluded the Oath of Allegiance.[39] He maintained that the agreement could not reconcile with Irish national aspirations.[40] His opponents talked of the pragmatism of the Treaty; for them the Republic must be sacrificed in order to save the people of Ireland from immediate war.[41]

Markievicz had opposed both the Home Rule Bill in 1912 and the Government of Ireland Act in 1920. In September 1921, she made speeches promising a Republic.[42] Reading the first copy of the Treaty it came to her "like a bolt from the blue." For her, the Oath of Allegiance constituted the greatest obstacle to any acceptance of the Treaty. According to her, swearing such an oath would be dishonest

> " first, before God and my own soul, and, secondly, before the men who died for Ireland in all the generations and, thirdly, to my constituency in St. Patrick's and the poor and the humble. They are nearly all poor now and each one has said to me,'You will be true to the Republic'."[43]

Thus, the poor and the humble – again, " the men of no property" – were those whose voice had to be heard when new Ireland was being envisioned and, even more importantly, to accept the Treaty would mean giving up the power that already had been taken. In Markievicz's words, the oath would mean pledging oneself to an authority other than that of the Irish Republic.[44] It was also a question of honour, because being "an honourable woman", Markievicz would "sooner die than give a declaration of fidelity to King George or the

---

36   Marreco, 267.
37   Dáil Eireann. Debate on the Treaty between Great Britain and Ireland signed in London on 6th December 1921, Dublin 1922, 32; Pakenham, Frank, Peace by Ordeal. With an introduction by Tim Pat Coogan and a preface by the author, London 1993 (First published 1935, new edition 1972), 225; see also Collins, Michael, The Path to Freedom. Dublin 1922, 30.
38   Collins in Cabinet Meeting, 3.12.1921, DE 1/3, 177, NAI.
39   See Foster 1985, 505-506.
40   Dáil Eireann. Debate on the Treaty..., 19.12.1921, 24-25.
41   See for instance the speech of Gavan Duffy, 21.12.1921, ibid.,87.
42   Murphy, Daniel J. (ed.), Lady Gregory's Journals, 294-295.
43   Dáil Eireann. Private Sessions of Second Dáil..., 16.12.1921, 204.
44   Dáil Eireann. Debate on the Treaty..., 16.12.1921, 204; Markievicz asserted that she would have created "some kind of trouble outside the Cabinet" if she had thought that de Valera would have accepted the Oath, ibid., 189.

British Empire."[45] In that respect Markievicz differed from Connolly, who had seen the oath of allegiance to the British Monarchy as a mere formality which was in no way binding.[46]

The Oath of Allegiance was the most important of the symbols which were discussed in the Treaty debate. At the previous annual meeting of Sinn Fein de Valera had given an assurance that whatever concessions the negotiations might bring, an oath of allegiance would not be one of them, even though the awful alternative might be war.[47] The oath involved a question of honour and this made it unacceptable to very many of the Volunteers.[48]

Markievicz made an emotional appeal for the rejection of the Treaty on 3 January 1922 in the Dáil. She declared that she would stand true to her principles both as a Republican and as one "pledged to the teeth for the freedom of Ireland." The republic she defended was "a Government by the consent of the people". That meant that she relied on the support of the majority of the Irish who had given their support to Sinn Fein and Dáil Eireann, and who would now vote against the proposed Treaty. Markievicz was committed to the "prosperity of the many, for the happiness and content of the workers, for ...James Connolly's ideal of a Workers' republic - co-operative commonwealth." Drawing together ideas from the Declaration of the Easter Rising, she indicated that this meant a state run by the Irish people for the people, a Government that looked after the rights of the people before the rights of property.[49]

For Markievicz, to accept the Treaty would also mean giving up idealism, even giving up "the spirit and the soul of Ireland." [50] She defined republicans as "idealists believing in and loving Ireland", those who were ready to take the "stony road" that led to ultimate freedom.[51] Were they not in power, the situation would be dramatically changed.

Markievicz attacked the Unionists, but not on the grounds of partition, which was an important issue to many other members. In her view, they should not be given any special treatment since they had not internalised Irish ideals and had not rejected their connections with Britain. She predicted gloomily that if the Unionists joined in the proposed government they would block every ideal. The Governor-General – who would be the representative of the Crown in Ireland – would be the centre from which anti-Irish ideals could circulate through Ireland, with English ideals to replace them: "love of luxury, love of wealth, love of competition, trample on your neighbours to get to the top, immorality

---

45 Dáil Eireann. Debate on the Treaty..., 3.1.1922, 183.
46 Anderson 1994, 119. It has been suggested that Markievicz resented the Treaty because it left Britain in sole possession of all the naval ports and military strongholds, Sebastyen, xxiv. In fact, she compared discussing the giving up of ports and "other things" to the oath, and held that whereas the former was possible, the latter was not, Dáil Eireann. Private Sessions of Second Dáil..., 16.12.1921, 204.
47 de Valera on 28 October 1921, in Moynihan, 74-75.
48 Coogan 1993, 307.
49 Dáil Eireann. Debate on the Treaty..., 181, 184-185.
50 Markievicz, Constance de, Peace with Honour, Poblacht na hEireann. The Republic of Ireland, 3.1.1922.
51 Dáil Eireann. Debate on the Treaty..., 3.1.1922, 186.

and divorce laws of the English nation."[52] Her concern was shared by other republicans as well; at that time it was feared that people would lose their idealism and their ideas of freedom and of a free nation would be submerged in the concerns of mere industrial and material undertakings. [53]

While discussing the role of Southern Unionists in Ireland Markievicz displayed an immense antipathy towards them. They had left people dying on the roadsides, had combined together against the workers, ruined the farmer and "sent the people to drift in the emigrant ships and to die of horrible disease or to sink to the bottom of the Atlantic."[54] The last accusation derived from Markievicz's own family history; the peasants her grand-father Robert Gore-Booth had evicted were said to have been drowned with the ship that was carrying them.[55] She made another reference to her own background when she told the Dáil that the English should not be trusted, and claimed to know because of the "black drop of English blood in me." It is interesting, however, that she explained her "black drop" by reference to her ancestors who had come to Ireland centuries earlier rather than to her English mother.[56] Nevertheless, her writings show that her personal view of the English was more complicated than her political speeches indicate.[57]

However, to attack English characteristics and declare that the goal was in fact a co-operative commonwealth where workers would be equal to other classes, and to object to any plan to establish an Upper Chamber[58] showed that mere independence was not enough for Markievicz. She strove for social equality, which is shown in her fear of the Unionists who, when in power, would block the education of the poorer classes and every bit of the progress that every man and woman amongst the working people of Ireland desired to see put into force.[59] Her antipathy towards Southern Unionists echo the words of James Connolly written on the eve of the Easter Rising:

> " We are out for the Ireland for the Irish. But who are the Irish? Not the rack-renting,slum-owning landlord; not the sweating, profit-grinding capitalist; not the sleek and oily lawyer; not the prostitute pressman - the hired liars of the enemy... Not these, but the Irish working class, the only secure foundation upon which a free nation can be reared."[60]

---

52   Dáil Eireann. Debate on the Treaty..., 3.1.1922, 182,184.
53   The opinion of Frank Gallaghers who had discussed with AE, Murphy, Daniel J. (ed.), Lady Gregory's Journals, 11.1.1922, 319.
54   Dáil Eireann. Debate on the Treaty..., 3.1.1922, 181.
55   Sebastyen, xi. The event was described in a ballad which was sung in Sligo, Haverty, 10-11.
56   Dáil Eireann. Debate on the Treaty..., 3.1.1922, 184.
57   She wrote about the decent people among "the enemy", Markievicz to Eva Gore-Booth, 1.4.1921, PL, 269-270 and described one Mr. Nevinson as "one of the real nice, honourable men who are so often found among the English", Markievicz to Eva Gore-Booth, 26.11.1920, PL, 255.
58   Dáil Eireann. Debate on the Treaty..., 3.1.1922, 181, 184-185.
59   Ibid., 182.
60   Connolly, James, The Irish Flag, *Workers' Republic*, 8 April 1916, in James Connolly:Selected Works, 145.

During the debate on the Treaty Markievicz was the only one who brought the workers and Connolly into the arena.[61] Her opinion that the "happiness and content" of the workers entailed another solution than the proposed Treaty was certainly not the opinion of pro-Treaty representatives of the Dáil. According to Piaras Beaslai it would still be possible to have industries built up on lines which would assure the worker a fair share. He was supported by Joseph McGrath, who had worked in the Ministry of Labour, and who held that the Democratic Programme could be put into force under the Treaty.[62]

Views on to the threat of war, should the Treaty be rejected, were another divisive factor among both the pro-and anti-Treatyites. Those who did not fear continuing warfare were to be found on both camps.[63] The anti-Treatyites as a whole stressed their desire for a real peace, not a peace which would give away the independence of Ireland.[64] According to some, war was not the worst evil, since no physical victory could compensate for a spiritual surrender[65], a view reflecting much of the history of Irish republicanism that depended on not caring about failures.[66]

Speaking of defeat made Markievicz angry as well:

> "Ireland has suffered more defeats than any other small nation, and it is because she cannot yet visualise defeat that she remains undefeated... The spirit is unconquerable, for as long as we are unconquerable the powers of Hell cannot prevail against a soul that is true...this "Treaty" is the price for English Government have offered to pay for the silencing of the guns of the IRA. It is the price she would pay for a peace...I say that there is an alternative...a real treaty that left us alone to make our own laws and manage our own affairs without the constant bitterness. We desire peace with England and friendship with the English people; they desire peace and friendship with us..."[67]

But were peace not to come, the Irish would once again be willing to sacrifice themselves. During the Dáil debate Markievicz quoted Connolly, who had never wanted to prevent the men and women of Ireland from fighting and dying if they were so minded. Markievicz was, according to her own words,"quite a pacific mind", who did not like to kill. However, because she claimed that she was not afraid to die, she seemed to take it for granted that the Irish people shared her view and were also ready to die as well. In any case, death was for her preferable to dishonour.[68] Her words bring to mind Pearse,

---

61 Norman, 232, and Haverty, 210, claim that Liam Mellows also spoke on behalf of the workers. In fact Mellows did not explicitly refer to workers at all, see Dáil Eireann. Debate on the Treaty..., 4.1.1922, 227-234.
62 Dáil Eireann. Debate on the Treaty..., 3.1.1922, 179; 6.1.1922, 306.
63 For instance Collins explained that he had not signed the Treaty because he feared the war, but because he did not want to the draw Irish into war without their agreement, Dáil Eireann. Debate on the Treaty..., 34.
64 Ada English, Dáil Eireann. Debate on the Treaty.., 4.1.1922, 248.
65 Mary MacSwiney, Dáil Eireann. Debate on the Treaty..., 21.12.1921, 119.
66 Fanning, Ronan, Independent Ireland. Dublin 1983, 11.
67 Markievicz, Constance de, Peace with Honour, Poblacht na hEireann. The Republic of Ireland, 3.1.1922.
68 Dáil Eireann. Debate on the Treaty..., 3.1.1922, 185.

who asserted that "We have the stregth and the peace of mind of those who never compromise."[69]

It is interesting to note that Markievicz's belief in the Irish people's willingness to die has been ignored in most of the biographies[70], though her unyielding position was reflected in the speeches of other women members of the Dáil. Because they had all lost a family member in the nationalist struggle in 1916 or afterwards, they were regarded as merely embittered, an accusation which they themselves denied. The women proclaimed that they rejected the Treaty because on principle; on questions of right and wrong.[71]

After an emotional and long discussion, the Anglo-Irish Treaty was finally accepted by Dáil Eireann on 7th January 1922 by 64 votes to 57.[72] De Valera announced the resignation of himself and the Cabinet. Griffith, who was elected Prime Minister, promised that Free State elections would then be arranged.[73]

Markievicz was among those who rejected the Treaty. The abrupt exchange of insults between her and Collins, happening when de Valera with his supporters marched out of the Dáil, has been carefully reported.[74] However, she was very much concerned about the division. Previously, in discussing the first proposal of Lloyd George on 25 July 1921, she did not condemn the terms outright, but wanted the documents circulated so that more time could be given to their consideration.[75] In December 1921, she expressed her understanding and sympathy for the delegates, although she disagreed with them. She hoped that in the end they could all work together for the good of Ireland.[76] After the Treaty had been accepted, she stressed that order and peace were needed; disruption and disagreement would lead to very serious results.[77] These words have usually been left unnoticed when the attitude of Markievicz to the Treaty split has been discussed.

To highlight the unyielding attitude of Markievicz and to ignore her calmer words illluminates the way in which the split has often been treated. Knowing all the violence that was to come, it is difficult to try and concentrate on the view of an 'open future' that both the pro-and the anti- Treatyites had at that time. It has been suggested that in the absence of an acceptable political system, many had pledged themselves to symbols which they were not prepared to sacrifice even when the real essence of their demands was granted.[78] According

---

69   Quoted in English 1993, 165.
70   Only Marreco emphasizes it, 270-271.
71   See Kate O'Callaghen, Dáil Eireann. Debate on the Treaty..., 20.12.1921, 59; Kathleen Clarke, ibid., 22.12.1921, 141.
72   Dáil Eireann. Debate on the Treaty..., 7.1.1922, 345-346.
73   Dáil Eireann. Debate on the Treaty..., 9.1.1922, 349, 381.
74   Collins called those who left deserters and foreigners, Markievicz replied by calling those who were for Treaty oath-breakers, cowards and Lloyd Georgites, Dáil Eireann. Debate on the Treaty..., 10.1.1922, 410.
75   " En route to the discussion Countess Markievicz had met the mother of a boy killed in the fighting, and had been swayed towards an aversion to doing anything which might bring similar anguish to any other mother.", Coogan 1993, 239.
76   Dáil Eireann. Private Sessions of Second Dáil..., 16.12.1921, 204.
77   Dáil Eireann. Debate on the Treaty..., 9.1.1922, 362.
78   Rumpf & Hepburn, 33.

to recent research, the principal reason why symbolism was so important in the Treaty controversy was because Sinn Fein, indeed Ireland, had been living in a world of political theatre. Also, there were many people in Ireland who recognised the great progress that had been achieved by militant nationalism. Sinn Fein and the Dáil government could both rightly claim mass political support.[79]

To advocate a republic has been seen as one of the symbols. It has been rightly stated that the 'Republic' became a sacred object and goal, sanctified both by the higher meaning invested in it, and by the blood sacrifices of the men and women who had died for its establishment.[80] However, division concerning the principle or formal establishment of a republic was to be discerned in Sinn Fein from the beginning.[81] In fact, the republic was not mentioned in the 1919 constitution passed by the shadow Government. [82] As has been discussed earlier, republicanism in Ireland has been seen as representing a "somewhat unstructured wish for indenpendence."[83]

It is clear, that Markievicz saw an independent republic as her goal. It was not merely a symbol, it was the framework in which decisions leading to social equality could be made. Her idea was that only in a sovereign republic would the freedom of different sections of Irish people be achieved. That idea resembled the notion of Pearse written in spring 1916:

> "The end of freedom is human happiness. The end of national freedom is individual freedom; therefore individual happiness. National freedom implies national sovereignty. National sovereignty implies control of all the moral and material resources of the nation." [84]

Thus, there could be no force superior to an independent republic. Accordingly, Markievicz wanted to persuade as many Irish groups as possible to resist the Treaty. Her belief that Irish women strongly opposed to Treaty was given some support when the Executive of Cumann na mBan, whose President she was, rejected it as the first of radical nationalist organisations and reaffirmed its allegiance to the Irish Republic.[85] In February the members of the Cumann supported the Executive by 419 to 63 votes, but simultaneously the organisation lost many important members, such as Jenny Wyse-Power.[86] As the second organisation under the guidance of Markievicz, the Fianna also objected to the agreement and lent its support to the opponents of the Treaty. Markievicz was unanimously re-elected Chief Scout.[87] During her period as a Minister she had

---

79   Mitchell 1995, 327-328.
80   Anderson 1994, 123-124.
81   Murphy, Brian P., Patrick Pearse and the Lost Republican Ideal. Dublin 1991, 104-105.
82   Garvin 1996, 55.
83   Garvin 1995, 11.
84   Cronin, 109.
85   The Women of Ireland, *Poblacht na hEireann*, 17.1.1922.
86   The Cumann na mBan Convention, *Poblacht na hEireann*, 14.2.1922; Ward 1983, 172.
87   Van Voris, 313.

constantly worked with the organisation[88] and, in a similar way, she tried to get support for resistance to the Treaty from the ICA.[89]

Seeking a reward for young women

In spite of the split, Sinn Fein strove to prevent division when it assembled for a general meeting in February 1922.[90] In the same month the anti-Treatyites attended the meeting of the Dáil whose departments were to work normally until the forthcoming elections[91] and the members who had resigned were replaced by new ones. Markievicz was thus working in a parliament, where she, along with other anti-Treatyites, could pose provocative questions to those supproting the agreement.[92]

The issue that got her strongest support was a motion to give the vote to young women. Earlier, during the war, she had praised the women for their braveness, though they suffered both mentally and physically.[93] Nevertheless, she was never fully happy about the political attitudes of women and did not accept their sometimes passive approach to matters. However, once more the war-like conditions gave her hope in the same way they had given her hope during the Great War:

> "This is being an education to ...[women] here...There has been less physical restraint on the actions of women in Ireland than in any other country, but mentally the restrictions seem to me to be very oppressive. It is hard to understand why they took so little interest in politics as a sex, when you consider that both Catholics and Dissenters (men) laboured under all their disabilities and yet remained politicians."[94]

To compare the situation with that in which Tone had operated, shows that Markievicz did not quite grasp the more complex situation of women in modern society. After the Treaty split, Markievicz put the women on a pedestal once again. Their vision had been

> "...keen and direct...no terror could cow them, and today the grief of the women is not for their loved ones who died true, but for those who were weak and who have not the clear vision."[95]

---

88 See e.g. letter to Patrick MacCartan in America, May 1920, Frank Gallagher Papers, MS 21 246, NLI.
89 Fox 1943, 215.
90 See The Ard-Fheis, *Poblacht na hEireann*,28.2.1922.
91 Dáil Eireann. Official Report, 28.2.1922, 91.
92 For instance about propaganda and strikes, Dáil Eireann. Official report, 28.2.1922, 99; 1.3.1922, 142-143.
93 Markievicz to Eva Gore-Booth, 1.1.1921, PL, 266.
94 Markievicz to Eva Gore-Booth, 6.12.1920, PL, 256.
95 Markievicz, A typescript of speech, Joseph McGarrity Papers, MS 17 463, NLI.

Her fellow opponents of the Treaty also assumed that women were, in main, against the Treaty.[96] It was recalled that women had not "cried surrender"; but had inspired the men to resist during the whole period of the terror. In the previous century it was the women who handed on the tradition of independence from generation to generation, to Pearse and Eamon de Valera, for example.[97] It is important to note in this context that the special characteristics of women – their purity, idealism, their nurturing capacities – were never used to develop the image of women as peace-makers and pacifists,[98] but rather their image as morally stronger warriors than most of the men. Thus, the traditional division of labour between the sexes in the nationalist fight was not only used by the opponents of women's emancipation but by the supporters of it as well. In the same way, the notion of the special nature of women could on occasions be used to support violence, rather than suggesting that because of their nature women in the politics would create a more peaceful and equal world.

Markievicz saw herself as a speaker on behald of women[99], whose capacities she firmly believed in. Not only had they been pure and unyielding in their moral and principles but they had taken the responsibilities which men had left behind while on the run. Relating to a motion advocating the dividing of lands and the giving of them to the members of the IRA, she wanted land to be given to women as well. In Markievicz's view, they were as capable of running farms as men "as I have seen demonstrated myself."[100] Now was the time to reward them.

Accordingly, Markievicz supported the motion which proposed giving the vote to young women between 21 and 30 years. The motion was justified by the Declaration of the Easter Rising and by the work of women during the war. Markievicz said that her

> "...first realisation of tyranny came from some chance words spoken in favour of women's suffrage and it raised a question of tyranny it was intended to prevent...That was my first bite, you may say, at the apple of freedom and soon I got on to the other freedoms, freedom to the nation, freedom to the workers. "

The question of votes for women, together with the bigger question of freedom for women and opening all professions to them, had always been important to her. One of the crying wrongs of the world was that women, because of their

---

96 Hanna Sheehy-Skeffington in a letter to Alice Park in California, 25.2.1922, quoted in Levenson, 139-140.
97 The Women of Ireland, *Poblacht na hEireann*,17.1.1922. In fact, de Valera had not got his nationalist ideology from his mother, she had sent her boy from America to be raised with her relatives in Ireland when he was very young.
98 About affinity between men and war and women and peace, see Bethke Elshtain , Jean, Women and War: With a New Epilogue, Chicago 1995.
99 When the sufferings of women, who were understood to be waiting for peace, were used as an argument during the debate on the Treaty, Markievicz forbade the speaker to speak for the women, Dáil Eireann. Debate on the Treaty..., 4.1.1922, 216.
100 Dáil Eireann. Official Report, 1.3.1922, 145.

sex, could be debarred from any position or any right that their brains entitled them to, continued Markievicz.[101]

She accused Griffith – who stood against the motion – for adopting a position similar to that of the English parties: when it suited them, they ran the Suffrage question, but when they were in a position to do something, they always found something more important. Markievicz pointed out that she was speaking on behalf of young women whom she counted in every way as her superiors. They had high ideals, education that had been denied her and furthermore, they had proved their valour during the years of terror, which had dragged them out of their shells more effectively than many years of work in the Franchise Societies. She appealed to the men of IRA to see that justice was done.[102] On another occasion, Markievicz remarked that women everywhere throughout the country were of the opinion that if they were good enough to take part in the fight, they were good enough to vote.[103]

Even though some members of the Dáil felt that the Declaration of the Easter Rising bound them to support the vote for young women,[104] the motion was rejected by 47 votes to 38.[105] The failure was partly due to the uncompromising attitude of women deputies who opposed the Treaty and partly because of the stand Cumann na mBan had taken. The views of these women were thought to represent the views of Irish women in general, which gave the pro-Treaty side a reason for refusing to concede any measure of franchise reform before the election.[106] For instance, Markievicz's opinion on women was in contradiction of the idea of P.S.O'Hegarty, who condemned women in the strongest terms when speaking of the war of independence:

> "...the worst effect was on the women...They took to their hearts every catch-cry and every narrowness and every bitterness, and steadily eliminated from themselves every womanly feeling...War, and the thing which war breeds - intolerance, swagger, hardness, unwomanliness - captured the women, turned them into unlovely, destructive-minded, arid begetters of violence.' "[107]

In the context of the split, female violence could be seen too personal and vindictive, whereas male violence could be given moral stature as a structured activity -war- and thus made less personal and idealised.[108] Irish women, who took the side of the opponents of the Free State were treated more critically after the split than before.

---

101 Dáil Eireann. Official Report, 2.3.1922, 206.
102 Dáil Eireann. Official Report, 2.3.1922, 206-207. She praised the courage of women in Cumann na mBan also in a letter to Miss Donnelly, no date, Joseph McGarrity Papers, MS 17 463, NLI.
103 Markievicz to Eva Gore-Booth, undated letter, PL, 298.
104 For instance Cathal Brugha, Dáil Eireann. Official Report, 2.3.1922, 208.
105 Dáil Eireann. Official report, 214.
106 Ward 1983, 174.
107 Farrell, 227.
108 See the ideas of Bethke Elshtain 1995, 169.

Although the hopes for an independent republic were crushed for the time being, and despite the negative response in the Dáil to motions on social reform -votes for young women or division of lands, for example,- Markievicz continued to work for the rejection of the Treaty. In April 1922 she travelled to America together with Kathleen Barry, who was a member of Cumann na mBan. America had always been important for Irish nationalists and after the Treaty split, both camps sent delegations there.

Markievicz was not too happy to go. She found ships the next worst thing to jail, and thought it awful not to be home at such a moment. She described the difficulties ahead as colossal, and anticipated that for a long time each and all of them would be suspicious of everything and everyone. She wondered if the rank and file would ever trust a leader again. Also, she thought it possible that the Army (the IRA) would "start out doing things on its own." In this context, Markievicz seemed to find comfort only in de Valera, whom she described as a strong person who had always used his influence for unity, toleration, sanity and turning people's minds from a desire for vengeance to higher things.[109] De Valera, who had gone through the Easter Rising and prison was for her the exemplary leader; straigth, true and honourable,[110] even too noble to understand crooks.[111]

Hence, the Treaty Split had strengthened the suspicions concerning the leaders that Markievicz was often expressing earlier. To her step-son she wrote:

> "...I begin to believe that all governments are the same, and that men in power use that power for themselves and are absolutely unscrupulous in their dealings with those who disagree with them..."[112]

It is important to note, however, that despite her mistrust of the leaders, Markievicz always had someone to see place on a higher level than the others. After Connolly, she could point to de Valera, who also met the requirements she set for a nationalist leader: he had fought, suffered and had not compromised his principles.

Opinion among Irish-Americans over the Treaty was just as divided as it was in Ireland. For instance *The Gaelic American* criticized the speeches of de Valera and did not write about Markievicz's trip at all. [113] Even though Markievicz was received with great receptions in different places, [114] she was

---

109 Markievicz to Eva Gore-Booth, On Board the 'Aquitania', 1922, PL, 285-286.

110 Dáil Eireann. Private Sessions of Second Dáil..., 9.1.1922, 362.

111 Markievicz to Joseph McGarrity, no date, Joseph McGarrity Papers, MS 17 627, NLI; about her appreciation towards de Valera, see also C de M, A Note on Eamon de Valera, *Eire*, 13.10.1923. It was common feature for de Valera's followers to beliebe that he was 'straight' and that he met 'crookedness with straight dealing', Coogan 1993, 297.

112 Markievicz to Stanislaus Dunin-Markievicz, New York, May 1922, Ms 13 778, NLI.

113 On de Valera, see e.g. De Valera Fomenting Civil War in Ireland, 15.4.1922; De Valera's Civil War Has Come, 22.4.1922; De Valera Fast Losing Ground in Ireland, 13.5.1922.

114 Markievicz to Eva Gore-Booth, No date, 1922, PL, 287,290.

also called a communist.[115] Markievicz tried to gain understanding for the anti-Treaty side by comparing the Easter Rising with the battle of Bunker Hill in the American War of Independence. True to her republican principles, she celebrated the American Revolution together with the French Revolution as the two greatest struggles in world history.[116] Yet it was important for Americans to understand that the Irish revolution was not completed. Markievicz quoted Liam Mellows who had rejected the Free State by stating that

> "The very words 'Irish Free State' constitute a catch-phrase. It is not a state, it is part of a state; it is not free, because England controls every vital point, it is not Irish, because the people of Ireland established a Republic."[117]

She stressed that the Treaty was unacceptable first and foremost because of the Oath, but also because of Partitition[118], which was a new addition to the obstacles she had tackled during the Dáil debate.

While Markievicz travelled through America, the nationalists strove for unity at home. In May of the year 1922 Collins and de Valera agreed on an electoral pact, whereby there would be a national coalition panel for the Third Dáil, the number of candidates being determined by the existing strength of each faction. After that, a coalition government would be formed. However, the British government would accept neither that idea nor the original constitution as drafted by the provisional government. That forced the Irish, who had sought for compromise, to change the draft for the Constitution to emphasise the British allegiance. Republicans argued against the holding of an election with an out-of-date register and maintained that the proposed consitution of the new state be submitted to the people before the election. In fact, it was only published in detailed form on the morning of the June election itself. In that election, the pro-Treaty panel won 58 seats against 35 for the anti-Treaty group. For the first time Labour took part in an election, winning 17 seats. Farmers and independents won 7 seats each.[119] Markievicz lost her seat for the first time

---

115 See Marreco, 278.
116 C de M, A typescript of speech, Joseph McGarrity Papers, MS 17 463, NLI. Markievicz had used the comparison also a few years earlier, *Cork Examiner*,13.8.1917. The battle of Bunker Hill had been used as an example in the republican press as well, see for example The True Analogy: The American Revolution and the Irish War of Independece, *Irish Bulletin*, 18 and 19.7.1921.
117 Van Voris, 311.
118 C de M, A typescript of speech, Joseph McGarrity Papers, MS 17 463, NLI. She had also condemned Partition in her election address, see Holloway Prison, Countess Markievicz, To The Director of Elections (Sinn Fein), 6 Harcourt St., Dublin, Ireland, 6.12.18, CO 904/164, page 33, (PRO).
119 Ward 1983, 180-181; See Prager, Jeffrey, Building Democracy in Ireland: Political Order and Cultural Integration in a Newly Independent Nation, New York 1986, 71-89. Markievicz descreibed the Register as a farce, Markievicz to Eva Gore-Booth, no date, PL, 298. The Third Dáil – according to the pact – was to be the heir and successor of the First and Second Dáil Eireann, not a Provisional Parliament. However, in May 1922 it was referred to as the Provisional Government, Macardle, 713, 718. Of the Panel Candidates 94 had been returned, 58 pro-Treaty and 36 Republican, ibid, 722. The new constitution was made subordinate ot the Treaty. The King had the power of veto over all legislation. The representative of the Crown was to be styled Governor-General of the Irish Free State, ibid, 723. With the publication of the Constitution cleavages between the pro-Treaty and anti-Treaty sections became wider, ibid, 734.

since she had been an election candidate, possibly because she did not have much time for her campaign.[120]

The result of the elections supported peace with Britain, but did not bring peace in Ireland. After getting back from her trip to America, Markievicz painted a bleak picture of the situation: " Things are awful here. There are more people being killed weekly than before the truce."[121] The anti-Treaty members of the IRA (the Irregulars) had in April taken over the Four Courts in Dublin and were determined to reject the Treaty. Collins described the situation more chaotic than before.[122] The unrest between winners and losers after the elections developed eventually into a Civil War when Collins – facing pressure on both the Irish and the British side – commanded the troops of the Free State Department to attack the Four Courts on 28th June 1922.[123]

The outbreak of the Civil War was a shattering experience for all those who had fought for a new Ireland.[124] The Treaty separated the Irish: rightists from rightists, leftists from leftists and democrats from a democrat. The unity of the independence movement had depended upon pressure from the British.[125] The result of the election did not impress the Irregulars, who were determined to oppose the Treaty with all the power at their disposal. Behind this may well be have lain the assumption that for people raised in the Fenian tradition, who had participated in the Easter Rising and who had witnessed gunmen getting impossible concessions which were unattainable for politicians, the results of elections were "not a big deal."[126] On the other hand, some have pondered on whether there would have been anything more than a relatively minor faction fight had de Valera not thrown his enormous prestige on the anti-Treaty side.[127]

Before the Civil War Markievicz had believed that if the people had enough time before the election on the Treaty they would chose what she considered right. However, she pointed out that unity was possible, but only if there was a common enemy.[128] The common enemy had now disappeared and the people had accepted the Treaty. When the war in Dublin broke out, there was no alternative for her.

Markievicz took part in the fight side by side with Irregulars because she most certainly felt it her duty, even if it meant fighting against former comrades, fellow Irishmen. She was extremely loyal to her commandants, first to Connolly and then to de Valera. She had earlier opened contacts between the Irregulars and the ICA, and accordingly, those members of the ICA who rejected the Treaty, were now helping the Irregulars.[129] In the same way as during the Easter

---

120 Haverty, 215.
121 Markievicz to Eva Gore-Booth, undated letter, PL, 298.
122 Coogan 1990, 315; Hopkinson, 89-91.
123 See Coogan 1990, 330; Hopkinson, 112-118; Fanning, 15.
124 MacCurtain 1989, 242-243.
125 Garvin 1987, 123-124, 141-142.
126 Laffan, Michael, Violence and Terror in Twentieth-Century Ireland: IRB and IRA, in Mommsen, Wolfgang J. & Hirschfeld, Gerhard, Social Protest, Violence and Terror in Nineteenth-and Twentieth-Century Europe, London 1982, 164.
127 Coogan 1993, 295.
128 Markievicz, A typescript of speech, Joseph McGarrity Papers, MS 17 463, NLI.
129 Fox 1943, 222.

Rising, the fight in Dublin only lasted about a week, but the bitter war in other parts of Ireland went on for almost a year. Markievicz, who as a markswoman gained an almost legendary reputation during the few days of struggle,[130] hid in Dublin after the surrender. It is important to note, however, that she fought only for one week and left the violent path after surrendering in Dublin. From thereon she concentrated on fighting with words.

---

130 See O'Faolain, 198; Van Voris, 325; O'Malley, Ernie, The Singing Flame, Dublin 1978, 158. There are some contradictonary assertions about the movements of Markievicz in the year 1922; Hopkinson states incorrectly that she was in America late autumn, Hopkinson, 253; O'Faolain claims that Markievicz left for Glasgow in August 1922 and stayed there for a year, which is also inaccurate, O'Faolain, 199.

Searching for a New Path

Fighting "for liberty"

After the lost Dublin fight, until the late autumn of 1922 Markievicz concentrated on making propaganda against the Free Staters. She wrote, printed and circulated a newspaper and drew political cartoons which were published in the republican papers.[1] In her drawings Markievicz represented a kind of social Darwinist way of thinking: she pictured the Free Staters as dull, untidy, fat and either mean or stupid. Their faces resembled those depicted in British cartoons about the Irish; they had low brows, small eyes and in general almost ape-like facial features. In contrast the republicans had clear features and a good posture and were represented as idealistic heroes.[2]

The message Markievicz spread was simple and clear: the Free Staters, who falsely called themselves the Government, had no moral or legal authority to rule.[3] She felt disillusioned:"...Our people have had a bitter lesson, every pact has been broken & no Free Stater's word is sacred. The air is gradually clearing now, & the removal of their two cornerstones will help much..."[4] By cornerstones she meant Griffith, who died of a brain haemorrhage on 12 August, and Collins, who was killed in an ambush soon after that. Her blunt words imply that she shed no tears for her former comrades. The division had been complete.

Like some other republicans, Markievicz also tried to gain support of her own abroad. She arrived in Scotland on 20 January 1923 and spoke on different occasions under the auspices of Sinn Fein both in Scotland and near London.[5] In Glasgow she helped to edit the republican paper *Eire*.[6] Although she had left in order to work for the Republicans, she seemed to be relieved to be away from Ireland and from the possibility of winding up in prison again. However, she told de Valera that she was willing to do "anything" he ordered her to do either there or in Ireland.[7]

---

1   In late autumn she lost her printing machine in a raid, Sheehy-Skeffington, Hanna, Countess Markievicz, Sheehy-Skeffington Papers, MS 24 189, NLI ; Roper, 99. From now on the term 'republican' refers to the group led by de Valera which opposed the Free State.

2   See for instance the cartoons in *The Republican War Bulletin*, 19.9.1922; 28.9.1922;13.10.1922; Curtis, L.Perry Jr., Apes and Angels:The Irishman in Victorian Caricature, Washington 1971.

3   Markievicz, Constance, By What Authority, *Poblacht na hEireann*, 26.8.1922.

4   Markievicz to Joseph McGarrity, no date, Joseph McGarrity Papers, MS 17 627, NLI.

5   Information about her movements from *Eire* in January-April 1923.

6   The paper was smuggled to Ireland and was circulated by Cumann na mBan and the Fianna, O'Faolain, 199.

7   Art O'Brien Papers, To the President from Countess Markievicz, 26.2.1923, MS 8424, NLI.

In her speeches Markievicz sought to convince her audience of the uncompromising idealism of the Republicans. They were fighting and dying for liberty, something that was deepest and strongest in human nature. She argued that the question was about

> ".... an ancient Gaelic Civilisation [versus] modern, moral anarchy of industrialism... The Gaelic Civilisation was founded on ideas of co-operation and de-centralisation, and the ambitions and talents of the people were directed towards learning art, beauty and holiness which alone can bring happiness and a lasting greatness to a people, and away from the terrible compensation for luxury which had led to all the miseries and vices of an industrial nation..."[8]

Markievicz confronted the Free Staters with arguments similar to those she had employed against the British. Thus, the struggle was not merely about different tactics or diverse opinions but about reconstructing Irish society. Despite her argument that the struggle was about the future of Ireland, she did not base her case against the Free State on social and economic politics – which, in fact, would have been quite difficult at that stage – but stuck with the most important symbol, the oath. She simplified her reasons for opposing the IPP earlier by claiming that her principal objection to it had derived from their taking an oath of allegiance, which she believed to be wrong and unprincipled.[9] She linked her objection to the oath to the teachings of Christianity and pointed out that there were many people in Ireland who had the same standard of honour as she had.[10]

The arguments Markievicz employed were the guiding line for the Republicans after the Civil War. In May 1923 the War ended and the Republicans dumped their arms after months of great difficulties.[11] According to de Valera,

> "Further sacrifice of life would now be vain and continuance of the struggle in arms unwise in the national interest and prejudical to the future of our cause... Other means must be sought to safeguard the nation's right...Seven years of intense effort have exhausted our people...A little time and you will see them recover and rally again to the standard. They will then quickly discover who have been selfless and who selfish - who have spoken truth and who falsehood..."[12]

The assertion that people eventually would come to the side with the Republicans reflected the strong tendency of the Sinn Fein leadership to tell people, what they should think.[13] During the Treaty debate de Valera – who assumed he knew what the Irish people wanted by examining his heart – had

---

8   (Scottish News) Madame Markievicz contrasts the Republic with the "Free State", *Eire*, 10.2.1923
9   C de M, De Valera's Oath – The Truth, *Eire*, 21.4.1923
10   C de M, The 2nd Commandement. Obligation of an Oath, *Sinn Fein*, 29.9.1923.
11   Hopkinson, 221,228.
12   See Moynihan, 114.
13   About this "Robespierrist" vision, see Townshend, 329.

seen that it was possible that "[a] war-weary people will take things which are not in accordance with their aspirations."[14] But Markievicz had found comfort in believing that there was a limit to the extent that people could be cheated.[15] She was confident that if all threat of a future were removed, and people were allowed to vote, they would give a mandate for the Republic. Then, a lasting peace on the basis of "Document No 2" could be made.[16]

In order to enable people to do "the right thing" republicans focused on the coming general elections. They reorganised the party and nominated 87 candidates, most of them on the run.[17] Markievicz, who had during the Civil War accused the Free State of stealing the symbols of the Republic and had called the President of the Executive Council of the Free State, W.T. Cosgrave, a puppet of the English Cabinet[18], now concentrated on proving that in all the elections since 1919 people had voted to send delegates to represent them in the Parliament of the Republic, Dáil Eireann. In the first three elections "the only mandate that we received was to maintain and defend the Republic with our lives. In the last election the mandate given by the people was for peace." Furthermore, Markievicz stubbornly clung to the idea that people were only temporarily distracted: she declared that the people believed they were voting for delegates to Dáil Eireann, not some other Parliament.[19] She broadened her criticism of the policy of her opponents by claiming that the Free State Constitution was drawn up to prevent the development of Gaelic ideals in Ireland.[20]

The success of the Sinn Feiners in the election was greater than expected; they gained 8 further seats and now held 44 seats in Free State Parliament. However, the people cast even more voters for the Free Staters, who had established a new party, Cumann Na nGaedheal. They gained 63 seats.[21] The election did not change the political situation. Markievicz, who was one of those elected, refused along with other Sinn Feiners to take her seat in parliament because of the oath of allegiance.

Nonetheless, Markievicz intended to continue to work outside the Parliament and urged Sinn Fein to put its programme into "immediate operation." She declared that a co-operative idea for building up of a Gaelic state should be adopted, instead of the English system of competition.[22] Her demands were the same as before the Civil War, even though the situation had changed

---

14   Dáil Debate on Treaty, 19.12.1921, 24. Also later, in 1925, de Valera asserted that people had not declared their will "as we know it to be their will", de Valera in 18 March 1925, quoted in Dunphy, 65; Coogan 1993,362.
15   Stop Thief by Madame Markievicz, *Eire*, 10.2.1923.
16   C de M, An Open Letter to the Independent Labour Party, 28.4.1923, *Eire*. She also expressed similar ideas in Scotland, see Madame in Scotland, *Eire*, 14.4.1923.
17   Van Voris, 330.
18   Stop Thief by Madame Markievicz, *Eire*, 10.2.1923.
19   Madame Markievicz Challenges O'Higgins, *Eire*, 7.7.1923 . She had used similar arguments in the previous year, see Markievicz, Constance, By What Authority, *Poblacht na hEireann*, 26.8.1922.
20   *Sinn Fein*, 18.8.1923.
21   Lee 1989, 94-95.
22   Great Dublin Rally, *Sinn Fein*, 8.9.1923,

dramatically. There was no real chance of ignoring the Free State and creating an alternative goverment. But to weigh the real chances and then propose a new programme had never been Markievicz's style. Her involvement with politics had started as a member of a tiny group seeking influence without any hope of real success in the near future. Now, when the Irish were divided in two, she again and again talked and wrote about her vision in the hope that it eventually would gain support.

"What Irish Republicans Stand For"

In the Treaty elections of June 1922 the republicans did not present any economic or social programme for the future. Sinn Fein had until 1922 symphatised with the methods and goals of co-operative movement, but after that time its members – whether Free Staters of Republicans – did little to encourage it.[23] In contrast to the lack of interest in social issues shown by the republicans, Labour had devised a moderate reformist programme, with their goal the creation of a republic run on the lines of a co-operative commonwealth. The aims of Labour therefore represented those of Markievicz, but there was an essential difference: Labour was pro-Treaty, and before the elections some republicans had argued that it was also pro-British.[24] In 1923 also the election programme of republicans paid only vague attention to unemployment, which they felt was a problem that could be solved by public works and support for home industries.[25]

As in the period before the Civil War, Markievicz sought to combine the goals of Labour and Sinn Fein. She had appealed to Labour both in England and in Ireland to help crush the Free State.[26] Her goals resembled those of the executed Liam Mellows, who in autumn of 1922 had demanded the translation of the Democratic Programme of 1919 into something definite, and who had seen it as important that Irish Labour should be kept on the side of the republicans.[27] Together with Mellows, Markievicz had in vain appealed to the IRA to activate a social policy.[28]

In a pamphlet, consisting of her writings for the British Labour paper *Forward*, Markievicz described in more careful detail what was the Republic that she wanted. She quoted James Connolly:

---

23   Mitchell 1974, 226.
24   Mitchell 1974, 152- 55; Anderson 1994, 120.
25   Mitchell 1974, 188.
26   She anticipated in a gloomy tone that while the republicans were being flogged today, the workers would be flogged tomorrow, *Sinn Fein*, 17.8.1923; 'Flogging Bill' meant Public Safety Act, which legalised the further detention of those in captivity,Macardle, 862. In Britain, Markievicz appealed to the Independent Labour Party. If it desired peace with Ireland, it should call on the British government to stop promoting war and should cease financing the Free State "Junta." C de M, An Open Letter to the Independent Labour Party, *Eire*, 28.4.1923.
27   English 1994, 52-53.
28   O'Connor 1992, 125.

"The conquest of Ireland has meant the social and political servitude of the Irish masses, and therefore the reconquest of Ireland must mean the social as well as the political independence from servitude of every man, woman and child."

Markievicz dedicated her leaflet to the memories of Wolfe Tone, Mitchell, Lawler [Lalor] and James Connolly, to whom she felt indebted for the faith and the knowledge that inspired it.

The quotation indicated once again that for Markievicz the struggle was not merely about political sovereignty but also about reconstructing Irish society in social terms. She saw the Free State as a further attempt to impose the English social and economic system on the Irish people, who "cling instinctively and with a passionate loyalty to the ideals of a better civilisation, the tradition of which is part of their subconscious spiritual and mental selves" and who were developing a co-operative commonwealth in Ireland. For that reason, claimed Markievicz, the Free State could never be acceptable to the people of Ireland. Moreover, that was the key that opened the door to a thorough understanding of the Irish question.[29]

Depending on studies of Irish history by Alice Stopford Green and James Connolly, Markievicz reminded her readers of the ancient democratic Irish clan organisation, which, according to Connolly, foreshadowed "the more perfect organisation of the free society of the future." [30] Drawing on the history and the subconscious of the Irish people, Markievicz presented the Republic as an ideal answer to their expectations.[31] She supported her claim by pointing out that the proclamation of the Easter Rising had been based on Gaelic ideals, which were further emphasized and developed in the Democratic Programme which she claimed had been drawn up by de Valera. In reality, de Valera had no part in devising the programme but obviously Markievicz wanted on the one hand to support de Valera, the leader of republicans and on the other hand, she probably wanted to damage Labour, whose representatives sat in the Free State Parliament. Furthermore, Markievicz sought to add de Valera's glory by drawing attention to the fact that he had refused a rise in his salary as President. In the same way, during the period of shadow government, the higher officials had received less money than in any country of the world – except Switzerland –, stressed Markievicz.[32]

The question of salaries and wages served to underline the idealistic and non-materialist nature of those who had worked in the Republican Government. In a similar vein Markievicz championed the Republican Government which, according to her, had become step by step de facto Government of Ireland. She picked out two examples to show the egalitarian and socially conscious nature of Dáil Eireann. Firstly, she drew attention to the republican justices, who

29   Markievicz, Constance, What Irish Republicans Stand For, Glasgow 1923, 1.
30   Ibid., 1.
31   Ibid.,1- 2.
32   Ibid., 2; See also Markievicz speaking during the Republican election campaign of de Valera, who without profit, stood loyal to the cause, Sinn Fein,17.8.1923.

were elected in compliance with "the old Gaelic custom", which meant choosing persons irrespective of sex or age. Another example she chose concerned rents, which were kept lower than in Britain.[33]

From celebrating the ideals behind the Dáil and pointing out its achievements in preventing an economic war in rural districts, Markievicz moved on to criticise the prevailing situation. Not surprisingly, she laid the primary blame on Britain, which had for centuries prevented the industrial development of Ireland. Accordingly, she was left with a small population and with little work for them. If things were left as they were, foreign enterprises and big farmers would capture and ruin their smaller and weaker Irish competitors.[34]

Yet there was another course, "the only sane course", the course of co-operation. Farmers had learned the lesson from the IAOS, remarked Markievicz, and they must now be taught to extend the principle that had organised the creameries to every branch of farming. They should also include the workers and shopkeepers in their co-operative societies. With the whole country organised, they should guard against the conquest of Ireland by foreign capital in order to prevent the development of the kind of villages that had created the "Black Country".[35] What she was advocating had been the economic policy of the Republic, asserted Markievicz. She admitted that few realised or understood it, but the sub-conscious soul of the nation instinctively recognised and approved it. Similarly, the British understood it, since they had wrecked and burnt the co-operative creameries.[36]

True to her black-and-white style, Markievicz described those opposing the co-operative schemes as individual climbers, drones and bloodsuckers. They were found both in the British garrison and among "renegade Irishmen" who were content to enrich themselves through an alliance with capitalism and imperialism and the government of Britain. She believed that the men who induced the people of Ireland to accept the Free State, did so, because they saw opportunities to grasp wealth and to accumulate power by so doing. [37] Fellow republicans used harsh language as well. Ireland was seen as ruled by a British garrison, speaking through the Free State parliament, whose Senate was seen as yet one more example of how the Free State was attempting to keep in step with the manners, customs, and values of the British Commercial interests were seen to be on the side of the Treaty. [38]

Thus the obstacles for giving expression to the special national characteristics of the Irish were found to spring from external causes, from the uncompleted nature of the struggle for freedom. From early on, Markievicz had articulated

---

33   Markievicz 1923, 2-3.
34   Ibid, 3-4.
35   Ibid., 4.
36   Ibid., 4. Also AE had expressed his concern at the attacks against co-operative societies, see AE, Thought for British Co-operators. Being a further demand for a Public Enquiry into the Attacks on Co-operative Societies in Ireland, Dublin 1920.
37   Markievicz 1923, 4-5,8.
38   Sean Lemass in February 1925, quoted in Dunphy, 64; Todd Andrews, in Andrews, C.S., Man of No Property, Dublin 1982, 13, quoted in Dunphy, 42; English 1994, 52-53.

both the political and social aspects of co-operation; the idea of self-help –
which was an essential part of both co-operative ideas and the ideas of Sinn
Fein – had been incorporated into her thought and activism at every level.
Markievicz had declared that one should 'live an Irish life. " The Irish would
live their Irish lives, would find their material fulfillment, if they focused on
supporting home industries and organising factories, shops and farms together,
on co-operative lines.

Markievicz did not highlight the activity of the industrial sector or
governmental support as a way of realising the co-operative ideal. In that she
agreed with AE and Aodh de Blacam, who after 1918 became the leading
spokesmen for co-operation. Both of them emphasized the small rural enterprise
and its individual aspects while Labour looked to the urban industrial sector
and argued the need for state participation in the realization of the co-operative
ideal. On the contrary, AE and de Blacam did not see this as being necessary.[39]
Markievicz also understood the question as one concerning the methods and
will of the Irish alone; unlike Connolly, she did not see the development of the
international economy as a precondition for Ireland.[40] Her nationalist
protectionism ignored the influence of international events, even though she
condemned the power of international finance[41] and demanded a knowledge
of the world economy in order to pursue an alternative policy to that of the
Free State.[42]

In her pamphlet, Markievicz attempted to prove that the creation of the Free
State was not a fortunate development for the working classes, either. She
maintained that its policies encouraged British capitalism instead of trying to
develop Ireland's own industries and trade. It created unemployment in areas
where labour was active and well-organised, and provided employment where
labour was unorganised. Continuing, Markievicz drew attention to the fact that
large contracts had been sent away from Ireland to England,in contradiction of
what the international Labour movement stood for.[43]

Moreover, the Free State was not a "Half-Way House" to a Republic, as,
according to Markievicz, could be seen by looking at the Constitution. She
went through the different articles, and condemned them one by one. A further
proof of moral decline was the raising of the salaries of the Governor-General,
the President and Ministers, while other wages were on a downward path, and
newspapers reported nothing but strikes and misery. The "Flogging Bill" brought
Ireland back to the times of the Penal Laws, asserted Markievicz. The calculated
policy of the Free State was to root the social and economic system of England
in Irish soil, and to eliminate all Labour-Republican ideas by force.[44] Markievicz

---

39   Mitchell 1974, 135.
40   According to Connolly, international competition would force the peasants to see the limits of
     individual ownership, Patterson, 9.
41   See letter from Markievicz to McGarrity, no date, McGarrity Papers, MS 17 463, NLI; also C
     de M, The Fianna, Eire, 9.6.1923.
42   C de M, Our Economic Policy, *Sinn Fein*, 2.2.1924.
43   Markievicz 1923, 6-7.
44   Ibid., 8. The 11 articles of Free State Constitution, acknowledging the king, were a part of
     republican folklore, see Murphy, 158; see also e.g. *Sinn Fein* 1.9.1923 and "Flashpoints " -
     The Free State Constititution, which touched on several articles in the Constitution.

labelled the Free Staters unprincipled, unidealistic materialists – a powerful accusation when one bears in mind the stereo-typed juxtaposition of the idealistic Irish and the materialistic British. It is important to note that she condemned the negotiators of the Treaty, not the people who had voted for it after being led on to a sidetrack. To lead them in the right way, she once again went into the streets to protest against the policy of those in power.

Reorganising republican opposition among women and Na Fianna Eireann

After the Civil War and the elections Markievicz continued her work in a new arena. She collected names for a petition for the release of the prisoners on behalf of the "Women's Prisoners' Defence League" (WPDL) which had been established in 1922 by Maud Gonne and an elderly suffragette and socialist Charlotte Despard. The organisation held Sunday meetings to protest against overcrowding and brutality in jails, mounted vigils outside prison walls and traced missing men and women. The women, who were relatives of the prisoners, became an institution in Dublin and embarrassed the Free State government. [45]

Markievicz went around Dublin with three girls who gave out bills and spoke to crowds wherever they gathered.[46] The radical and open propaganda of WPDL against the Free State most obviously satisfied Markievicz, who had protested in the streets against the visit of the King over ten years before. Her actions also echoed those promoted at Sinn Fein's Annual Convention in 1923. After the lost and bitter Civil War Sinn Fein stressed the need for passive resistance, which had been an essential part of its policy from the very beginning. The Convention paid particular attention to prisoners and propaganda,[47] which matched well with the activities of Markievicz at this period. In the next year, de Valera was also reported as saying that publicity should be put before everything else. [48] However, her activities with the WPDL led to the arrest of Markievicz. She was taken to an Internment Camp, where she went on hunger-strike. At the same time thousands of republican prisoners were using the same tactic, but after two prisoners died, the hunger-strikers decided to stop. Luckily for Markivicz, that happenend when she had only reached her third day and she was released just before Christmas.Given her previous comments on hunger-strikes, however, it must have taken a lot of personal courage to start one.[49]

---

45   Ward 1983, 190.
46   Markievicz to Eva Gore-Booth, Undated (Nov. or Dec. 1923), PL, 281. She was disappointed at the fact that no-one continued her work while she was away, Marreco, 293.
47   Sinn Fein Ard-Fheis, *Sinn Fein*, 20.10.1923. In July 1923 de Valera said that the present purpose was now to work through the Sinn Fein organisation, to devote themselves to social reform and to education, and to developing the economic and material strength of the nation, Macardle, 863.
48   Coogan 1993, 362.
49   Markievicz was arrested on 20 November 1923, Van Voris, 331. She told that she had not suffered at all, that she had been perfectly happy and had no regrets, Markievicz to Eva Gore-Booth, 1923, PL, 304-305; about her fears, see PL, 304 and letter to Eva Gore-Booth,

By collecting names and speaking on the streets against the Free State Markievicz was organising resistance in a similar way to that used before the Easter Rising. It has been asserted that protesting in the streets and going on hunger-strike were out-dated and histrionic methods in the Ireland of the 1920s.[50] Yet they were now the only possible ways of drawing attention to the problems of the prevailing situation.

In the activities of Markievicz, women were constantly an important group. In her view, their action had no limits set by radiation: one of her cartoons showed a woman situated on a roof with a gun in her hand. However, the text of the picture – "With the Dublin Brigade I.R.A"[51] - showed that the woman in the picture was not just anyone, but Markievicz herself. Another of the drawings illustrated the complexity there was regarding the proper place of women. In the picture she showed a vision of "a republican home" where a man, holding a rifle was about to kiss a little child that her mother held in her arms. The mother said: "Kiss daddy goodbye, darling, he's going off to fight for the Republic."[52] The latter picture demonstrated better than the former the traditional view relating to the role of women. Although they were prepared to labour night and day, and were often more capable than men of detecting evil and treason, they were finally represented as auxiliaries – albeit powerful auxiliaries – to the IRA.[53] The role of women of Cumann na mBan resembles in many ways women's participation in other national liberation struggles.[54]

A speech Markievicz gave in connection with the reorganising of Cumann na mBan, seemed to be somewhat at odds with the passive policies the republicans – at least through their party Sinn Fein – were currently supposed to be pursuing. Markievicz reminded her audience that no one knew when they might be attacked again: "Peace is beautiful and we want peace; but we cannot shirk the fight if it is the only way to win..." She bade the women to feel encouraged by the success that would ultimately come and pointed out the weak position of the corrupt Free State Administration, and the problems within the Free State government and the army. [55]

However, evoking a combative spirit in an organisation that was a part of the IRA, was not the main issue for Markievicz. Once again, she pointed out the need to work, because "we cannot afford to sit still and do nothing..." She

26.9.1917, PL, 295. After the hunger strike, she had wanted to hang out wanted to hang out Red Cross flags from the windows and to make a propaganda display in the temporary hospital run by Maud Gonne, but this idea was abandoned, Fox 1935, 19-20.

50   Haverty, 218.
51   C de M, *The Republican War Bulletin*, 3.10.1922.
52   C de M, A Republican Home, *The Republican War Bulletin*, 5.10.1922.
53   The Women of Ireland, anonymous, *The Republican War Bulletin*,5.10.1922
54   For instance in Cyprus women, who joined the extremist nationalist Greek-Cypriot group EOKA B in the 70's,acted as foils for EOKA fighters. They did not carry weapons, but transported them. They carried information and acted as messengers, and there were a number of women's units who threw or carried bombs after dark, In the public consciousness, however, the image of women that predominated during this period was the one of 'mother of our young martyrs', a tragic,black-clothed woman, willing to offer her sons, for the motherland., Anthias, Floya, Women and Nationalism in Cyprus, in Yuval-Davis (ed), 159-160.
55   Meeting of Dublin branches of Cumann na mBan, *Eire*, 31.5.1924. Markievicz was referring to the army mutiny crisis that had weakened the government in March 1924.

wanted the women to be prepared for elections; they should study social, civic and economic problems and also learn the Irish language. They should focus on making concrete suggestions on how work could be provided for the unemployed. One effective way to do this method was, of course, to build up co-operatives. The new plans of Cumann na mBan still depended on the old programme; the members were given military and physical drill and classes in first aid. However, more emphasis was put on other, less military activities such as forming a choir or camogie and rounders teams and giving lectures on historical, social and economic subjects.[56]

Appealing to the women of the Cumann to relieve unemployment by establishing co-operatives related to Markievicz's demand during the previous elections; that the economic programme of Sinn Fein should become a reality. Taking the "only sane course" was not merely the task of Sinn Fein, but of every individual as well. Rather than just being ready for battle – despite the rather militaristic tone in which she chose to begin her speech –, being prepared should also mean that one should educate oneself and act in a way that would promote co-operative Gaelic activity. Thus eventually, individuals would together form a powerful group that could work for the reconstruction of the whole of society.

Besides helping in reorganising the women's organisation whose president she was, Markievicz considered it important to strengthen Fianna na Eireann. She stressed the educational views of the former Fianna organiser Liam Mellows and pointed out the need for great intellects rather than just men of military ability.[57] The work with the Fianna was important to her; she said that they were working very hard, and that they had to start again from the very beginning – with nothing.[58]

In order to make the "new" Fianna as inviting as possible, an appeal, signed by Markievicz, emphasized that it was now being organised on an

> "...entirely new basis, making it a complete scouting and educational organisation, similar to the Boy Scout organisation throughout the world, teaching and training the boys to be good citizens and good Irishmen..."[59]

On the other hand this Irish organisation was seen as "a counterforce to the Imperialist English scout movement", which had been recruiting members in the schools. That the boys of Ireland should be banded into an organisation whose outlook was Irish in every aspect, was considered a "matter of urgent national importance."[60] Furthermore, the stigma of protestantism was attached to the other scout movements. Catholic boys were advised to join Na Fianna Eireann and Catholic girls should turn to similar organisations, both of which

---

56   Meeting of Dublin branches of Cumann na mBan, *Eire*, 31.5.1924.
57   Fianna Eireann. Report of the 12th Annual Ard-Fheis, *Sinn Fein*, 29.3.1924.
58   Markievicz to McHugh in Glasgow, 1.12. 1925, Constance Markievicz Papers, MS 13 778, NLI.
59   *An Phoblacht*, 20.11.1925.
60   *An Phoblacht*, 27.11.1925

should be kept strictly educational and breath "the spirit of uncompromising Nationality."[61]

Markievicz had taken a new interest in the girls movement during the Civil War when she started the"Clan Maeve", an organisation for Irish girls along the lines of the Fianna.[62] It was, however, a one-off attempt which never bore fruit, even later, when the reorganising of the Fianna was under way. Possibly it had been her trust in the pure morals of the female sex, which she had seen as the explanation of the unyielding attitude of the anti-Treaty women, had provided the impulse to start something new for the girls. Boys or girls, the goal was no longer to re-establish the lost Irish Republic. Now the object was to be pursued on an individual level by constructing model citizens. The need for education had also been articulated even before the Easter Rising and had been stressed after the Anglo-Irish War.[63] Following the goals of Cumann na mBan, members should now be occupied with educating themselves mentally rather than militarily.

The Progressive programme of Sinn Fein

The Republicans, who had withdrawn from parliament, had established a shadow Government in the autumn of 1922. This "Second Dáil" consisted of the Sinn Feiners elected at elections, though de Valera admitted that it could not function in reality. What mattered for some republicans, was merely that it had been kept alive.[64] No Department of Labour was established, and Markievicz had no role in the Cabinet. In addition, the republicans who formed Sinn Fein wanted to gain the support of the people. The tone of de Valera in summer 1924 was not a new one: quoting Wolfe Tone he addressed the need to unite Ireland, something which could happen only through the establishment of the Republic and only when the Irish were able to choose what they wanted without any threat from outside.[65]

The goals of Sinn Fein were, nevertheless, more elaborate than before. The party stood for a progressive policy on economic and social issues; its goals were to improve working conditions, impose tariffs, divide large land-holdings and establish a national housing authority. Nearly all of these suggestions derived from Labour. De Valera emphasized the essential duty of the state to see that work was supplied for its citizens and declared his allegiance to the Democratic

---

61   To the People of Ireland, no date, anonymous, NLI.
62   Fox 1935, 19.
63   Tone Commemoration Number. *Fianna: The Official Organ of Fianna Eireann*, June 1922, Vol. I No 1,3.
64   Murphy, 140; Hopkinson, 187; Macardle, 779-780. On September 9th 1922 Cosgrave was elected President and he appointed his Ministry, Macardle, 783. In December 1923 the Irish Free State came into existence officially. The Members of the Provisional Parliament met as the Lower House of the Oireachtas -the Parliament of the Irish Free State. This House continued to designate itself "the Dàil", Macardle, 820.
65   Moynihan, Speaking in Ennis, 15 August 1924, 115-116.

Programme of the First Dáil.[66] In addition, Sinn Fein again articulated its support for co-operatives.[67]

Labour, which shared many of the goals of Sinn Fein, had not been able to gain more support in the Free State, nor had the trade union movement been prepared to attack conservative Government policies.[68] Moreover, Labour had to struggle with a split in the trade union movement after Jim Larkin returned to Ireland in April 1923. Markievicz regarded the split as deplorable and strongly criticised Larkin, whom she had previously greatly respected:

> " He has no policy as far as one can see, and is conducting a very vicious personal vendetta against the individual men of the Labour Party. They reply in the same vicious personal manner, and meantime strikes are lost and the movement is suffering...[Larkin's] present attitude...is.:.the attitude of a child in a temper who tries to break up all the things it wants to play with and cannot get..."[69]

According to Markievicz, some Sinn Feiners saw in the split an advantage for their own party. Personally, she saw no such thing, and feared that the whole Labour organisation could finally break.[70] It was plausible that members of Sinn Fein counted on winning back those who voted Labour, if their programme showed enough concern on social and economic issues. The republicans directly attacked the Labour Party by reminding workers of the example of Connolly - the militant nationalist and socialist.[71]

Markievicz, who had urged Sinn Fein to put forward social and economic policies, suggested studying the social and economic systems of the past and present in order to create a policy that was efficient. Depending on the conception of the economy that nationalists had in common, she spoke in favour of developing home industries and supported protection wherever it was proved to be the best policy. However, she also pointed out the need to examine what "progressive and co-operative lines" meant.[72]

In Markievicz's view, the need for a new economic policy was evident everywhere:

> "There is starvation on every side, not only among the very poor, but among the people who were quite well off...All the small businesses here are heading for ruin, and the farmers are in a bad way. The list of bankrupts is something appalling. The list of highly paid officials for whom jobs are made by those at present in power is daily increasing. To meet these expenses the old-age pensioners have been docked 1 s per week off their pensions, as well as their bag of coal per fortnight. Taxes are awful, food prices are daily rising and rents are wicked..."[73]

---

66   Mitchell 1974, 235.
67   Sinn Fein Standing Committee Minutes, 15.1.1925, 2B/82/117, p.111, NAI.
68   Brown, 81.
69   Markievicz to Charles Diamond, 9.6.1924, P 5482, NLI.
70   Markievicz to Charles Diamond, 9.6.1924, P 5482, NLI.
71   Mitchell 1974, 174.
72   C de M, Our Economic Policy, *Sinn Fein*, 2.2.1924.
73   Markievicz to Stanislaus Dunin-Markievicz, August 1924, Constance Markievicz Papers, MS 13 778, NLI

Visiting Limerick a couple of months before had given her the same feeling:

"...I never saw worse slums or met nicer people. Don't talk to me about politics, tell me how to get bread for the children was a very general cry. If one could only get the people to understand that politics ought to be nothing more or less than the organisation of food, clothes, housing & transit of every unit of the nation one would get a lot further. Also if they would only learn and watch their leaders, aye, and distrust them, fear them even more than their opponents... If the people would only read, study and make up their minds as to where they wanted to go and as to how to get there, we would easily win out, but alas, it's always their impulse to get behind some idol, let him do all the thinking for them and then be surprised when he leads them all wrong." [74]

Although Markievicz described the work situation in Limerick as desperate, she at the same time believed that the "tide has really turned," but it meant a lot of work and no rest. Each by-election went better and they had high hopes.[75] To improve the situation of her party, she spoke about Sinn Fein programme regarding unemployment and pensions.[76] She attacked the Free State Minister of Home Affairs Kevin O'Higgins, who held that the promises of Sinn Fein concerning housing and pensions were unattainable in prevailing conditions. Markievicz asserted that workers, small farmers and small business people were facing ruin and starvation. She described the actions of the Free State as anti-nationalist and anti-Christian and referred to the words of Pope Leo XIII which set as the purpose of the government of the state the bringing of benefits to the people over whom it was placed.[77]

Markievicz was impatient with the Irish people, who did not – as they to her mind should – see the connection between everyday misery and politics. She was concerned about the question of how power could be evenly distributed and how "the foolish and uneducated" could be avoid being grouped into unthinking battalions, which was something that "all lovers of freedom" were looking for.[78] While a "life is politics" remained as a guide line in her work, she found it hard to understand why the people did not simply take action of their own, instead of passively forsaking politics. Yet she wanted to believe that people would finally open their eyes and would finish the work of Easter Week once they saw that the "English rule us still."[79]

Markievicz's criticism of the policy of Free State did not derive from mere political opposition. The truth was that economic and social issues were not of primary importance to the Cosgrave government. In the Constitution, those elements were almost left out. The objectives of Pearse included in the Democratic Programme were rejected as a "Communist Doctrine."Government

---

74   Markievicz to Charles Diamond, 9.6.1924, P 5483, NLI.
75   Markievicz to Eva Gore-Booth, Limerick 1924, PL,298.
76   Sinn Fein, 22.11.1924; *Sinn Fein*, 10.1.1925.
77   C de M, Definite Reply to Mr. O'Higgins, *Sinn Fein*, 15.11.1924
78   Markievicz to Eva Gore Booth, 1923, Pl, 303.
79   Markievicz, Constance de, Some Women in Easter Week, PL, 41.

policy since autumn 1923 had been to cut down public spending and deflation; it demanded a lowering of salaries and benefits; a cut in pensions and in the salaries of teachers as well as in unemployment benefit. In fact, unemployment continued to be a serious problem and was little helped by the small public work programme. The Government did not grasp the educational or housing issues promoted by Labour and considered its suggestions unrealistic.[80] The policies of Cumann na nGaedheal favoured large farmers at the small holders' expense and in the summer of 1923 there were strikes and fights against the wage cuts.[81]

As the Government gave full effect to its policy of keeping wages down and giving the current assistance to agriculture only, poverty escalated, both unemployment and emigration rose, and the trade-union movement was greatly weakened. The Government refused to contemplate state intervention to bring about even the mildest of social reform as a means of alleviating the economic plight ot the poor. In north Dublin the slum conditions were among the worst in Europe, with high infant mortality rates. The Free State government started to relieve distress only in the 1930s. [82] Markievicz, who lived in Dublin and lamented "the appalling poverty that meets one everywhere,"[83] daily met the deterioration of the poor, which reinforced her view of the Free State's failure.

Connolly – A Catholic Republican and Socialist

As for Markievicz, the new course of politics entailed depending on the teachings of James Connolly. In June 1924 she was busily finishing her pamphlet on him and was thrilled that Sinn Fein intended to publish it. She took it as a sign that "at last everybody is slowly beginning to move ahead on the right lines."[84]

Markievicz was careful to place Connolly in the republican camp by quoting his own definition of himself as a Republican and a Socialist. Furthermore, she explained his class consciousness not by reference to his socialism but to his nationalism. Hence it was "great and self-sacrificing love for the men and women of his class, which was co-existent with and co-ordinate with a great love of his country." Markievicz stressed that for Connolly the freedom of Ireland did not mean mere political freedom, which would leave the Irish enslaved mentally to English ideals of civilisation, and enslaved materially under the English capitalist system. [85] She ignored class issues, which some nationalists like Aodh de Blacam had seen to lie behind the Irish Question. However, he also explained the class struggle in Ireland as a nationalist struggle

---

80   Mitchell, 177–202.
81   Dunphy, 53. At the same time the Labour Party refused to give political leadership to outbursts of defensive agitation by sections of the working class, Dunphy, 55.
82   Dunphy, 56–59; Brown, 13-16; Fanning, 100. About housing and poverty, see also Dunphy, 99,101.
83   Markievicz to Eva Gore-Booth in 1923, PL, 304.
84   Markievicz to Charles Diamond, 9.6.1924, Synge Papers, P 5482, NLI.
85   Markievicz, Constance, James Connolly's Policy and Catholic Doctrine, 1924, 4.

where the only class which stood in the way of freedom was the class which stood for the Union.[86]

Regarding the present situation, Markievicz painted a bleak picture of the struggle of the poor and the life of unemployed fathers, hungry mothers and children living in one-room tenements. She quoted Connolly's passionate words that Ireland, as distinct from her people, was nothing to him.[87] Maintaining the status quo meant maintaining the miseries and injustices among a large percentage of the poor. Ignoring their sufferings contradicted the Christian standpoint as well.[88]

Drawing on Connolly's writings Markievicz strove to explain what could be the alternative to the present situation. She was quick to point out that what Connolly had suggested was not state socialism or socialism deriving from foreign theories, but simply "application of the social principle which underlay the Brehon laws of our ancestor." Accordingly, Connolly was not a disciple of Marx or any man, but stood for the socialism of James Connolly and of nobody else.[89]

In order to achieve an ideal situation, where workers would have co-operative control over the machinery of production and where the state would be a social instrument in the hands of its men and women organised into unions; those same workers would then form the industrial administration of the national government of the country[90]. But for this to be achieved, mental development would be necessary. Markievicz highlighted the need for education and declared that Connolly dreamt of schools where the "ideals and principles of Christ would be the guiding rule, where culture, refinement and learning would be striven for." [91] The schools Markivicz envisioned resembled those of Pearse which had blended together nationalism and the Catholic faith.

Obviously noting the need to stress the differences between Connolly's policy and those of recent Russian revolution, Markievicz pointed out that the contemplated development was not likely to be sudden, rather it would come through the gradual reorganisation and reconstruction of the whole system of production and of distribution, through organising the co-operatives, the one big union and the local boards and political machine.[92] Markievicz, who promoted co-operative principles, reminded her readers that Connolly had praised the work of the IAOS and that he had pointed out the necessity of co-operation between the town workers and working farmers.[93]

By comparing the ideas of Griffith and Connolly Markievicz sought yet again to demonstrate the difference between the politics of the Free Staters and those of the Republicans. She asserted that Griffith, despite his "original

---

86 de Blacam, Aodh, What Sinn Fein Stands For, Dublin 1921, 107.
87 Markievicz 1924, 4-6.
88 Markievicz 1924, 34, 41.
89 Markievicz 1924, 3, 7-9.
90 Markievicz 1924, 7-8.
91 Markievicz 1924, 31-33.
92 Markievicz 1924, 29.
93 Markievicz 1924, 16.

scheme" to build up "a Free Ireland", merely wanted to revive the status of 1782 – the time of the Grattan parliament – and that his policies, which aimed to create opportunities for Irish businessmen, in fact meant accepting the British system. In opposition to that, Connolly had set out to do away with British capitalism and imperialism and to gaelicise Ireland. [94] Focusing hostile attention on Griffith in particular was common among Socialist republicans. They were convinced, like Markievicz, that capitalist interests and Irish republican aspirations were fundamentally incompatible.[95] However, it is essential to remember that in the case of Markievicz, this rejection of Griffith only occured after he accepted the Treaty.

Markievicz strove to validate Connolly's resolute republicanism by claiming that his "internationalism" – by which she obviously meant the idea of international socialism – meant only a "Free Federation of Free Nations to maintain international affairs so as to avoid wars." Hence, in her view, internationalism supported a world consisting of nation-states. To emphasize the nationalism of Connolly she defined it as the inspiration of his life, as "the great whole that included his social, political and international politics." Again, Markievicz pointed out that Connolly had wanted Ireland to be built on the foundation of its traditions and on the insticts of the Irish people that were thrown up in each popular movement and inspired the people to self-sacrifice. She crystallised the meaning of Connolly by defining his writings as "the gospels of our Nationality".[96] Markievicz's words clearly reflected her own ideas on the relationship between nationalism and socialism as intertwined in the Irish historical heritage and as the guiding light for the politics of the present, which should secure the formation of a socially, economically and culturally distinctive nation-state.

However, to portray Connolly as a moderate socialist and as a devoted nationalist was not enough in Ireland, where, according to the words of Markievicz herself, most Catholics shuddered at the word 'socialist'. [97] No wonder, therefore, that she took pains to assure her readers that the teachings of Connolly and the Catholic Church did not contradict each other. The relationship of Connolly to the Church had been dealt with earlier by two Catholic priests, whose writings Markievicz referred to.[98] Her concern was also a reflection of that current of mild anti-clericalism in the separatist movement, a kind of a belief that the priests were failing in their duty by not supporting purist republicans wholeheartedly.[99]

---

94 Markievicz 1924, 28-29.
95 English 1994, 32; about nationalists condemning capitalism, see also Daly, Mary E., 1994, 84.
96 Markievicz 1924, 42-46.
97 Markievicz 1924, 6.
98 Rev. P. Coffery, James Connolly's Campaign against Capitalism, in the Light of Catholic Teaching, *Catholic Bulletin*, vol. 20; The Social Teaching of James Connolly by Lambert McKenna, edited with commentary and introduction by Thomas J. Morrissy, SJ, Dublin 1991.
99 See Garvin 1987, 127-128; Ward 1983, 284, note 56. During the Civil War the Catholic Church had excommunicated all Republicans, Ward 1983, 192.

Markievicz lamented the contemporary situation in the churches and sects, which according to her were controlled by juntas of priests and clergy who acted in a way that Christ would have disliked.[100] She criticised the representatives of Catholic Church during the election campaigns for taking the Free State side and emphasized that she herself was speaking as a Catholic.[101] Markievicz carefully expounded out Connolly's critique of those sections of the church who took part in politics, thus avoiding any general critique of the Catholic religion itself. She referred to the Encyclical of Pope Leo XIII, which had approved the principle of working men's unions and pointed out that according to Connolly, the Holy See did not in principle wish to prevent a single Catholic from working for the bettering of his conditions.[102]

Markievicz's view of socialism has been criticised as naive and emotional rather than theoretical. She has been accused of not giving priority to over socialism after the Easter Rising.[103] It is true that Markievicz did not show a great interest in the field of socialist theory. Moreover, in her prison letters she expressed a certain reluctance to adhere to theories in general. However, there is no evidence to disprove her stout commitment to realising the goals that the Proclamation of the Easter Rising and the Democratic Programme of 1919 envisaged. The words of Peadar O'Donnell – another republican advocating socialism – that "Theory with me is the interpretation of the situation that bursts in my face..."[104] aptly illuminate Markievicz's way of thinking. She was first and foremost a practical politician, busy attending meetings, giving speeches and helping those in need. It is essential to note that the man who was her mentor was Connolly, whose socialism was greened with Irish nationalism. Markievicz understood his policy through her own ideas, which encompassed the need for social reform as well. Connollyian socialism was for her at one and the same time both a way and an aim to inspire the Irish people in the struggle for independence. She was not campaigning for the small Communist Party of Ireland, led by Roderick Connolly, son of James Connolly.[105]

To raise the people, she also portrayed Wolfe Tone as a radical revolutionary, whose aims in her view were as revolutionary as bolshevism. Moreover, she transferred the ideas of Connolly to Tone by claiming that he gave his life to break the subtle and cruel oppression and enslavement that resulted from the establishment of the English social and economic system. Finally, Markievicz claimed that in fact Tone's cry was to link up the oppressed peoples and classes of the world.[106] While writing these words, Markievicz was growing more and more critical of the course adopted by her own party.

---

100   Markievicz to Eva Gore-Booth, 1923, PL, 303.
101   C de M , A Comment on the Folly of Dr. Fogarty, *Eire*, 1.9.1923
102   Markievicz 1924, 10-12,17. In a pamphlet "How the Republic Will Deal With Poverty" (NLI), later in year 1924, the Christianity and democratic principles of Republicans were highlighted and they were also backed with the views of Leo XIII. James Connolly also referred to the Pope Leo XIII, see Connolly, The Rights of Life and the Rights of Property, 1897.
103   See Metscher, 456; O'Connor, 93, also Patterson who describes her pamphlet containing whimsical mystifications, Patterson, 25.
104   Quoted in English 1994, 66
105   Only in one letter she mentions co-operating with communists, presumably in Glasgow, writing "Please try and get that article on education that I gave to the Communists and that they didn't use...", Markievicz to Charles Diamond, 9.6.1924, P 5482, Synge Papers, NLI.
106   Constance de Markievicz ,Wolfe Tone's Ideals of Democracy, *An Phoblacht*, 26.6.1925.

■ Warrior of Destiny –
Markievicz and Fianna Fail

Critisizing Sinn Fein

Markievicz, who in public directed her strongest criticism at the Free State, was at the same time also critical when it came to the actions of Sinn Fein. When the question of the legal standing of the Second Dáil was discussed at a meeting on 15 January 1924 she maintained that it was mere pretence and play-acting to pose as the Government of the Republic and went on to argue that it "was nonsense to call ourselves a Government when the people have turned us down. We have the majority against us and until we have the majority of the people with us again we are not a Government." Her views evoked a critical response from most of the other members present. It was agreed unanimously that the Cabinet would continue as the Cabinet of the Republic, which implied that Markievicz also accepted the decision.[1] Unlike after the elections in 1923, she now maintained that all properly constituted governments should be based on the consent of the governed.[2]

The Republicans strove to continue double government as they had done with the First Dàil[3], but in reality the situation was very different. The people's support for the policy of Sinn Fein had declined compared to the situation before the Treaty. Because of that, Markievicz regarded the First and the Second Dàil as two completely different phenomena. Another important policy-maker shared her frustration, De Valera, who had been released from prison in the summer of 1924 and had begun to have doubts about the policy of abstentionism and about keeping the Second Dáil alive.[4]

To regain the support of the people Markievicz constantly reminded her fellow republicans of the importance of having definite social policy, thus continuing the appeal of Liam Mellows in 1922. In the January of 1924, she supported the practical amendments to the Democratic Programme made by Mary MacSwiney.[5] Later in the same year Markievicz argued that the people wanted to know whether they stood for "the Liam Mellows programme -the Connolly and Pearse idea or do we merely stand for camouflaged British capitalism and imperialism?" Moving forward from merely stressing the

---

1   Murphy, 142-143.
2   In the resumed meeting of Comhairle na d'Teachtai in 8.8.1924. The body was formed of the anti-Treaty members elected at elections. Meeting of 7.8.1924, Gaugham, 357.
3   Pyne, 40.
4   Coogan 1993, 372.
5   Murphy, 143.

illegality of the Free State as such, she pointed out that commercial and industrial dependence would be as bad as anything.[6] Again, at the Sinn Fein Annual Meeting in 1925, she requested a policy which would clear the "English" economic system out of the country. The Democratic Programme, which "was perfect in the abstract" was not enough. She remarked that many people at the time of Tone fell away because they did not understand that the Republic meant the obtaining by the people not only of their full political rights, but also their economic rights. Now half the people did not support them because they did not know what the Republican programme was. What was wanted was a definite statement of policy showing what Acts they should pass with the object of controlling the wealth of the country. Finally, Markievicz referred to the workers who wanted a "distinctive policy as opposed to the present economic programme." She anticipated that workers and others, who suffered in the prevailing conditions, would join republicans if they would only give concrete suggestions instead of merely expounding principles.[7] That had been the goal of Liam Mellows as well: he had maintained that Irish Labour should be kept on the side of republicans; who thus were "back to Tone...relying on...'the men of no property.' "[8]

Markievicz's view recalled the contradiction that there was between the Free State policy which depended on a free-trade economy and the nationalist economic politics which involved government intervention and protectionism. In much the same way de Valera stressed the need to concentrate on "the economic side", to devise means of helping the Irish in economic terms.[9] Another important figure among the republicans, Sean Lemass asserted that England's economic grip was more dangerous than her political grip on the country.[10] He appealed to Dublin voters by stating, that the interests of the Republicans were the interests of the whole Irish people and not those of a small priviliged class.[11] Markievicz's response to the situation was thus a similar one to that of those who were to found the most influential party in an independent Ireland.

However, the most important issue that highlighted the weakness of the republicans at the end of year 1925 was that of partition. The Unionists, supported by the British, were the winners. The Boundary Agreement left the border between north and south unaltered. Nationalists on both sides of the border were disappointed, even bitter.[12] Republican Deputies protested against partition and signed a declaration, Markievicz amongst them.[13] It was becoming

---

6   In the resumed meeting of Comhairle na d'Teachtai in 8.8.1924, Gaugham, 333.
7   Sinn Fein Ard Fheis, *An Phoblacht*, , 20.11.1925.
8   English 1994, 52-53.
9   Ibid.
10   Lemass in *Irish Times* 5.1.1925, quoted in Dunphy, 66.
11   Dunphy, 20. See also Pyne, Peter, The third Sinn Fein Party 1923-26, *Economic and Social review*, vol.I (1969-1970), 50.
12   Laffan 1983, 104-105. In the agreement the Free State was released from the payment to Britain, which had been a part of the Treaty, ibid; Dunphy, 70.
13   Macardle, 895.

obvious that the new programme of Sinn Fein was not enough at that stage. The Free State had been internationally recognised and was supported by the majority of Irish voters. Sinn Fein had lost members, some elections and its finances were not in a good condition.[14] Unemployment, poverty and pressure forced thousands of young republicans to emigrate. For some of Sinn Fein the solution was to be found in the words of Sean Lemass, who asserted, " There are some who would have us sit by the roadside and debate abstruse points about a 'de jure' this and a 'de facto' that, but the reality we want is away in the distance...and we cannot get there unless we move."[15]

Markievicz was among those republicans who were becoming ready to work in the Free State parliament. In November 1925 de Valera suggested that republicans should consider doing so. His idea did not gain enough support, however, and the meeting did not discuss the oath or change the policy of Sinn Fein in that respect. Markievicz, together with Mary MacSwiney, devised a compromise proposal when de Valera threatened to resign.[16] A division in the ranks of Sinn Fein was nonetheless inevitable. In March 1926 de Valera proposed again that Sinn Fein should try to get rid of the oath of allegiance. After that participating in the work of the Free State Parliament would no longer be a question of principle but of politics and the action would be peaceful and effective. Furthermore, a social and economic programme would be linked with a political one, and that would stress the duty of Sinn Fein to watch over and to safeguard the interests of the labouring classes and the working small farmers. His idea led to a quarrel and was rejected by 223-218. Following this de Valera left Sinn Fein[17] and established a new party, Fianna Fail. As a background to the split was the contradiction of two viewpoints. Some, including Markievicz and Sean Lemass, shared the view that the republican Second Dàil was merely a symbol which did not offer any real prospect for the future. Others, like Mary MacSwiney and Count Plunkett, regarded it as a government de jure.[18]

A New Departure – Fianna Fail

Markievicz presided over the meeting at which the new party was formally launched in the La Scala Theatre on 16 May 1925. At that meeting de Valera explained his ideas as to the new party more broadly. After abolishing the oath, he asserted, it would be possible to end all other forms of foreign influence. He expressed his sympathy with Connolly as regards taking care of the less fortunate, but went on, somewhat tritely, to say that for him political independence meant that "our people may live happily and rightly, freedom to

---

14 Pyne, 40-42.
15 Quoted in Prager, 200; Dunphy, 68-69.
16 *An Phoblacht*, 20.11.1925; Murphy, 150-151.
17 Moynihan, 127-128.
18 Murphy, 167.

make this nation of ours great in well-being and noble doing." He also pointed out several issues which were still to be dealt with, like securing employment for a large number of young men, reorganising transport, reafforestation, the development of water and for power as well as fisheries and housing.[19] Privately de Valera was less concerned at the lack of a social policy. Rather, he worried about the possibililty that Free State members would be replaced by farmers and labourers and other class interests, which in his view would mean that the national interest as a whole would be submerged in a clash of rival economic groups.[20]

The organisational success of Fianna Fail was immediate and impressive. By November 1926 the party had 460 *cumainn* and by the next summer there were more than 1000 party units. By November 1926 more than 400 public meetings had been held with party speakers present.[21] Over 500 representatives took part in the first Convention. De Valera was unanimously elected President. Markievicz was one of the 16 members of the Executive and one of the six women.[22] She explained her views to Eva quite frankly:

> " I sometimes think people get rather mad when they go in for politics...Dev., I say like a wise man, has announced that he will go into the Free State Parliament if there is no oath and this has caused an unholy row. I myself have always said that the oath made it absolutely impossible for an honourable person who was a Republican, to go in, and that if it were removed, it would then be simply a question of policy with no principle involved, whether we went in or stayed out. Dev thinks the moment has come to start out attacking the oath and demanding its removal. Some unlogical persons are howling. They stand for principle and for the honour of the Republic and prefer to do nothing but shout continually 'The Republic lives!'...Such a queer lot of people who are taking this stand. It's quite surprising. I think the ordinary man and woman in the street will agree with us. I don't think that we'll get the oath removed, at any rate for a long time, but anyhow it is something to go with a chance of success, and something outside Ireland might help."[23]

Using de Valera's expressions Markievicz highlighted the importance of the oath even though it had for quite some time been of secondary importance in her criticism at the Free State. In a situation where she was obviously deeply frustrated at the group's lack of influence, she found her former comrades who chose otherwise, to be illogical. In spite of the difficulties there might be in getting the oath removed, the new direction finally enabled concrete development. That she believed it was time to act and not merely to talk in

19   Moynihan, 135–142.
20   de Valera in a letter to Joe McGarrity in 1926, quoted in English 1994, 97.
21   Dunphy, 82. About the early years of Fianna Fail, see also Dunphy, Richard, The Soldiers Set Out: Reflections on the Formation of Fianna Fail, in Hannon, Philip & Gallagher, Jackie, Taking the Long View. 70 Years of Fianna Fail, Dublin 1996, 7-20.
22   The First Convention of Fianna Fail, *Irish Independent*, 25.11.1926; Ward 1983,202.
23   Markievicz to Eva Gore-Booth, About May or June 1926, PL, 307.

opposition, was evident in her light remark to her sister:" One blessed thing about this row is that I have got out of a great deal of awful meetings."[24]

Accepting the programme of Fianna Fail was not difficult for a former member of Sinn Fein. In its founding constitution Fianna Fail showed its continuity with traditional Sinn Fein thinking, reiterating the belief that Ireland could flourish as an independent country and calling for industrial development behind protective tariffs along with programmes of reforestation, transport, land distribution, and a state development bank.[25] Moreover, Fianna Fail strove to secure the political independence of a united Ireland as a republic; it wanted to restore the Irish language and to develop a native Irish culture.[26] One important thing with regards to priorities of Markievicz was that Fianna Fail really should portray itself as a follower of the Irish nationalist revolution and its programme included a great deal of nationalist rhetoric and anti-British utterances.[27]

Even though Markievicz might not have been satisfied with the vague remark that in Fianna Fail the development of a social system was to be based on the equal opportunity for every Irish citizen to live "a noble and useful Christian life"[28] , she most probably found the declaration that the resources and wealth of Ireland would be subservient to the needs and welfare of all the people[29] as a step in the right direction. After all, she had asserted that there could be no freedom in any country where wealth was accumulated in the hands of the few.[30] Moreover, while Fianna Fail's election programme in 1927 was built to attract the agricultural and industrial workers – to a extent that gave Labour leader Thomas Johnson reason to accuse Fianna Fail of stealing Labour's clothes[31] – and while it linked poverty and hunger to a government in the pay of "Imperialists"[32], the new party was heading in just the way that Markievicz found necessary. For her "life was politics", and politics meant being concerned with the everyday life, as we have seen before. She shared the view of Sean Lemass who argued that people would join Fianna Fail, if they were taught that national independence meant real concrete advantages for the common people and not merely an idealists' paradise. However, there is no proof that she helped in shaping that economic policy of Fianna Fail, even though she participated in the meetings and accepted the policy.[33]

24   Markievicz to Eva Gore-Booth, About May or June 1926, PL,308.
25   Daly, Mary E., Industrial Development and the Irish National Identity 1922-39, Dublin 1992, quoted in English 1994, 96-97.
26   Moynihan, Aims of Fianna Fail. Press Statement 17 April 1926, 131.
27   Prager, 200,203-206;words of Lemass, Dunphy, 69.
28   Moynihan, 131.
29   Mitchell 1974, 236.
30   *An Phoblacht*, 20.11.1925.
31   Mitchell 1974, 244.
32   Dunphy, 119.
33   Haverty has argued that Markievicz might have been helping, because she and de Valera sometimes met to discuss such things, Haverty, 227. However, she has named no source regarding this.

The continuing, various activities in the nationalist arena[34] in which Markievicz participated indicate her commitment to changing the tide for the republicans. Joining the new party increased the enthusiasm of Markievicz[35], but it also led to the forsaking of old ties. Markievicz resigned from the Cumann na mBan, whose President she had been for a several years because her membership of Fianna Fail contravened the constitution of the Cumann, which was pledged to work with the IRA. On November 1925 the IRA had severed its connection with the Second Dáil, declaring that it would act under an independent executive, which was given the power to declare war when a suitable opportunity arose to "rid the Republic of its enemies."[36] That was the path Markievicz chose not to take. A member of the Cumann said that "it nearly broke their hearts to lose her."[37] It was not easy for Markievicz, either.[38]

Markievicz's joining Fianna Fail has been interpreted her foresaking the violent path for constitutional methods.[39] However, that assumption is hardly justified when her whole career is examined. Despite her acceptance of the Rising and of war if necessary, she herself actually joined in the battle for only two weeks during a career of almost 20 years. Furthermore, she had shown her appreciation of at least the aim of parliamentiarism in the first Dàil Eireann. The question was much more one of who ruled the parliament. It has also been suggested that the Civil War had matured Markievicz and caused her to strive for honour through elections, constitutional opposition and debate and that she had forsaken the use of guns once Irish people began to kill other Irish people.[40] It is obviously true that she did not personally use guns any more, but she was willing to retain provision for military training in the Constitutions of both Fianna Eireann and Cumann na mBan even after the Civil War. Certainly the experience of Civil War was a hard thing for her, but the reasons for her joining Fianna Fail are not to be found merely in her rejection of violence but rather in question of strategy for safeguarding republican interests in the Free State.

The greatest loss for Markievicz had been the support that the republicans had achieved after the Easter Rising. She had managed to convince herself that

---

34 She participated in the meetings of the Sinn Fein Committee, was a member of its publicity and economic committee and reported to Sinn Fein on the activities of the Prisoners' Committee, Meetings of Sinn Fein Standing Committee from December 1924 to January 1926, 2b/82/117; 2B/82/119; *Sinn Fein*, 20.12.1924; she participated in the activities of Cumann na mBan and Fianna Eireann, see Annual Meeting of Cumann na mBan, *Sinn Fein*, 24.11.1924; about Fianna e.g. *An Phoblacht*,12.3., 9.4.,7.5.,4.6. 1926. Furthermore, she lectured to working class girls and boys, O'Faolain, 203-204, 212. In addition to this, she worked on different city councils , in committees focused on housing, health, pensions and small children and helped the hospital for small children, St. Ultans, See Roper, 97; Van Voris, 341; Marreco, 297.

35 Markievicz to Stanislaus Dunin-Markievicz, 14.1.1926, MS 13 778, NLI

36 Patterson, 28; English 1994, 67-68.

37 Ward 1983, 201.

38 Descriptions of her anxiety at that time by contemporaries, see O'Faolain, 207-208; Comerford, Maire, Women in the Irish Struggle, *The Irish Democrat*, May 1968, Maire Comerford Papers, MS 24 896, NLI.

39 Haverty, 226.

40 Norman, 270.

the election of June 1922 did not articulate the wishes of the Irish people, but the following elections had simply confirmed the position of the Free State. Markievicz, who constantly demanded a policy on social and economic questions could not influence Irish domestic politics outside the parliament; she could not ease poverty and unemployment on the scale she wished for. The establishment of the Free State had returned her to a situation where her involvement in political decision making was no longer possible. Facing that reality Markievicz was willing to accept the new parliament if only the oath were rejected. But the possibility of introducing new social and economic policies was not the only reason for her turn. For Markievicz Fianna Fail's ideas reflected the national heritage which was now in danger.

The Political testament of Markievicz – her faith in the women and in the youth of Ireland

Even though Markievicz was busy with the new party, she found time to write a play which demonstrated her understanding of the past and her forecast of the future of Ireland. Markievicz, who had often played a leading role in the plays of her husband, had herself written some earlier pieces.[41] "*Broken Dreams*" which she described as "not literary, only just a thrilling story during the Tan war and in Sligo, but...human and natural",[42] clearly bore witness to her commitment and showed she had no regrets about the policies of the past.

Eileen, the heroine of the play, is a modern and independent woman. She is like an ideal picture of young Markievicz herself both in her looks and attire.

> "Eileen is tall, slim and goodlooking with short brown hair softly and naturally curling round a striking face...There is little suggestion of sex in her, she is more like a young boy in her manner, even with the men who love her, she is so simple and frank. She wears well made a short tweed skirt and coat, with shirt blouse or jumper, simple hat and good country walking shoes with low heels. She does not affect either marcel wave or manicured hands, nor does her face give the effect of being powdered..."[43]

But even she, despite her reluctance, has to follow the path that her mother wants – that is, to get married. And as in a true tragedy, she is married to a cruel drunkard Seamus , whose unprincipled nature is shown not only in his low brow and fondness for foreign clothes, but also in his personal history. He, the villain of the play has in the same way as Michael Collins left his work in London and travelled to Dublin to fight at the G.P.O in the Easter Rising.

---

41 " A one act play of mine was played last night with great success!", Markievicz to Casimir Dunin-Markievicz, Constance Markievicz Papers, around 1921, MS 13 778, NLI; she had also organised "The Republic Players Dramatic Society' which in a year produced 12 plays, two of them which were hers, 'The Invicible Mother" and "Blood Money".
42 Markievicz to Eva Gore-Booth, About May or June 1926, PL, 306.
43 Markievicz, Constance, Broken Dreams, Sheehy Skeffington Papers, MS 24 185, NLI.

Eileen, who holds the struggle for Irish independence as more important than marriage, accepts Seamus after hearing about his bravery during the war.

However, life with Seamus is anything but happy and as the last straw Eileen is accused of killing him, because she is known to be a good shot. She is rescued by the hero, Eamon – conveniently named after de Valera – who solemnly expresses his judgment on Seamus, now found to be a traitor:

> "Weak and vain men trying to exalt themselves only lose themselves. He lost himself in treachery. With self-respect went hope and faith and courage. Love became a delusion and a mockery. All that made life worth while to him was gone. Men like him are their own slayers. God only gives happiness to those who give all; it is only where there is no self that there is God."

Again, the words of Eamon echo the words of Yeats' Cathleen ni Houlihan.

In a similar way, another play of Markievicz portrayed a pure-minded young woman who had to struggle not only with an English officer but with drunk and cowardly Irish traitors. In this play, the heroine called Peggy saves the hero, who of course had been fighting for Irish independence in 1798. This play, written before *Broken Dreams*, is more unforgiving regarding Irish traitors who surrendered to the temptation of money; their only destiny is death.[44]

The dialogue of Markievicz is quite awkwardly – for instance Eileen says "But I am quite comfortable. At least as comfortable as a girl can be in a country that has not its freedom" – but her message can't be avoided. The true heroes of the Irish people are first and foremost women, who never give up their principles, whereas Irish men must be divided into the "bad" and the "good." However, the women cannot survive by their own efforts alone. They are still confronted with limitations on their sex in a traditional society and, interestingly, in her plays it is usually the men who are given the final words which sum up true republican principles.

Markievicz herself was a woman who not only preached the need for self-help but was quick to do something concrete when it was necessary. During the shortage of coal in the winter of 1926-27 she helped the Dublin poor by making them food, giving them money – which she partially raised by selling her own remaining jewels – and collecting turf for them in the mountains.[45] Her philanthrophy was not a new thing in her politics. It was a heritage from her childhood, when she had accompanied her mother to help the peasants and when she had first been introduced to the duties of the better-off towards the less fortunate. Her readiness to work resembled the attitude of of militant feminists in Victorian Britain. It has been argued that they, in much the same way as was characteristic of British socialism, adopted a dedicated responsibility for achieving the 'good life' through their own actions.[46] However, her actions should not be oversimplified by assuming that her work during the winter was

---

44   Markievicz, Constance, Blood Money, O'Mullane Papers, MS 22 636, NLI.
45   O'Faolain, 210-211; Van Voris, 345; Roper, 108.
46   Stanley, 88.

a protest against the prevailing politics and that she attended meetings only because they were the only form of politics then available to her.[47] If she had wanted to concentrate on philanthrophy, she could abandoned politics. However, she chose to try and exert her influence within a larger arena.

The message of Markievicz was now one of forgiveness,[48] even though she continued to celebrate the heroism of the Easter Rising as giving comfort "as the years went mournfully by, each bearing its sorrowful tale of wrong triumphant."[49] But there was no need to despair as long as there were young people in Ireland. Writing to members of Fianna Eireann Markievicz gave her own views on what to do and how to proceed in the Free State.

According to Markievicz, the first real step in citizenship was taken joining the Fianna. There one was learnt to obey laws by obeying rules and how to govern and how to change laws by taking an interest in the working of the organisation. She remarked that even though one might not agree with all the rules, they must be obeyed and while doing that one could think over how they could be changed for the better. These ideas could be discussed and later they could be brought forward as motions in conventions. By electing delegates one learnt to choose the best men – those who were the straightest and had the noblest ideas – just as one chose T.D.s and councillors when one became an adult. If one were chosen to fill a position, one would learn to look on it as a duty that one had been given, and not an empty honour.

But the citizenship Markievicz described not only entailed a knowledge of organisational rules and democracy. It also meant adopting the principle "Love your neighbour as yourself." Those who believed in that could not bear to see someone living in misery, while others were idle and rich. Therefore one's duty as a good citizen was to try and end the tyranny and misery. The one weapon at hand was the vote. Only a careless, bad citizen neglected to register to vote and so cut himself off from taking any part in the government of his country. Those who had been trained in the Fianna, "mentally and physically" to free Ireland and the people of Ireland, should not let any opportunity be missed and should not leave any weapon carelessly aside.

Finally, Markievicz posed questions to the boys, in the manner of a republican catechism. They should ask about freedom, about why Britain partioned Ireland and made them speak English instead of our own language, why the people who worked hardest had the smallest and most miserable homes and why the idlers had big houses and owned great stretches of land, and ask whether a country was really free when foreigners owned all the big factories and business houses?[50]

---

47   Haverty, 227. Sawyer contradicts the view that Markievicz was in a way carrying the family tradition a stage further and recalls to the not so good relations that existed between her and her family, Sawyer, 42. This, however, does not exlude the importance of the heritage itself.
48   Speech of Markievicz on the grave of two republican soldiers, *An Phoblacht*, 17.12.1926; Cole and Colley Commemoration, *Sinn Fein*,13.9.1924.
49   Markievicz, Constance, 1916, *The Nation*,24.3.1927.
50   Citizenship, By the late Madame Markievicz. Written for Fianna Eireann, *The Nation*, 13.8.1927.

The method of Markievicz were based on education in nationalist-minded organisations, on active participation in politics and on using the vote. The young person who loved his neighbour would grow to be a citizen who strove to make society more equal by constitutional methods in parliament. However, there could be often a heavy price to pay, and a Fianna boy might face the need for self-sacrifice just like Christ, who himself in his childhood was just like any other boy. [51] This message to the youth of Ireland brought up again the themes of Markievicz's early political speeches to women, which expressed her belief in the great moral power of the vote.

The vote was the weapon in which her new party Fianna Fail trusted.[52] Its goal was victory in the general elections of July 1927. Markievicz participated in the election campaign with her characteristic vigour. Her main themes were nothing particularly new; they focused on blaming the Free State for economic chaos while arguing that the policy of Fianna Fail would save Ireland from extinction as a nation and her people from ruin and starvation. She promised that her party would not cut the old age pension and would concentrate on providing work for all.[53] She was also in favour of a pension for mothers and was constantly concerned with the situation of the children.[54]

Fianna Fail won 44 seats in the election. Its success was considerable compared with that of Sinn Fein which had got only 5 succesful candidates.[55] Markievicz was among those elected but she died soon afterwards on 15th July as a result of the peritonitis that followed an operation for appendicitis.[56] She did not have to make the choice of whether to take the oath in order to get into parliament, a new rule following the murder of Deputy prime Minister Kevin O'Higgins. Markievicz had lost her mother in January of the same year and her sister Eva in 1926, but she had her husband and daughter by her side when she died in hospital. People had gathered outside to pray for her. One woman wondered what the people in the slums would do without her.[57]

Her funeral was a big occasion in Dublin. In his speech de Valera praised Markievicz:

"Madame Markievicz is gone from us, Madame, the friend of the toiler, the lover of the poor. Ease and station she put aside, and took the hard way of service with the weak and the down-trodden. Sacrifice, misunderstanding and scorn lay on the road she adopted, but she trod it unflinchingly..."[58]

---

51 C de M, A Christmas Message to the Fianna, *An Phoblacht*, 18.12.1925.
52 Fianna Fail was, from the beginning, totally electorally orientated, Dunphy 1996, 10.
53 Free State Failure. Speech of Countess Markievicz at the opening of the election campaign in South Dublin, *The Nation*, 14.5.1927; C de M, Return of Eamon de Valera to Ireland. Triumphal Greetings in Cork and Dublin, *The Nation*, 21.5.1927.
54 Markievicz to J.P. Dunne, June 1927, Markievicz Papers, MS 13 778, NLI.
55 O'Neill, Thomas P., In Search of a Political Path. Irish Republicanism 1922 to 1927. In *Historical Studies X*, ed. By G.A. Hayes-McCoy. Dublin 1976,170.
56 Norman, 276.
57 Roper, 108.
58 Van Voris, 349.

Markievicz would have liked to know that she was described as " a pure gold link in our chain of great patriots."[59] After all, patriotism was, according to her, perhaps the greatest of Irish national charasteristics.[60]

59   A Patriot at Rest, *The Nation,* 23.7.1927.
60   Article on Patriotism, Markievicz Papers, MS 15 065, NLI.

■ Markievicz – a Freedom Fighter

Constance Markievicz was born among the privileged Anglo-Irish but dedicated her life to ending British government in Ireland. Many people from her class were at this same time interested in cherishing the Irish language and culture but only few combined armed rebellion against British government with these nationalistic cultural goals. And even fewer fought to improve the status of workers and women, in the way that Markievicz did.

Constance Markievicz was a nationalist whose aim was to make Ireland an independent nation. Already in her youth she was inspired by the Irish cultural legacy and worked to maintain it. Markievicz's conception of Ireland was based on an ideology that romanticized the past of "Irish Ireland". She found justification for her claim for independence on the one hand in looking back to a golden age of the past and trusting in permanent national characteristics, but on the other hand also in the history of Ireland's sufferings. Those elements were in a more central position in her thinking than emphasizing the significance of the nation's own language.

Markievicz emphasized the significance of a shared history and environment as a uniting factor for the Irish, -including Anglo-Irish-, and this was a natural basis related to her own background. Those elements together with the national characteristics had formed an Irish "race" that was unlike any other. The Irish did not care for material things; idealism and the spirit of self sacrifice as well as instinct were characteristic of them in the same way as emotionality was a characteristic of their language. For Markievicz, supporting the republic was also "instinctive", a proof of the race's memory. Thus it was natural and characteristic for the Irish to strive for independence, towards a new society. Markievicz's concept of the characteristics of Ireland were partly shaped by contradictions. Compared to Britain Ireland was small and materially poor but on the other hand spiritually rich and equal. The social Darwinist thinking of that time was reflected in Markievicz's speeches, too: she described the British as unpleasant even in their appearance.

Religion was one of the most important features that was believed to distinguish the Irish from the British. Even before converting to Catholicism Markievicz used religious metaphors as part of her polemic. The fight against Britain was for Markievicz a fight against a prosperous, arrogant, materialistic empire, David's fight against Goliath. But like David, Ireland had a righteous God on its side, as Markievicz suggested in her poems. Religious metaphors and comparisons of nationalists to the martyrs of the early church were a constant feature of Markievicz's speeches and writings: she compared Larkin to Christ and the Fianna-boys to the Christ Child. It was possible and permitted for a man to compare his life to Him; every one had to bear his cross. The Irish nationalists that fought against British materialism were like a small Christian vanguard to Markievicz. They shared a high spiritual idealism that would finally break the enemy. Markievicz even linked the Last Judgment with nationalism: then the life of every Irishman would be weighed as well as the way they had paid their debt to the martyrs of nationalism.

Converting to Catholicism was not only Markievicz' personal choice but an important feature in the portrait of any perfect Irish patriot after the Easter Rising. The conversion showed in her work in public writings where she could use religion as a weapon against the supporters of the Irish Free State or against employers and at the same time emphasize the right religion and the Christian morality of the republicans. In trying to persuade the people to support James Connolly's ideas after the civil war and after election defeat she emphasized his Christian principles and the harmony and the combatibility of Connolly's ideology with the doctrines of the church. The Christian idea of salvation was reflected in the description of her own two conversions: first to the nationalist movement and, second, to Catholicism, both of them happening in a situation where sudden enlightenment made Markievicz a person who had found a new path.

For Markievicz the republic of Ireland meant unambiguously the island of Ireland but over time the definition of the Irish people had become a more complex issue. Like many other nationalists Markievicz disregarded the problem of Ulster and hoped that every one that had experienced the common past and environment of the island of Ireland could join together regardless of different background, class or religion. Markievicz strongly criticized those Irishmen who overlooked that goal; in other words those unionists and those who worked for Great Britain and were on the whole indifferent to nationalism.

To achieve political goals was even more important to her than the revival of the national culture: Ireland had to regain the independence that it had lost when it became part of the United Kingdom. It must become a republic that would guarantee equal citizenship to all its citizens regardless of class and gender. In Markievicz's view, only the independent republic could offer the necessary framework for social and economic reforms. Ireland was entitled to strive for republic because it was a community quite separate from Great Britain and it had the features of a nation-state; it had a unique culture, history and language that the people living on the island of Ireland shared.

According to Markievicz part of the characteristics of the Irish "race", like sacrificing one self and heroism, had already shown themselves over a long period of time. One could rely on them also when planning the future, because creating an independent nation was not possible without sacrifices. Markievicz thought that because of the necessity of violence and suffering the desire to sacrifice one self had to be roused in Irishmen. Gaining independence was seen as the right object of a small and noble nation's fight. Markievicz accepted the republican doctrine according to which the use of force was the only possible way to independence. The Irish were to be educated with might and main, with speeches, writings, demonstrations and actions, to see the fact that the connection with Britain had to be broken even if violence proved necessary. Markievicz founded a youth organization Na Fianna Eireann just for that purpose.

Markievicz wanted to arouse all Irishmen to resistance but did not imagine the eventual rebellion would have the widest possible support. She believed in the arousing power of an exemplary vanguard, just like IRB which relied on the traditional nature of rebellion in Ireland and Markievicz accepted the IRB's separatist republicanism, although she did not like the conservatism of the organization. However, accepting the tradition of past rebellions and reviving it in the modern world were important to Markievicz. But even if she supported traditional rebellion: people marching to battle with waving banners and uniforms and shouting the slogans of bygone patriots, the "army" that she had planned for this battle was an exceptionally radical group of women, young people and workers.

Before the Easter Rising in 1916 the guiding line in the politics of Markievicz was through passive resistance and cultural nationalism to create wide support for a violent rebellion by which the connection to Great Britain would be broken and a republic of Ireland founded. The defeat in the Easter Rising was a victory in the view of Markievicz because it fulfilled her wish: it changed people's opinion and made them resist the British government. When that goal had been reached and when the republican shadow government, Dáil Eireann had been formed, she worked as a minister in it. In that role Markievicz followed the decisions of Dáil Eireann which she saw as made by representatives democratically chosen by the Irish people. One of the themes of her speeches became the hope that the republic would be acknowledged in the peace negotiations at Versailles, and when that hope faded, the improving of social defects and the creating of an economic policy capable of coping with Ireland's problems became most central in her work.

When the possiblity of promoting independence improved after the Easter Rising and having gained the support of the people, the republic became the goal of the nationalist movement. Not every one, however, saw the founding of the republic as the main goal, as Markievicz did. Her aim was an independent republic of Ireland, precisely the worker's republic that James Connolly had worked for, a co-operative nation. It was a republic people had died for, a republic where preference was given to the rights of those -poor people, women and workers- that at that moment had no influence at all. During the first Dáil Eireann she built the image of the future republic on the basis of an agrarian ideal. In the future land would be given to both landless men and women; the ideal was a patriot family living in the country and raising a lively and healthy generation with the products of the land. Markievicz put emphasis also on the way of life in that future home: a good home was like the nation in miniature. She was fascinated with the idea of home and women's role in the building of ideal homes in ideal Ireland.

The idea of co-operation that was part of Markievicz's ideal republic had been familiar to her since her youth, and in spite of the success of co-operative movements all over Europe she considered it an Irish idea. A small-scale experiment with the Fianna-boys proved to Markievicz that co-operation was an idea worth supporting and that the rising generation of Ireland should adopt it. Quoting the Democratic Programme that the shadow parliament promulgated in 1919, Markievicz emphasized co-operation as a true characteristic of the republic: co-operation was the only sensible way and the only possible alternative to the former economic policy that was so alien to the Irish mind. She thought that accepting the Free State spelt not only political defeat but did a great deal of harm to the economic structure, because it meant the rejection of the idea of co-ooperation which was characteristic of the Irish and which distinguished the Irish from the British way of thinking.

For Markievicz it had always been a great challenge that she had to act in a situation where Ireland was more or less a part of Great Britain. She did not trouble herself about that after the republicans had formed their shadow parliament: that and the people's support gave her hope of impending victory and a feeling that the ties with Britain had been severed. That is why she so strongly condemned the oath of allegiance that was accepted in the compact of the Irish Free State. Markievicz did not wish for divisions in the nationalist ranks but when the civil war broke out she considered it her duty to join battle alongside the troops of the republicans rebelling against the Free State for she had sworn allegiance to the republic. The war and defeat in the election in which she had hoped the people "awakened" by the Easter Rising would show their "instinctive" judgment with regard to the Free State, were a bitter disappointment for her. In that hopeless situation she returned to the streets to speak directly to the people. As a weapon against the Free State she used now, in the middle of a depression, the proclamation of a new, stronger reformating politics. Markievicz also demanded that her own party, Sinn Fein should emphasize similar things.

However, Sinn Fein was not the only forum for Markievicz, not even when it was at its most popular just after the Easter Rising. The nationalist movement gathered around Sinn Fein did not in itself quite fulfill Markievicz's social and political aims. Her concept of the idea of equality that was a central part of being Irish made it also possible for her to work in the women's and worker's movements as well. The problems that these movements emphasized had also an impact on Markievicz's vision of future, and she did not reject or postpone the resolving of these problems as the mainstream of the national movement did. It was also important for her to awaken women and workers to the national fight because if they were organized they could better watch and demand their rights in the future.

Markievicz had already supported the suffragette movement in an earlier phase. Organizing and educating herself particularly for public life and proclaiming the movement's demands in public were already familiar means of political action for her in her early days in the suffragette movement. When

Markievicz became an active member of the nationalist movement, the suffrage had still to be gained in a situation where an independent Irish parliament still could not act. She therefore worked to improve women's situation through those movements which at that time strove for political independence. As a basis for this she had, regardless of her disappointments, her concept of the naturally egalitarian morals of the Irish race and on the other hand the memory of the country's past when women were active in every field of social life. The best advocate for women's rights among men she found in James Connolly. Among women's organizations Markievicz's ideas were best fulfilled first in the radical Inghinidhe na hEireann which declared open rebellion and demanded that the people should be awakened, educated and trained, and in later Cumann na mBan which became in practice a part of the IRA after the Easter Rising. On the other hand, organizing girls to act in the Fianna or organizing women to act in their own union IWWU was only a minor part of Markievicz' work. Most important for an independence fighter was to organizing women for the national fight and this was not a principal aim of the IWWU. On the other hand, the improvement of the conditions of working women and mothers was close to Markievicz's heart; she always preserved the habit, familiar to her since her childhood, of holding out a helping hand to poor families.

In the shadow government, furthering the cause of women was left to Markievicz. As a minister Markievicz tried to increase women's influence by appointing them arbitrators in her own ministry and giving them assignments that she thought would suit them because of their gender, like taking care of child abuse cases. She hoped for women candidates in the elections and tried to carry through the initiatives of giving them land. Although Markievicz considered men's attitudes and even the principles of the Catholic church which maintained the inequality between genders to some of be the reasons for women's poor situation at that time, she found women's passivity to be the biggest reason. This could be due to personal experience, breaking our of her background. Her amazement at women's passivity was also due to her knowledge of the past when women's activity had been both possible and natural. Now that women lacked independence, they had simply forgotten. But because women's activity had once existed and was now only "slumbering", it was possible to awaken the women with the help of speeches, writings and her own example.

Markievicz emphasized the historical example of the fighting woman, even if she did not demand that every woman should be in a leading position. Every one had her own place and her own duties, but one had to keep in mind the goal of independence and every action had to be aimed at that goal. The fact that to Markievicz the woman of the past was a fighter was not important only because she could thus justify women's participation but also because in this way she could encourage women to strike a new course and to cross their limits. To Markievicz wrong ideals of femininity were those that defined a woman only as a housewife and a mother and shut her out of politics. The rejected aspects of both genders – the feminine side of a man's soul and the masculine side of a woman's soul should be emphasized more freely. In the education of women and girls she was not inspired by the role of a domestic or a nurse: because the women had taken part in battles they were entitled to get the franchise and a place among the decision-makers – just as she herself was entitled to be a minister. Thus Markievicz did not emphasize those "feminine qualities" of women with the help of which they would in the name of the general good best serve society by staying at home, even though she did remind women of the necessity of creating a good home during the first Dáil Eireann, when she according to her own view was already working for the future republic. However, Markievicz could hardly have accepted Fianna Fail's conservative concept of a woman's place.

In her way of dressing and acting Markievicz liked to emphasize the masculine, even aggressive side of woman. In an Inghinidhe na hEireann play she appeared as an armour-clad Joan of Arc who would fight to free Ireland. Joan of Arc was not a mother and motherhood was not a primary issue for Markievicz. She did not direct her words to mothers in particular but spoke to women as women and to the Irish in general. Also when claiming improvements in the conditions of working women, she was, in spite of her sympathy, more like their leader and organizer than like a mother understanding the problems of another mother. By encouraging women in the role of a fighter and choosing that role voluntarily herself, Markievicz certainly broke the traditional rules which may explain the fact that she was often seen as a hysterical, fanatic and also a bad mother. Alertness and heroism were characteristic of her writings about women, as well in her writings such as her historical plays, where women had a central role and where they were firm and righteous. Markievicz who in the beginning of her career emphasized the pure ideals of women which they had kept outside party politics, saw the same kind of hope in those women who had rejected the compact of the Free State and by that action had proved the dependability of their principles. By emphasizing women's qualifications and possibilities, Markievicz was also justifying her own actions, because it was relatively rare for a woman to be active in politics at that time.

Women were a group that had to be recruited to fight but they were not by any means the only group. By educating the children of Irish mothers a generation could be created with the help of which the battle could be started. Like Patrick Pearse and the women of Inghinide na hEireann Markievicz paid attention to the education of the rising generation. Unique to her methods was the fact that the boys in Fianna na hEireann were trained to be soldiers. The essence of the education that was offered to the boys was that of preparing for the extreme sacrifice; morals and spiritual training were specially emphasized. Although Markievicz trusted in the power of education and enlightenment to such an extent that she considered social evolution to be inevitable when the amount of knowledge increased, the solving of the national question could not be left to rest upon it alone. For solving that question people had to be organised and trained even to take arms.

In addition to women and children Markievicz wanted to take also into the front ranks of the fighters those workers whose living conditions needed to be improved. For her the labour question was opened up by Larkin and Connolly both of whom wanted to create an independent labour movement which would cover the whole of Ireland. For Markievicz suffering people were always worthy of respect, and during the Lock-Out she saw in the Irish labour movement a small national army which had fought against Britain without sparing itself. Their fight against British capitalists was the same battle about the same things as Ireland's fight against British supremacy. For her Larkin and Connolly were living legends of the independence fight whom she certainly and especially considered to be nationalists.

Markievicz did not by any means see socialism as a strange idea to the Irish as, for example, Arthur Griffith did. On the contrary it was an idea that emphasized national uniqueness and was based on the Irish history and character, and she defined it as "James Connolly's socialism". For Markievicz the labour movement was not so much about a revolution that would change the structures dramatically, as about rearranging and rebuilding, in other words about reformism. It was crucial that the labour issue had opened up for her just through Connolly who thought that it was impossible to separate the national and the labour issues from each other. However, Connolly was not the only person close to Markievicz who tried to forward the worker's cause; her sister's life's work among women workers was also significant in the development of her thinking.

Markievicz did not want to postpone the resolving of social problems as the mainstream of the national movement did. The problems that the labour movement had brought up had to be solved and the workers had to be given a chance to be a part of solving them. Co-operation was the key to a truly succesful establishment of national independence and it had to be extended to all groups of society. Thus Markievicz as minister acted as a conciliator between workers and employers trying to avoid confrontations among the Irish.

After the Easter Rising Markievicz believed that the workers would support the nationalist politics of Sinn Fein. She made it clear that she supported both movements because her concept of a free Ireland was both "economic and political". Markievicz wanted the Irish to get organized both economically and politically - in trade unions, co-operative associations and republican organizations. Markievicz connected economic freedom with political freedom: it meant supporting Irish industry, strengthening the Irish trade union movement and nationalizing Irish business life in every way. Economic freedom did not mean government-led socialism, which Markievicz denied was Connolly's goal. She explained Connolly's aim to take command of factories, farms and political organs rather as giving of authority to Irish representatives than as a central feature of syndicalism. Neither the contents of Markievicz' speeches nor her aims changed essentially, although she sometimes talked about class and capitalism. Gaining full national independence was central for her all the time.

For Markievicz Wolfe Tone's phrase: "men of no property have to support rebellion" did not mean only the landless but also the workers. Thus, Markievicz wanted the workers to take part in the national fight but not necessarily to lead it. In a situation where the Irish republic was about to be founded labour had to take its share of the burden. Although Markievicz saw hope in the Bolshevik revolution, she did not regard the success of the Bolsheviks as a victory for socialism; in her writings it was more like an example worth following: it was as if the great French revolution that had had so much influence on the Irish republicanism, had broken out again.

*   *   *

The established image of Markievicz as an impatient and bloodthirsty weathercock is too simple. She worked in politics tirelessly for almost twenty years and in spite of her rebellious attitude and her colourful speeches, she spent only two weeks of that time in physical fighting. For Markievicz the most important thing was to work in organizations and parties in order to make the Irish accept her programme. Her basic principles did not change with every new contact, but she made choices, she rejected Hobson, for example, when he proved to be over careful in her judgment; she rejected Larkin when he disbanded the workers' front and she rejected the compact of the Free State. After the founding of the Free State when the policy of Sinn Fein prohibited her from taking part in politics and prevented her from gaining the people's support, Markievicz disengaged herself from that part of the radical republicans that still held out against the treaty and joined Fianna Fail party that de Valera had founded. Her choices tell us a lot about what Ireland would be like in the future and what she thought were the means to achieve it.

The franchise was a necessary weapon for Markievicz throughout her career. She believed in the moral power of the franchise. In spite of her suspicion of parlamentarianism she wanted a republic to follow the rebellion, a republic where representatives chosen by the people would gather together to make the decisions. Voting and fulfilling other obligations of citizenship gave the basis for actions which had to be backed up by an idea - thus Markievicz did not want the dictatorship of a small vanguard to follow the rebellion. On several occasions she demanded that people trust themselves and distrust their leaders. In the background there was the idea of a deliberative person seeing the situation the way Markievicz did. Once she was out of politics in prison, she emphasized that she had done enough, now it was some one else's turn. However, she was conscious of the importance of her work, which was manifested in her claim to the post of Minister of Labour.

The fact that she polled a large number of votes in almost every election proves that her person and her politics were received with sympathy among the voters. By that standard she was a successful politician. Certainly she was also the first woman to be elected to the House of Commons but as a minister in the shadow government she was not, however, among the most important or the most appreciated. Her programme was too radical and her aim, a republic that would cover the whole island of Ireland did not come true. To her contemporaries and to succeeding generations her goals were often left in the shadow by her colourful actions and personality. However, Markievicz worked tirelessly for wide social reforms throughout her career. A dream of liberty united and sustained up her actions and thinking.

The basis of Markievicz' political career is crystallized in her remark "Life is politics". That idea was the basis of her own actions, too. For her politics consisted not only of being a member of an organization or a party but also taking of action personally when needed. Her idea of what a society should guarantee its members was reflected in her own charity work for she continually raised money and food for the poor. In a broader sense, that observation was not only personal but was also connected with the programme that she advanced. The Irish national ideology had to reveal itself publicly in every action - not just in a certain sphere of politics or not only through the leaders' example.

The emphasizing of self-action that was part of the co-operative idea, had characterized the ideas of Markievicz at all times. Markievicz hoped that the Irish would themselves understand the necessity of a national struggle without being compelled to do so. As Irishwomen or Irishmen, workers or children, individuals had their own duties to perform. Supporting independent agriculture and Irish industry would create work and wealth for the ordinary Irishmen who would take part in decision-making and change their circumstances through organizing. Markievicz' citizen was someone who depended on the republican tradition: it was his duty to forward good government and his duties to his community were more important than the privileges that he expected and was granted. The freedom of an individual could only be achieved through the gaining of national freedom, freedom regardless gender or class, and only national freedom could offer the possibility of living a "true Irish life": the life of a useful, independent citizen.

■ Abbreviations

AIL= All for Ireland League
Bean=Bean na hEireann
Cumann= Cumann na mBan
Dáil= Dáil Eireann
Fianna = Na Fianna Eireann
IAOS= Irish Agricultural Organisation Society
ICA= Irish Citizen Army
Inghinidhe = Inghinidhe na hEireann
IPP=Irish Parliamentary Party
IRA = Irish Republican Army
IRB = Irish Republican Brotherhood
ISRP= Irish Socialist Republican Party
ITGWU= Irish Transport and General Workers Union
ITUCLP= Irish Trade Union Congress and Labour Party
IV= Irish Volunteers
IWFL= Irish Women's Franchise League
IWSLGA = Irish Women's Suffrage and Local Government Association
IWWU= Irish Women Workers' Union
MS= Manuscript
NAI= National Archives of Ireland
NLI= National Library of Ireland
PL= Prison Letters of Countess Markievicz
SPI= Socialist Party of Ireland
UVF= Ulster Volunteer Force
WPDL= Women's Prisoners' Defence League

■ Bibliography

MANUSCRIPT SOURCES

ENGLAND

Public Record Office, (PRO)London

Countess Markievicz, CO 904/164

IRELAND

National Archives of Ireland, (NAI) Dublin

Copy Minutes of Sinn Fein Standing Committee 1919-1922. 999/40.
Dáil Eireann Papers relating to First Dáil. Ministry & Cabinet Minutes 1919-1921. DE 1/1, 1/2, 1/3, 1/4.
Dáil Eireann Papers relating to First Dáil. Department of Finance. DE 4/2/6, DE 4/2/8.
Dáil Eireann Papers relating to First Dáil.Department of Labour.DE 2/5.
Meetings of the Sinn Fein Standing Committee 1918-1925 2B/82/116, 2B/82/117.

National Library of Ireland, (NLI) Dublin

Roger Casement Papers
Maire Comerford Papers.
Frank Gallagher Papers.
Irish National Aid Association and Volunteer Dependents'Correspondence.
Joseph McGarrity Papers.
Constance Markievicz Papers.
Colonel Maurice Moore Papers.
Art O'Brian Papers.
William O'Brien Papers.
O'Mullane Papers.
Count Plunkett Papers.
Hanna Sheehy Skeffington Papers.
Synge Papers. [7 Letters of Countess Markievicz to Charles Diamond,Glasgow 1917-1924 and 3 n.d. with an article in the Irish National Interest (by C.M.?)]mf.P 5482.

Typescript report of Sinn Fein Annual Convention 1917.

National Museum,Dublin

Prison Notebook of Constance Markievicz

UNITED STATES OF AMERICA

Library of Congress, Washington d.c.

Ella Young Papers

National Archives, Washington d.c.

Records of Department of State. Relating to Internal Affairs of Great Britain, 1910-1929. American Consulate, Dublin, Ireland .

Penn State University, College Park, Pennsylvania.

Eva Gore-Booth Collection.

PRINTED MATERIAL

Newspapers and journals

An Phoblacht 1925-26
Bean na hEireann 1909-1911
Catholic Bulletin 1917.
Cork Examiner 1917
Eire 1923-1924
Fianna 1915-1916
Fianna Christmas Number 1914
The Gaelic American 1916
Irish Bulletin 1919-21
Irish Citizen 1912-1920
Irish Freedom 1910-1914
Irish Opinion. Voice of Labour 1917-1919
Irish Volunteer 1914

Irish Worker 1911-1914
The Nation 1927
Nationality 1917-1919
New Ireland 1918, 1922
Old Ireland 1920
Poblacht na hEireann 1922
The Republican War Bulletin 1922.
Sinn Fein 1908-1913, 1923-25
Tone Commemoration Number.Fianna. The
    Official Organ of Fianna Eireann 1922.
Watchword of Labour 1920.
Workers' Republic 1915-1916.

Official publications and printed documents

Correspondence Relating to the Proposals of
    His Majesty's Government for An Irish
    Settlement. Presented By Parliament By
    Command of His Majesty. London 1921.
Dáil Eireann. Debate on the Treaty between
    Great Britain and Ireland signed in London
    on 6th December 1921. Dublin 1922.
Dáil Eireann. Minutes of Proceedings of the
    First Parliament of the Republic of Ireland
    1919-1921.Official Record. Dublin 1922.
Dáil Eireann. Official Report. For Periods 16
    August to 26 August 1921 and 28 February
    1922 to 8 June 1922. Dublin 1922.
Dáil Eireann. Private Sessions of Second Dáil.
    Minutes of Proceedings 18 August 1921 to
    14 September 1921 and Report of Debates
    14 December 1921 to 6 January 1922.
    Dublin 1972.
Irish Historical Documents since 1800. Ed. by
    Alan O'Day & John Stevenson. Dublin
    1992.

Contemporary material and reminiscences

AE[George Russell], The National Being.
    Dublin 1918.
AE, Nationality and Imperialism, in Lady
    Gregory (ed.), Ideals in Ireland. London
    1901.
AE, Thought for British Co-operators.Being a
    Further Demand for a Public Enquiry into
    the Attacks on Co-operative Societies in
    Ireland. Dublin 1920.
Amusing Proceedings, *Sligo Champion*
    26.12.1896
Berresford Ellis, P., James Connolly: Selected
    Writings. London 1988.
Boyle, John F., The Irish Rebellion of 1916. A
    Brief History of the Revolt and its
    Suppression. London 1916.
"Charles Russell". Should the Workers of
    Ireland Support Sinn Fein? (1918) in Sinn
    Fein and Socialism. Historical reprints no
    19. Cork 1977.

Collins, Michael, The Path to Freedom. Dublin
    1922.
Connolly-Heron, Ina, James Connolly. A
    Biography, Liberty June-July 1966.
Connolly O'Brien, Nora, Portrait of a Rebel
    Father. Dublin 1935.
Connolly, James, Labour in Irish History.
    London 1987 (Dublin 1910).
Cousins, James H.& Margaret, We Two
    Together. Madras 1950.
Craig, E.T., An Irish Commune. The History
    of Ralahine with an Introduction by George
    Russell (AE) and Notes by Diarmuid ó
    Cobhthaigh. Dublin 1920.
Cumann na mBan. Annual Convention.
    October 22nd and 23rd 1921. Report.
Cumann na mBan Convention. September 28th
    & 29th 1918.
Cumann na mBan. Policy for 1917-1918.
    Dublin 1917.
Czira, Sydney, The Years Flew By. Dublin 1974
De Blacam, A, What Sinn Fein Stands For: The
    Irish Republican Movement; its History,
    Aims and Ideals, examined as to their
    Significance to the World. Dublin 1921.
Denson, Alan (ed.), Letters from AE. Selected
    by Alan Denson. London 1961.
Dickinson, Page L., The Dublin of Yesterday.
    London 1929.
Doyle, Chrissie M., Women in Ancient and
    Modern Ireland. Dublin 1917.
The Ethics of Sinn Fein. [pamphlet] 1917.
Fianna Handbook. Dublin 1914.
Figgis, Darrell, Recollections of the Irish War.
    London 1927.
The First Convention of Fianna Fail. *Irish
    Independent* 25.11.1926
Fox, R.M., The History of the Irish Citizen
    Army. Dublin 1943.
Fox, R.M., Rebel Irishwomen. Dublin 1935.
Gifford, Sydney, Countess de Markievicz, in
    Joy, Maurice (ed.), The Irish Rebellion of
    1916 And Its martyrs: Erin's Tragic Easter,
    New York 1916.
Green, Alice Stopford, Irish Nationality.
    London and New York, 1911.
Hobson, Bulmer, Defensive Warfare. Belfast
    1909.
Hobson, Bulmer, Ireland Yesterday and
    Tomorrow. Tralee 1968.
Hobson, Bulmer, To the Whole People of
    Ireland. The Manifesto of the Dungannon
    Club. Belfast 1905.
Hyde, Douglas, What Ireland is Asking For, in
    Lady Gregory (ed.), Ideals in Ireland.
    London 1901.
Ireland's Joan of Arc, *The Literary Digest for
    July 15*, 1916.
Jones, Francis P., History of the Sinn Fein
    Movement and the Irish Question of 1916.
    New York 1919.
Joy, Maurice, Introduction in Joy, Maurice
    (ed.), The Irish Rebellion of 1916 And Its
    Martyrs: Erin's Tragic Easter. New York
    1916.

Kelly, John (ed.), The Collected Letters of W.B.Yeats. Volume one.1865-1895. Oxford 1986.

Litten, Helen (ed.), Revolutionary Woman. Kathleen Clarke 1878-1972. An Autobiography. Dublin 1991.

Macardle, Dorothy, The Irish Republic. A Documented Chronicle of the Anglo-Irish Conflict and the Partioning of Ireland with a detailed account of the period 1916-1923. Dublin 1951 (First published 1937).

MacLachlainn, Piaras F. (ed.), Last Words. Letters and Statements of the Leaders Executed After the Rising at Easter 1916. Dublin 1971.

McMullen, William, Introduction in Ryan, Desmond (ed.), Connolly: Workers' Republic. Dublin 1951.

Markievicz, Casimir Dunin, The Memory of the Dead: A Romantic drama of '98 in Three Acts. Dublin 1910.

Markievicz, Constance de, Introduction, in Fianna Handbook. Dublin 1914.

Markievicz, Constance, James Connolly's Policy and Catholic Doctrine. 1924.

Markievicz, Constance de, Some Women in Easter Week, in Prison Letters of Countess Markievicz. London 1986 (London 1934)

Markievicz, Constance de, What Irish Republicans Stand For. Glasgow 1923.

Madame Markievicz and Liberty Hall. [pamphlet] 1913.

Markievicz, Count S., Memories of My Father. Irish Times 17.12.1937.

Martin, F.X.(ed.), The Irish Volunteers 1913-1915. Recollections and Documents. Dublin 1963.

The Memory of the Dead: A Romantic drama of '98 in Three Acts. By Casimir Dunin Markievicz. Dublin 1910.

Milligan, Alice, Irish Heroines, in Dunn, Joseph and Lennox, P.J. (eds.), The Glories of Ireland, Washington 1914.

Moran, D.P., The Battle of Two Civilizations, in Lady Gregory (ed.), The Ideals in Ireland. London 1901.

Moran, D.P., The Ideals in Ireland. Dublin 1905.

Moynihan, Maurice (ed.), Speeches and Statements by Eamon de Valera 1917-73. Dublin 1980.

Murphy, Daniel J. (ed.), Lady Gregory's Journals. Volume One. Books One to Twenty-Nine. New York 1978.

Murphy, H.L., Irish Leaders in Our Time: Countess de Markievicz. An Cosantoir June 1946. Dublin.

O'Brien, William, Introduction in Ryan, Desmond (ed.), James Connolly: Labour and Easter Week. A Selection from the Writings of James Connolly. Dublin 1949.

O'Brien &Ryan, Desmond (eds.), Devoy's Post Bag. Dublin 1953.

O Cathasaigh,P.(Sean O'Casey), The History of the Irish Citizen Army. Dublin 1919.

O'Donnell, Frank J.Hugh, The Dawn-Mist. A Play of the Rebellion. Dublin 1922.

O'Faolain, Sean, Constance Markievicz. London 1987. (London 1934).

O'Hegarty, P.S., The Indestructible Nation. A Survey of Irish History from the English Invasion. The First Phase:The Overthrow of the clans. Dublin 1918.

O'Hegarty,P.S., The Victory of Sinn Fein. How it won it and how it used it. Dublin 1924.

A Painful necessity. [pamphlet] Dublin 1922/23.

Pankhurst, E. Sylvia, The Suffrage Movement. An Intimate Account of Persons and Ideals. London 1931

Pankhurst, E.Sylvia, The Suffragette: The History of the Women's Militant Suffrage Movement 1905-1910. New York 1911.

Phillips, W.Alison, The Revolution in Ireland. London 1923.

Plunkett, Sir Horace, Ireland in the New Century. Dublin 1982 (1905).

Plunkett, Horace, Pilkingon, Ellice and Russell, George ("AE"), The United Irishwomen. Their Place, Work and Ideals. With a Preface By the Rev. T.A. Finlay. Dublin 1911

The Present Duty of Irishwomen. [pamphet] 1918.

Prison Letters of Countess Markievicz. With a New Inroduction by Amanda Sebestyen. London 1987. (London 1935)

To the People of Ireland. [pamphlet]n.d.

Raeburn, Anthonia, The Militant Suffragettes. Introduction by J.B. Prestley, London 1973.

Roper, Esther, Biographical Sketch, in Prison Letters of Countess Markieivcz. London 1987 (London 1934).

Roper, Esther, Biographical Introduction, in Poems of Eva Gore-Booth. Complete edition with The Inner Life of a Child and Letters. London 1929.

R.U. Floinn, The Ethics of Sinn Fein, [pamphlet] n.d.

Ryan, Louise, Irish Feminism and the Vote. An anthology of the Irish Citizen Newspaper 1912-1920, Dublin 1996.

Ryan, Desmond (ed.), Connolly :Workers Republic. Dublin 1951.

Ryan, Desmond (ed.), James Connolly: Labour and Easter Week. A Selection from the Writings of James Connolly. Dublin 1949.

Ryan, Desmond, Remembering Sion. A Chronicle of Storm and Quiet. Edinburgh 1934.

Sheehy-Skeffington, Hanna, Constance Markievicz, An Phoblacht 5.5. 1928.

Sinn Fein and Socialism. The Cork Workers Club. Historical Reprints no 19. Cork 1977

Skinnider, Margaret, Doing My Bit for Ireland. New York 1917.

Smythe, Colin (ed.), Seventy Years. Being the Autobiography of Lady Gregory, London 1974.

The Social Teaching of James Connolly by Lambert McKenna, edited with commentary and introduction by Thomas J. Morrissy, SJ, Dublin 1991.

Stephens, James, The Insurrection in Dublin. New York 1916.

The Two Policies. Sinn Fein or ... Parliamentarianism. By a Western Priest. [pamphlet] 1918.

Woman's Suffrage. *Sligo Champion*. 19.12. 1896.

Women, Ideals and the Nation. A Lecture Delivered to the Students' National Literary Society, Dublin, by Constance de Markievicz. Dublin 1909.

Wyse-Power, Jenny, The Political Influence of Women in Modern Ireland, in Fitzgerald, William G.(ed.), The Voice of Ireland. A Survey of the Race and Nation from All Angles By the Foremost Leaders of Home and Abroad, Dublin 1922.

Yeats, William Butler, The Autobiography. Consisting of Reveries Over Childhood and Youth . The Trembling of the Veil and Dramatic Personae. New York 1953.

Yeats, W.B., Collected Plays. London 1982.

Young, Ella, Flowering Dusk. New York 1945.

SECONDARY SOURCES

Alter, Peter, Nationalism, London: New York 1989.

Anderson, Benedict, Imagined Communities. reflections on the Origin and Spread of Nationalism. (Rev. Edition.) London 1991 (1983).

Anderson, Bonnie S. and Zinsser, Judith P., (eds.), A History of Their Own: Women in Europe from Prehistory to the Present vol II. New York 1988.

Anderson,W.K., James Connolly and the Irish Left. Dublin 1994.

Anthias, Floya and Yuval-Davis, Nira, Women and the Nation-State, in Hutchinson, John & Smith, Anthony D. (eds.), Nationalism. Oxford 1994.

Anthias, Floya, Women and Nationalism in Cyprus, in Yuval-Davis, Nira and Anthias, Floya (eds.), Woman - Nation-State. New York 1989.

Asikainen, Sari, "Me toivomme ihannemaata." Hilja Pärssisen varhainen aatemaailma ennen kansanedustajuutta, Tampereen yliopisto. Yhteiskuntatieteiden tutkimus-laitos. Naistutkimusyksikkö. Julkaisuja - Sarja N 9/1994. Tampere 1994.

Ayling, Ronald, 'Two Words for Women': A Reassessment of O'Casey's Heroines, in Gallagher, S.F. (ed.),Women in Irish Legend, Life and Literature. Irish Literary Studies 14. Buckighamshire 1983.

Barker, Rodney, Political Ideas in Modern Britain. London 1978.

Ben-Israel, Hedva, From Ethnicity to Nationalism, in 18th International Congress of Historical Sciences from 27 August to 3 September. Proceedings. Montreal 1995.

Berresford Ellis, Peter, A History of the Irish Working Class. London 1985. (1st edition 1972)

Bethke Elshtain, Jean, Feminism and the Crisis of Contemporary Culture, in Melzer, Arthur M., Weinberger, Jerry and Zinman, M. Richard, History and the Idea of Progress. Ithaca and London 1995.

Bethke Elshtain, Joan, Women and War. With a New Epilogue. Chicago 1995 (1987).

Blom, Ida, Nation-Class-Gender. Scandinavia at the Turn of the Century. *Scandinavian Journal of History,* 1/1996.

Blom, Ida, World History as Gender History. The Case of the Nation State, in Tonnesson, Stein, Koponen, Juhani, Steensgaard, Niels and Svensson, Thommy (eds.), Between National Histories and Global History. Historiallinen Arkisto 110:4. Helsinki 1997.

Bourke, Marcus, The O'Rahilly. Tralee 1967.

Boyce , D.George, Nationalism in Ireland. (3rd edition). London 1995 (1982).

Boyd, Andrew, The Rise of the Irish Trade Unions 1729-1970. Tralee 1972.

Boyle, J.W., Connolly, the Citizen Army and the Rising, in Nowlan, Kevin B. (ed.), The Making of 1916. Studies in the History of the Rising. Dublin 1969.

Bradshaw, Brendan, Nationalism and Historical Scholarship in Modern Ireland, in Brady, Ciaran (ed.), Interpreting Irish History. The Debate on Historical Revisionsim. Dublin 1994.

Branca, Patricia, Women in Europe Since 1750. New York 1978

Braybon, Gail, Women and the War, in Constantine, Stephen, Kirby, Maurice W., Rose, Mary B., (eds), The First World War in British History, London 1995.

Brown, Terence, Ireland.A Social and Cultural History. 1922 to the Present. New York 1985.

Brunn, Gerhard, Historical Consciousness and Historical Myths, in Comparative Studies on Governments and Non-Dominant Ethnic Groups in Europe 1850-1940. Edited by Andreas Kappeler in collaboration with Fikret Adanir and Alan O'Day. Worcester 1992.

Brunn,Gerhard, Hroch,Miroslav, Kappeler, Andreas, Introduction in Comparative Studies on Governments and Non-Dominant Ethnic Groups in Europe 1850-1940. Edited by Andreas Kappeler in collaboration with Fikret Adanir and Alan O'Day. Worcester 1992.

Cahill, Liam, Forgotten Revolution. Limerick Soviet 1919: A Threat to British Power in Ireland. Dublin 1990.

Cardozo, Nancy. Maud Gonne. Lucky Eyes and A High Heart. London 1979.

Chatterjee, Partha, Colonialism, nationalism, and colonized women: the contest in India. *American Ethnologist* 1989, 622-633.

Clancy, Mary, Aspects of Women's Contribution to the Oireachtas Debate in the Irish Free State,1922-1937, in Luddy, Maria and Murphy, Cliona (eds.), Women Surviving. Studies in Irish Women's History in the 19th & 20th centuries. Dublin 1990.

Coffey, Thomas, Agony at Easter. New York 1969.

Collins, Peter, Irish Labour and Politics in The Nineteenth and Twentieth Centuries, in Collins, Peter (ed.), Nationalism & Unionism. Conflict in Ireland 1885-1921. Belfast 1994.

Colum, Padraic, Arthur Griffith. Dublin 1959.

Comerford, Maire, The First Dáil. Dublin 1971.

Condren, Mary, Sacrifice and Political Legitimation: The Production of a Gendered Social Order, *Journal of Women's History*. Vol. 6 No 4/Vol. 7 No 1(Winter/Spring) 1995.

Conlon, Lil, Cumann na mBan and the Women of Ireland 1913-1925. Kilkenny 1969.

Coogan, Tim Pat, De Valera. Long Fellow, Long Shadow. London 1993.

Coogan, Tim Pat, The I.R.A.. Glasgow 1987.

Coogan, Tim Pat, Michael Collins. A Biography. Dublin 1990.

Couldrey, B.M., Faith and Fatherland:The Christian Brothers and the Development of Irish Nationalism 1838-1921. Dublin 1988.

Cowell, John, Sligo. Land of Yeats' Desire. It's history, literature, folklore and landscape. Dublin 1989.

Coxhead, Elizabeth, Daughters of Erin. London 1965

Cronin, Sean, Irish Nationalism. A History of its Roots and Ideology. Dublin 1980.

Cronin, Sean, McGarrity Papers. Tralee 1972.

Cullen, L.M., Life in Ireland. London 1968.

Cullen Owens, Rosemary ,Smashing Times. A History of the Irish Women's Suffrage Movement 1889-1922. Dublin 1984.

Curious Journey. An Oral History of Ireland's Unfinished Revolution, ed. by Kenneth Griffith & Timothy E. O'Grady. London 1982.

Curtin, Nancy J., Women and Eighteenth-Century Irish Republicanism. In Margaret MacCurtain and Mary O'Dowd (eds.), Women in Early Modern Ireland. Edinburgh 1991

Curtis, Liz, The Cause of Ireland. From the Uniited Irishmen to Partition. Belfast 1994.

Curtis, L.Perry Jr., Apes and Angels:The Irishman in Victorian Caricature. Washington 1971.

Curtis, L.P., Jr., The Greening of Irish History, *Éire-Ireland*, 3/1994.

Dalton,G.F., The Tradition of Blood Sacrifice to the Goddess Éire. *Studies*. Winter1974.

Daly, Mary E., The Economic Ideals of Irish Nationalism: Frugal Comfort of Lavish Austerity?, *Éire-Ireland* 4/1994.

Dangerfield, George, The Damnable Question. Boston 1976.

Davis, Richard, Arthur Griffith and Non-Violent Sinn Fein. Tralee 1974.

Dudley Edwards, Owen, The Mind of an Activist. James Connolly. Dublin 1971.

Dudley Edwards, Ruth, Patrick Pearse. The Triumph of Failure. London 1977

Dunphy, Richard, The Making of Fianna Fáil Power in Ireland 1923-1948. Oxford 1995.

Dunphy, Richard, The Soldiers Set Out: Reflections on the Formation of Fianna Fail, in Hannon, Philip & Gallagher, Jackie, Taking the Long View. 70 Years of Fianna Fail, Dublin 1996.

Dwyer, T.Ryle, Eamon de Valera and the Partition Question, in O'Carroll, John P. and Murphy, John A. (eds.), De Valera and His Times.Cork 1983.

Eagleton, Terry, Heathcliff and the Great Hunger: Studies in Irish Culture. London and New York 1995.

Elliott, Marianne, Wolfe Tone. Prophet of Irish Independence. New Haven and London 1989.

English, Richard, Green on red; Two case studies in early twentieth-century Irish republican thought, in Boyce, George D., Eccleshall, Robert and Geogham, Vincent (eds.), Political Thought in Ireland Since the Seventeenth Century. London and New York 1993.

English, Richard, Radicals and the Republic. Socialist Republicanism in the Irish Free State 1925-1937. Oxford 1994.

Fallon, Charlotte H., Soul of Fire. A Biography of Mary MacSwiney. Dublin 1986.

Fanning, Ronan, Independent Ireland. Dublin 1983.

Farrell, Brian, Markievicz and the Women of the Revolution, in Martin, F.X. (ed.), Leaders and Men of the Easter Rising, Dublin 1916. London 1967.

Fitzgerald, Desmond, Memoirs 1913-1916. London 1968.

Fitzgerald, Garrett, Our Republicanism is more recent than we realise, Irish Times 29.5.1993.

Fitzpatrick, David, De Valera in 1917:the Undoing of the Easter Rising, in O'Carroll, John P. and Murphy, John A. (eds.), De Valera and His Times.Cork 1983.

Fitzpatrick, David (ed.), Ireland and The First World War. Dublin 1988.

Fitzpatrick, David, Ireland Since 1870, in Foster, R.F., The Oxford History of Ireland. Oxford 1989.

Foster, R.F., Ascendancy and Union, in Foster, R.F. (ed.), The Oxford History of Ireland, Oxford 1989.

Foster, R.F., Modern Ireland 1600-1972. London 1985.

Foster, R.F., Paddy and Mr Punch. Connections in Irish and English History. London 1993.

Foster, R.F., W.B.Yeats: A Life. I. The Apprentice Mage 1865-1914.Oxford 1997.

Fox, R.M., The History of the Irish Citizen Army. Dublin 1943.

Fox, R.M., Louie Bennett. Her Life and Times. Dublin 1958.

Gaitskell, Deborah & Unterhalter, Elaine, Mothers of the Nation: a Comparative Analysis of Nation, Race and Motherhood in Afrikaner Nationalism and the African National Congress, in Yuval-Davis, Nira and Anthias, Floya (eds.), Woman - Nation-State, New York 1989.

Gallagher, Michael, Socialism and Nationalist Tradition in Ireland 1798-1918. *Éire-Ireland* 2/1977.

Garner, Les, Stepping Stones to Women's Liberty. Feminist ideas in the women's suffrage movement 1900-1918. Rutherford 1984.

Garvin, Tom, The Evolution of Irish Nationalist Politics. Dublin 1981.

Garvin, Tom, Nationalist Revolutionaries in Ireland 1858-1928. Oxford 1987.

Garvin, Tom, The Rising and Irish Democracy, in Nì Dhonnchadha, Màirìn and Dorgan, Theo (eds), Revising the Rising. Dublin 1991.

Garvin, Tom, 1922. The Birth of Irish Democracy. Dublin 1996

Gaugham, J.Anthony, Austin Stack:Portrait of a Separatist. Naas 1977.

Gellner, Ernest, Nations and Nationalism. Oxford 1983.

Gilley,Sheridan, Pearses Sacrifice:Christ and Cuchulain Crucified and Risen in the Easter Rising,1916, in Alexander, Yonah and O'Day, Alan (eds.), Ireland's Terrorist Dilemma. Dordrecht 1986.

Godineau, Dominique, Daughters of Liberty and Revolutionary Citizens, in George Duby and Michelle Perrot, (General editors), A History of Women in the West IV. Emerging Feminism from Revolution to World War. Cambridge (MA) 1993.

Greaves, Charles D., The Irish Transport and General Workers Union. The Formative Years. Dublin 1982.

Greaves, C.Desmod, Liam Mellows and the Irish Revolution. Southampton 1988(1971).

Greaves, C.Desmond, The Life and Times of James Connolly. London 1961.

Greenfeld, Liah, Nationalism. Five Roads to Modernity. Cambridge (MA)& London 1992.

Grossman, Anton J.J., Irische Nationalbewegung 1884-1915. Füssen 1979.

Hall, Wayne E., Shadowy Heroes. Irish Literature of the 1890's. Syracuse 1980.

Halmesvirta, Anssi, Riiviöistä ritareiksi. Verneri Louhivuori, suomalaisen partioaatteen synty ja nuorkirkollinen luonteenmuokkausideologia 1910-1924, in Historiallinen Arkisto 19, Suomen Historiallinen Seura. Tampere 1997.

Harkness, David, Ireland in the Twentieth Century. Divided Island. Houndmills 1996.

Harrison, J.F.C., Robert Owen and the Owenites in Britain and America.The Quest for the New Moral World. Oxford 1969.

Haverty, Anne, Constance Markievicz. An Independent Life. London 1988.

Hawkins, Maureen S.G., The Dramatic Treatment of Robert Emmet and Sarah Curran, in Gallagher, S.F.,Women in Irish Legend, Life and Literature. Irish Literary Studies 14. Buckighamshire 1983.

Hearne, Dana, The Irish Citizen 1914-1916: Nationalism, Feminism and Militarism, *Canadian Journal of Irish Studies*, Volume 18, Number 1, December 1991,

Hetmann, Frederik, Eine Schwierige Tochter. Köln 1987.

Hickey, D.J.& Doherty, J.E., A Dictionary of Irish History 1800-1980. Dublin 1980.

Hobsbawm, E.J., Nations and Nationalism since 1780. Programme, Myth, Reality. Cambridge 1990.

Holton, Sandra Stanley, Feminism and Democracy. Women's Suffrage and Reform Politics in Britain 1900-1918. Cambridge 1986.

Holton, Sandra Stanley, In Sorrowful Wrath: Suffrage Militancy and the Romantic Feminism of Emmeline Pankhurst, in Smith, Harold L. (ed.), British Feminism in the Twentieth Century, Aldershot 1990.

Holton, Sandra Stanley, The Suffragist and the 'Average Woman', in *Women's History Review*, Volume 1, No 1, 1992.

Hopkinson, Michael, Green Against Green. The Irish Civil War. Dublin 1988.

Howard, Michael, War and Nations [The Lessons of History, Oxford 1991, 39-43], in Hutchinson, John & Smith, Anthony D., (eds.), Nationalism. Oxford 1994.

Hutchinson, John, The Dynamics of the Cultural Nationalism. The Gaelic Revival and the Creation of the Irish Nation State. London 1987.

Hyrkkänen, Markku, Aatehistorian mieli. *Historiallinen Aikakauskirja* 4/1989.

Immonen, Kari, Metodikirja, Turku 1993.

Innes, C.L., Woman and Nation in Irish Literature and Society, 1880-1935. London 1993.

Jeffreys, Sheila, The Spinster and Her Enemies: Feminism and Sexuality 1880-1930. London 1985.

Johnson, Paul, A History of the Modern World. From 1917 to the 1980s. London 1984.

Johansson, Rolf, Irish Labour and the Downfall of Home Rule 1916-1918, in Tammisto, Antero, Mustakallio, Katariina, Saarinen, Hannes (eds.), Miscallanea. Vammala 1989.

Joll, James, The Second International 1889-1914. Oxford 1974.

Jones, Mary, These Obstereperous Lassies. the History of the Irish Women Worker's Union. Dublin 1988.

Kee, Robert, The Bold Fenian Men. London 1972.

Kemiläinen, Aira, The Idea of Nationalism, *Scandinavian Journal of History* 1/ 1984,31-64.

Kemiläinen, Aira, Keskitetty valtio - historiallinen näkökulma, in Raento, Pauliina (ed.), Yhdessä erikseen. Kansalliset konfliktit Länsi-Euroopassa, Helsinki 1993, 213-232.

Kiberd,Declan,Inventing Irelands, *The Crane Bag*. Ireland:Dependence & Independence. Vol 8,no 1. Dublin 1984.

Kirby, Maurice W., Industry, Agriculture and Trade Unions, in Constantine, Stephen, Kirby, Maurice W., Rose, Mary B., (eds), The First World War in British History, London 1995.

Käppeli, Anne-Marie, Feminist Scenes, in George Duby and Michelle Perrot, (General editors), A History of Women in the West IV. Emerging Feminism from Revolution to World War. Cambridge (MA) 1993.

Laffan, Michael, Insular Attitudes:The Revisionists and their Critics, in Nì Dhonnchadha, Màirìn and Dorgan, Theo (eds), Revising the Rising. Dublin 1991.

Laffan, Michael, "Labour Must Wait." Ireland's Conservative Revolution. In Radicals, Rebels and Establishments. *Historical Studies XV.* Dublin 1985.

Laffan, Michael, The Partition of Ireland 1911-1925. Dublin 1983.

Laffan, Michael, The Unification of Sinn Fein in 1917, *Irish Historical Studies*, vol XVII,1970-1971.Dublin.

Laffan, Michael, Violence and Terror in Twentieth-Century Ireland: IRB and IRA, in Mommsen, Wolfgang J. and Hirschfeld, Gerhard (eds), Social Protest, Violence and Terror in Nineteenth-and Twentieth-Century Europe. London 1982.

Larkin, Emmet, James Larkin. Irish Labour Leader 1876-1947. London 1965.

Lawrence, John, The First World War and its Aftermath, in Johnson, Paul (ed.), Twentieth-Century Britain: Economic, Social and Cultural Change. London 1994.

Lee, J.J., Ireland 1912-1985. Politics and Society. Cambridge 1989.

Lee, Joseph, The Modernisation of Irish Society. Dublin 1973.

Levenson, Leah & Natterstedt, Jerry H., Hannah Sheehy-Skeffington. Irish Feminist. Syracuse 1986.

Levine, Philippa, Feminist Lives in Victorian England. Oxford 1990.

Lewis, Jane, Models of equality for women: the case of state support for children in twentieth-century Britain, in Bock, Gisela and Thane, Pat (eds.), Maternity and Gender Policies. Women and the Rise of the European Welfare States, 1880s -1950s. London 1991.

Lewis, Gifford, Eva Gore-Booth and Esther Roper. A Biography. London 1988.

Liddington, Jill & Norris, Jill, One Hand Tied Behind Us. The Rise of the Women's Suffrage Movement. London 1978.

Lindsay, Deirdre, Labur Against Conscription, in Fitzpatrick, David (ed.), Ireland and The First World War. Dublin 1988.

Luddy, Maria, Women and Charitable Organisations in Nineteenth Century Ireland, *Women's Studies International Forum*, Vol. 11, No 4,1988.

Lynch, Diarmuid (ed.by F.O'Donoghue), The IRB and the 1916 Rising. Cork 1957.

Lyons, F.S.L., Culture and Anarchy in Ireland 1890-1939. Oxford 1979.

Lyons, F.S.L., Ireland Since the Famine. Glasgow 1973.

MacAodha, Bréndan S., Was this a Social Revolution, in Ó Tuama, Sean (ed.), The Gaelic League Idea. Dublin 1972.

MacCarthy, Charles, The Impact of larkinism on the Irish Working Class. *Saothar* 4/1978. Dublin.

McCartney, Donal, Hyde, D.P.Moran and Irish Ireland, in Martin, F.X. (ed.), Leaders and Men of the Easter Rising, Dublin 1916. London 1967.

McClintock, Anne, Family Feuds:Gender, Nationalism and the Family, *Feminist Review* No 44, Nationalisms and National Identities. Summer 1993.

McCullough, Martin, Hobson, and Republican Ulster, in Martin, F.X. (ed.), Leaders and Men of the Easter Rising, Dublin 1916. London 1967.

McKillen, Beth, Irish Feminism and Nationalist Separatism1914-1923, *Éire-Ireland* 3/ 1981.

McKillen, Beth, Irish Feminism and Nationalist Separatism, 1914-1923, *Éire-Ireland*, 1/ 1982.

MacCurtain, Margaret, Fullness of Life: Defending Female Spirituality in Twentieth Century Ireland, in Luddy, Maria and Murphy, Cliona (eds.), Women Surviving. Studies in Irish Women's History in the 19th & 20th centuries. Dublin 1990.

MacCurtain, Margaret, Women, the Vote and Revolution, in MacCurtain, Margaret Ó Currain, Donncha (eds.), Women in Irish History. The Historical Dimension. Naas 1978.

MacDonagh, Oliver, States of Mind. A Study of Anglo-Irish Conflict 1780-1980. London 1983.

MacWhite, Eoin, A Russian Pamphlet on Ireland by Count Markievicz, in Irish University Review. A *Journal of Irish Studies*, Vol. I, 1, Autumn 1970.

Maley, Willy, Varieties of Nationalism:Post-Revisionist Irish Studies, *Irish Studies Review*, 15/ 1996.

Marreco, Anne, The Rebel Countess:The Life and Times of Countess Markievicz. London 1967.

Martin, F.X., 1916 - Myth, Fact and Mystery. *Studia Hibernica* 7/1967.

Martin, F.X.,1916 - Revolution or Evolution, in Martin, F.X. (ed.), Leaders and Men of the Easter Rising, Dublin 1916. London 1967.

Matossian, Mary, Ideologies of Delayed Development [Ideologies of "Delayed Industrialization": Some Tensions and Ambiguities, in J.H. Kautsky (ed.), Political Change in Underdeveloped Countries, New York 1962,256-64], in Hutchinson, John & Smith, Anthony D. (eds.), Nationalism. Oxford 1994.

Mauranen, Tapani, Osuustoiminta - kansanliikettä aatteen ja rahan vuoksi, in Alapuro, Risto- Liikanen, Ilkka-Smeds, Kerstin- Stenius, Henrik (eds.), Kansa liikkeessä. Helsinki 1987.

Metscher, Priscilla, Republicanism and Socialism in Ireland. A Study in the Relationship of Politics and Ideology from the United Irishmen to James Connolly. Frankfurt 1986.

Meyer, Donald, Sex and Power: The Rise of Women in America, Russia, Sweden, and Italy, Second Edition, with a New Introduction. Connecticut 1989.

Miller, David W., Church, State and Nation in Ireland 1898-1921. Dublin 1973.

Mitchell. Arthur, Labour in Irish Politics. Dublin 1974.

Mitchell, Arthur, Revolutionary Government in Ireland: Dáil Eireann 1919-22. Dublin 1995.

Mitchell, David, Women on the Warpath. The Story of the Women of the First World War. London 1966.

Moody, T.W., Irish History and Irish Mythology. In Brady, Ciaran (ed.), Interpreting Irish History. The Debate on Historical Revisionsim. Dublin 1994.

Moran, Sean Farrell, Patrick Pearse and the Politics of Redemption: The Mind of Easter Rising 1916, Washington d.c., 1994.

Morgan, Austen, James Connolly. A Political Biography. Manchester 1988.

Moriarty,Mary & Sweeney,Catherine, Markievicz. The Rebel Countess. Dublin 1991.

Morrow, Ann, Picnic in a Foreign Land: The Eccentric Lives of the Anglo-Irish. London 1989.

Moynahan, Julian, Anglo-Irish:The Literary Imagination in a Hyphenated Culture. Princeton 1995.

Murphy, Brian P., Patrick Pearse and the Lost Republican Ideal. Dublin 1991.

Nevin, Donal, The Irish Citizen Army in Nowlan, Kevin B. (ed.), The Making of 1916. Studies in the History of the Rising. Dublin 1969.

Newsinger, John, "As Catholic as the Pope". James Connolly and the Roman Catholic Church in Ireland. *Saothar* 11/1986.

Newsinger, John, Easter Rebellion - Defeat or Victory. *Monthly Review* 7/1982.

Newsinger, John, "I Bring Not peace But A Sword": The Religious Motif in the Irish War of Independence. *Journal of Contemporary History* Vol. 13 1978, 609-28..

Ni Eireamnoin, Eibhlin, Two Great Irishwomen: Maud Gonne MacBride and Constance Markievicz. Dublin 1972.

Norman, Diana, Terrible Beauty. A Life of Constance Markievicz. Dublin 1987.

Nowlan, Kevin B., The Gaelic League and Other National Movements, in Ó Tuama, Sean (ed.), The Gaelic League Idea. Dublin 1972.

Nowlan, Kevin B., Tom Clarke, MacDermott, and the I.R.B., in in Martin, F.X. (ed.), Leaders and Men of the Easter Rising, Dublin 1916. London 1967.

Nutt, Kathleen, Irish Identity and the Writing of History, *Éire-Ireland*, 3/1994.

Ó Briain, Liam, Saint Stephen's Green Area. *Capuchin Annual* 1966.

O'Brien, Conor Cruise, Ancestral Voices: Religion and Nationalism in Ireland. Chicago 1995.

O'Brien, Conor Cruise, Ireland's Fissures,and My Family's. *The Atlantic Monthly.* January 1994.

ÓBroin, Leon, Dublin Castle and the 1916 Rising. London 1970.

Ó Broin, Leon, Protestant Nationalists in Revolutionary Ireland: The Stopford Connection. Dublin 1985.

Ó Broin, Leon, W.E.Wylie and the Irish Revolution 1916-1921. Dublin 1989.

Ó Ceallaigh, Sean, Arthur Griffith, *Capuchin Annual* 1966.

O'Connor, Emmet, A Labour History of Ireland 1824-1960. Dublin 1992.

Ó Cuiv, Brian, The Gaelic Cultural Movements and the New Nationalism, in Nowlan, Kevin B. (ed.), The Making of 1916. Studies in the History of the Rising. Dublin 1969.

O'Day, Alan, Irish Catholics in the British State 1850-1922, in Kappeler, Andreas, Adanir, Fikret and O'Day, Alan (eds.), Comparative Studies on Governments and Non-Dominanat Ethnic Groups in Europe 1850-1940. Volume VI. Worcester 1992.

Offen, Karen, Defining Feminism: A Comparative Historical Approach, *Signs: Journal of Women in Culture and Society*, 1/1988.

Oikarinen, Sari, Gender, Nationality and War. Irish and Finnish Women and the Struggle for Independence in the Beginning of this Century in Gullikstad, B. & Heitmann, K., Kjønn, makt, Samfunn in Norden I et historisk perspektiv. Bid I. Konferanse-rapport fra det 5. nordiske kvinnehistorikermøte, Klækken 08-11.08.96, Trondheim 1997, 206-221.

Oikarinen, Sari, Hilja Pärssinen -Työväen-liikkeen runoilja ja poliitikko, in Yksi kamari – kaksi sukupuolta. Suomen edus-kunnan ensimmäiset naiset. Eduskunnan kirjaston tutkimuksia ja selvityksiä 4. Jyväskylä 1997.

Oikarinen, Sari, The Rebel Countess: Constance Markievicz, in Hannon, Philip and Gallagher, Jackie (eds.), Taking the Long View. 70 Years of Fianna Fail. Dublin 1996.

O'Malley,Ernie, The Singing Flame. Dublin 1978.

Ó Tuathaigh,Gearóid, Nationalist Ireland 1912-1922. Aspects of Continuity and Change, in Collins, Peter (ed.), Nationalism & Unionism. Conflict in Ireland 1885-1921. Belfast 1994.

O'Neill, Daniel J., The Cult of Self-Sacrifice. *Éire-Ireland* 1/1989.

O'Neill, Thomas P., In Search of a Political Path. Irish Republicanism 1922 to 1927. *Historical Studies X*. Dublin 1976.

Pakenham, Frank, Peace by Ordeal. With an introduction by Tim Pat Coogan and a preface by the author, London 1993 (First published 1935, new edition 1972).

Patterson, Henry, The Politics of Illusion: Republicanism and Socialism in Modern Ireland. London 1989.

Pelling, Henry, A History of British Trade Unionism. Harmondsworth 1992 (1st edition 1963).

Prager, Jeffrey, Building Democracy in Ireland. Political Order and Cultural Integration in a Newly Independent Nation. New York 1986.

Phillips, Gordon, The Social Impact, in Constantine, Stephen, Kirby, Maurice W., Rose, Mary B., (eds), The First World War in British History. London 1995.

Pugh, Martin, Domestic Politics, in Constantine, Stephen, Kirby, Maurice W., Rose, Mary B., (eds), The First World War in British History. London 1995.

Pyne, Peter, The third Sinn Fein Party 1923-26, *Economic and Social review*, vol.I (1969-1970)

Rauter,Anton, Co-operative principles and Their Importance for Co-operative Progress, in Co-operatives to-day. Selected Essays from Various Fields of Co-operative Activities. Genova 1986.

Renan, Ernest, Qu'est-ce qu'une nation? [Transl. Ida Mae Snyder, Paris 1882], in Nationalism, edited by John Hutchinson and Anthony D.Smith, Oxford 1994.

Rendall, Jane, The Origins of Modern Feminism: Women in Britain, France and the United States 1780-1860. London 1985.

Reynolds, Lorna, Irish Women in Legend, Literature and Life, in Gallagher, S.F. (ed.), Women in Irish Legend, Life and Literature.

Irish Literary Studies 14. Buckinghamshire 1983.

Robbins, Frank, Under the Starry Plough. Recollections of the Irish Citizen Army. Dublin 1977.

Romero, Patricia W., E. Sylvia Pankhurst. Portrait of a Radical. New Haven 1987.

Rose, Catherine, The Female Experience. The Story of the Women Movement in Ireland. Naas 1975.

Rosen, Andrew, Rise Up, Women! The Militant Campaign of the Women's Social and Political Union 1903-1914. London 1974.

Rumpf, E. & Hepburn, A.L. , Socialism and Nationalism in twentieth Century Ireland. Liverpool 1977.

Ryan, Desmond, The Rising. Dublin 1966.

Ryan, Louise, Traditions and Double Moral Standards: the Irish suffragists' critique of nationalism, *Women's History Review*. 4/1995.

Ryan, Louise, Women Without Votes:The Political Strategies of the Irish Suffrage Movement, *Irish Political Studies* 9/1994.

Sawyer, Roger,"We Are But Women'.Women in Ireland's History. London 1993.

Scott, Joan W., Gender: A Useful Category of Historical Analysis. *The American Historical Review*, 5/1986.

Scott, Joan W., Gender and the Politics of History, New York 1988.

Sebastyen, Amanda, Introduction in Prison Letters of Countess Markievicz. London 1986.

Sheehy-Skeffington, Hanna, Reminiscences of an Irish Suffragette, in Sheehy-Skeffington, Andree and Cullen Owens, Rosemary (eds.), Votes for Women. Irish Women's Struggle for the Vote, Dublin 1975.

Sihvo, Hannes, Suomalaisuuden pyhä tuli, in Tommila, Päiviö (ed.), Herää Suomi. Suomalaisuuliikkeen historia. Jyväskylä 1989.

The Social Teaching of James Connolly by Lambert McKenna SJ, Edited with commentary and introduction by Thomas J.Morrissey, SJ. Dublin 1991.

Somervell, D.C., English Thought in the Nineteenth Century. London 1929.

Stanley, Liz with Morley, Ann, The Life and Death of Emily Wilding Davison. A Biographical Detective Story. With Gertrude Colmore's The Life of Emily Davison, London 1988.

Tennberg, Monica, Etnisiä konflikteja selittävät teoriat ja niiden ongelmat, in Raento, Pauliina (ed.), Yhdessä erikseen. Kansalliset konfliktit Länsi-Euroopassa. Helsinki 1993, 27-40.

Thompson, William Irvin, The Imagination of an Insurrection. Dublin, Easter 1916. Massachusetts 1982(1967).

Tierney, Michael, Eoin MacNeill. Scholar and Man of Action 1867-1945. Oxford 1980.

Tosh, John, The Pursuit of History. Aims, Methods & New Directions in the Study of Modern History (2nd edition). London & New York 1991 (1984).

Townshend, Charles, Political Violence in Ireland. Government and Resistance Since 1848. Oxford 1983.

Van Voris, Jacqueline, Constance de Markievicz: In the Cause of Ireland. Vermont 1967.

Voices of Ireland. Conversation with Donncha Ó Dulaing. Dublin 1984.

Wall, Maureen, The Background of the Rising: from 1914 until the issue of the countermanding order on Easter Saturday 1916, in Nowlan, Kevin B., The Making of 1916. Studies in the History of the Rising. Dublin 1969.

Walsh, Oonagh, Testimony from Imprisoned Women, in Fitzpatrick, David (ed.), Revolution? Ireland 1917-1923. Dublin 1990.

Ward, Margaret, In Their Own Voice. Women and Irish Nationalism. Dublin 1995

Ward, Margaret, Irish Women and Nationalism, Irish Studies Review, No 17/1996/7.

Ward, Margaret, Maud Gonne. Ireland's Joan of Arc. London 1990.

Ward, Margaret, Unmanageable Revolutionaries. Dublin 1983.

Wardley, Peter, Edwardian Britain: Empire, Income and Political Discontent, in Johnson, Paul, 20th Century Britain. Economic, Social and Cultural Change. London 1994.

West, Trevor, Horace Plunkett:Co-operation and Politics. An Irish Biography. London 1986.

White, Terence de Vere, Mahaffy, the Anglo-Irish Ascendancy, and the Vice-Regal Lodge, in Martin,F.X. (ed.), Leaders and Men of the Easter Rising, Dublin 1916. London 1967.

Whyte, John H., 1916 - Revolution and Religion, in Martin, F.X. (ed.), Leaders and Men of the Easter Rising, Dublin 1916. London 1967.

Woolf Stuart, Introduction in Woolf, Stuart (ed.), Nationalism in Europe. 1815 to the present. A reader. London 1996.

■ Index